THE RELIGIOUS ARCHITECTURE
OF NEW MEXICO

QUARAI. THE CHURCH, FROM THE NORTHWEST. 1937.

THE RELIGIOUS ARCHITECTURE OF NEW MEXICO

In the Colonial Period and Since
the American Occupation

GEORGE KUBLER

Published for the

SCHOOL OF AMERICAN RESEARCH

by

UNIVERSITY OF NEW MEXICO PRESS
Albuquerque

Fourth printing, 1972. Manufactured in the United States of America.
Library of Congress Catalog Card No. 72-86823.

TO
E. B. BROWN

The temples . . . are not objects for admiration, nor are they sumptuous, for they are very small, with walls of mud and adobes, built without skill and at no expense.

GOVERNOR MENDIZABAL, 1663 (Hackett, C. W.,
Historical Documents Relating to New Mexico, III [1937], 213)

It is not amiss to say . . . that we waited too long to acknowledge the unique and very great heritage we had in the early New Mexican missions. We now see them as one of the country's painfully few genuine creative achievements; but we did not see it till they had been spoiled and many of them destroyed forever.

Sheldon Cheney and Martha Candler,
"Santos," *Parnassus*, VII (1935), 22–24

PREFACE TO FOURTH EDITION

Since 1940, knowledge of the architectural history of these buildings has been increased by the appearance of important documents, by new excavations, and by ethnographic studies. A chronological summary of printed and unpublished writings on these many discoveries follows.

DOCUMENTS

1942   The great history and documentary collection on the Pueblo revolt of 1680, by C. W. Hackett with translations by C. C. Shelby (*Revolt of the Pueblo Indians of New Mexico and Otermin's Attempted Reconquest, 1680–1682*, 2 vols., Coronado Historical Series, vols. 8, 9, Albuquerque, 1942), contains 32 more or less extended descriptions of the damages suffered by the missions. These can eventually be correlated with other sources to give a more exact estimate of the reconstructions by eighteenth-century builders.

1944   An archival study by F. V. Scholes and L. B. Bloom ("Friar Personnel and Mission Chronology," *New Mexico Historical Review* 19, 1944, 219–26; 20, 1945, 58–82) needs careful sifting for indirect information about architectural activity.

Professor Scholes also has redated the report he published in 1929 as being part of the work by Zarate Salmerón. In 1929 Scholes believed this was written in 1629, but in 1944 ("Correction," *New Mexico Historical Review* 19, 1944, 243–46) he proposed 1641–44 as its date of composition.

1945   The manuscript of the *Memorial* of 1634 by Alonso de Benavides has been known since its discovery in Rome by C. R. Fish in 1908–9, but it contains less information for architectural studies than the earlier version (1630) edited by E.A.B. Ayer in 1916. The *Memorial* of 1634 (F. W. Hodge, G. P. Hammond, and Agapito Rey, *Fray Alonso de Benavides' Revised Memorial of 1634*, Coronado Historical Series, vol. 4 Albuquerque, 1945) was annotated mainly by Hodge, who set in order the complicated question of the sequence of the missions among the Zuñi pueblos (pp. 191–92).

1947   Among documentary studies of single monuments, an article by Eleanor B. Adams is important ("The Chapel and Cofradía of Our Lady of Light in Santa Fe," *New Mexico Historical Review* 22, 1947, 327–41). This little chapel, planned in 1760 and inaugurated in 1761, was perhaps the design of Governor Marín del Valle, who was also its donor. The stone altarpiece, according to Domínguez writing in 1776, was made of stone from Ranchos de Pujuaque below Nambe (op. cit., pp. 32, 60). The name of the sculptor is still unknown, although Pál Kelemen has connected the altarpiece with "north Mexican carving" ("The Significance of the Stone Retablo of Cristo Rey," *El Palacio* 52, 1945, 243–72).

1949 A reconquest document of 1697–98 about repossessing the Franciscan friary in Santa Fe has led Fray Angelico Chavez to reconstruct in convincing detail the exact locations of the successive churches of 1629, 1717, and 1804 ("Santa Fe Church and Convent Sites in the Seventeenth and Eighteenth Centuries," *New Mexico Historical Review* 24, 1949, 85–93).

1954 Eleanor B. Adams brought out an extended study of eighteenth-century church politics ("Bishop Tamaron's Visitation to New Mexico, 1760," Historical Society of New Mexico Publications in History 15, 1954). The significance of this document was much enriched by her researches on the conflict of the friars with bishops and governors after the reconquest (also H. W. Kelly, *The Franciscan Missions of New Mexico, 1740–1760*, Historical Society of New Mexico Publications in History 10). Her translation follows the Mexican edition of 1935. She appended other documents, such as the record of Bishop Crespo's visitation in 1730, and a Franciscan reply to threats of secularization. For architectural studies, however, the documents themselves contain little information that has not already been used.

1956 The richest single addition to our knowledge of colonial New Mexico is the visitation in 1776 by Fray Atanasio Domínguez, edited by Eleanor B. Adams and Fray Angelico Chavez as *The Missions of New Mexico, 1776* (Albuquerque, University of New Mexico Press, 1956). The text contains the most complete colonial descriptions in existence of this architecture. Domínguez understood and loved architecture: his report surpasses all other surviving accounts, even those of Mexico proper. Architectural historians rarely if ever find such descriptions in colonial missionary histories. One technical error appears in the superb translation: *arco toral* is not "vaulted arch" (p. 13 and passim), but "chancel opening." Arches were almost never used. Each description of mission buildings is accompanied in this edition by a clear perspective freehand drawing of the church and friary by Horace T. Pierce.

EXCAVATIONS

1943 E. L. Hewett and R. Fisher (*Mission Monuments of New Mexico*, Albuquerque, 1943, 195–237) have assembled various reports on the reclamation and restoration of colonial monuments in New Mexico. Summaries of excavations by Albert G. Ely (1935) and Wesley Hurt (1930–40) at Quarai appear, as well as Joseph Toulouse's account of the excavation and repair of Abó, and William Witkind's on Pecos in 1939–40.

The full report by Toulouse on Abó appeared in 1949 ("The Mission of San Gregorio de Abó," Monographs of the School of American Research, no. 13). It is an exemplary brief account of excavations in colonial ruins. In the light of Mrs. Pinkley's discovery (see p. x), the buttressed structure of Abó now appears related to that of the second church at Pecos built in 1622.

1949   The western missions were poorly known until the appearance of Ross Montgomery's work on Awatovi (R. G. Montgomery, W. Smith, and J. O. Brew, *Franciscan Awatovi*, Papers, Peabody Museum, Harvard, vol. 26). As an architect and as a specialist on liturgy, Montgomery guided the excavation of the mission buildings, and his parts of the report are a handbook on mission life and building activity. Part IV, by Watson Smith, on mural decorations in the church is our most complete discussion of such a program, and it includes a section on glazed tiles.

1955   S. A. Stubbs and B. T. Ellis excavated in 1955 at San Miguel in Santa Fe (*Archaeological Investigations at the Chapel of San Miguel*, Monographs of the School of American Research, no. 20). They found a smaller, undated church beneath the present one, and therefore predating 1710. Thus San Miguel now is confirmed as a building of post-reconquest date by every line of evidence. In the same year Stubbs and Ellis also excavated on the site of the Castrense chapel, finding nothing earlier than 1760, but establishing a two-towered façade, which was not mentioned by Domínguez in 1776.

1959   Stanley A. Stubbs excavated the oldest church ruins at Quarai and Tabirá ("New 'Old' Churches found at Quarai and Tabirá," *El Palacio* 66, 1959, 162–69). He identified the ruin 150 feet southwest of the main walls as "the first Christian religious edifice erected at Quarai." At Pueblo Blanco, 15 miles northeast of Gran Quivira, another early chapel ruin was identified as being Tabirá, erected about 1629 and renovated in 1659.

1965   A. G. Ely has reported on the recent repairs and restorations carried out at S. José, Giusewa ("Stabilization of a Mission," *El Palacio* 72, 1965, 5–9). He regards the church as founded in 1621–22 and repaired in 1625 and 1628.

1966   The archaeology of Hawikuh remained practically unknown to the public until F. W. Hodge's excavations were published in 1966 with a chapter on church and friary by Watson Smith and Ross Montgomery (W. Smith, R. B. Woodbury, N.F.S. Woodbury, and Ross Montgomery, *The Excavation of Hawikuh by Frederick Webb Hodge . . . 1917–1923*, Contributions, Museum of the American Indian, Heye Foundation, vol. 20). These pages of intricate local detail avoid discussing the relationship of Hawikuh to the rest of Pueblo Mission architecture, by assuming that Montgomery's detailed work on Awatovi had already discharged that obligation. As a monograph this volume belongs among the masterpieces of southwestern archaeological writing.

1967   The major archaeological discovery in the world of the missions of seventeenth-century Mexico fell to the late Jean Pinkley at Pecos in 1967 (see John MacGregor, "Original Church Discovered at Pecos," *The New Mexican*, August 6, 1967, pp. D1–D2, Santa Fe). After Mrs. Pinkley's death in 1969, Alden C. Hayes and Roland S. Richert completed the excavations for the Southwest Archaeological Center. Mr. Hayes generously sent his manuscript to me before publication. He notes (*The Four Churches of Pecos*, n.d., p. 6) that as chief archaeologist at Pecos for the National Park Service, Mrs. Pinkley began by trenching for the walls of the porter's lodge described by Domínguez in 1776. Hayes's summary of her results follows. Mrs. Pinkley "encountered massive masonry foundations at a level immediately below the footings of the standing church. More exploration resulted in the realization that she had found the southwest bell-tower of an older and much larger church. The remaining walls were traced to reveal that the earlier structure had burned and that another church was built to stand almost entirely within its nave."

Hayes concludes that four churches were built at Pecos. The first in 1619 was the adobe nave about a quarter of a mile northeast of the main quadrangle of the pueblo on a narrow ridge (S. A. Stubbs, B. T. Ellis, and A. E. Dittert, "The 'Lost' Pecos Church," *El Palacio* 64, 1957, nos. 3–4). The excavators believe it was built there before 1620, as a shortlived trial effort by a tyro upon bedrock unsuited for use as a cemetery, and far outside the pueblo.

The second church was the large buttressed structure begun by Fray Andrés Soárez in 1622, and discovered by Mrs. Pinkley. It corresponds to Benavides's description in 1634 (p. 67) as "a convent and church of peculiar construction and beauty, very spacious," by spanning a nave 40 feet wide.

After the events of the rebellion of 1680 and the reconquest of 1692, Soárez's large church, which must have resembled Tepeaca in Mexico, or Huejotzingo, lay in ruins. To replace it (according to Hayes), a small temporary chapel was erected among the ruins of the convents as the third church at Pecos. It remained in use only until 1705. The fourth structure arose in 1705. This is the church whose walls still stand, built inside the plan of Soárez's church, but facing the other way, with the entrance near the old sanctuary, and the new sanctuary at the old entrance. Hence the actual church walls at Pecos are of early eighteenth-century date. Mr. Hayes points out that the arched doorways of the eighteenth-century sanctuary of the fourth church were not true arches, but corbelled and trimmed to give a rounded effect (p. 67).

1968   Alden C. Hayes has also solved the problem of the 1629 *convento* at Las Humanas ("The Missing Convento of San Isidro," *El Palacio* 75, 1968, 35–40). Benavides said in 1634 that Fray Francisco Letrado had built a rectory, but Gordon Vivian did not find it when he cleaned out the church ruin in 1951 ("Excavations in a 17th Century Jumano Pueblo, Gran Quivira," National Park Service Archaeological Research

Series, no. 8, Washington). When Hayes excavated Mound 7 in 1965, it had been regarded as a house block of the pueblo. Facing the church, however, the house block corner contained eight rooms that had been adapted for use as a *convento* in 1629. Later on eight more European rooms were added, two with large fireplaces. This instance of the missionary use of native rooms exemplifies the initial stages of the original conversions with unprecedented details.

1971   The restoration report by Odd S. Halseth for the Laguna church, dated 1923, is published in *El Palacio* 77, 1971, p. 21, with a commentary by E. Boyd on the oeuvre of the anonymous Laguna Santero, whom she postulates as having introduced Salomonic columns in Santa Fe about 1798 and spreading the fashion to the western pueblos.

ETHNOGRAPHIC STUDIES

1953   The late Stephen F. de Borhegyi made an ethnographic study of the Esquipulas cult near Copan which was transplanted to Chimayo ("The Miraculous Shrines of Our Lord of Esquipulas in Guatemala and Chimayo," *El Palacio* 60, 1953, 23–111). In the course of his study of the church at Chimayo, Borhegyi provides a correct reading of the church-door inscriptions (p. 95).

1955   S. Buenaventura at Chimayo has been discussed by E. Boyd ("Repair of the Oratorio of S. Buenaventura at Chimayo," *El Palacio* 62, 1955, 99–101). She reports a ceiling dated 1873, in this room built as a private chapel for the Ortega family, and now used by the Carmel cofradía.

1964   An unexpected *morada* was discovered by Bainbridge Bunting (*Taos Adobes*, Santa Fe, 1964) at Arroyo Hondo, built in the 1850s in forms of colonial ancestry. His date for it may enshrine it among the most ancient examples of the type.

1968   Richard E. Ahlborn, in "The Penitente Moradas of Abiquíu" (*Contributions from the Museum of History and Technology, Paper 63*, Smithsonian Institution, Washington, 1968) has clarified the history of the cult, and documented its architectural forms as well as the objects used in the *moradas*. He takes issue with Fray Angelico Chavez (A. Chavez, "The Penitentes of New Mexico," *New Mexico Historical Review* 29, 1954, 97–123, p. 100) who regards "penitentism" as an importation from Mexico early in the nineteenth century, lacking origins in the Third Order of St. Francis. Ahlborn notes that flagellation and other practices resembling "penitentism" were witnessed and approved at Abiquíu by Fray Atanasio Domínguez in 1776. Indeed he traces the beginning of such local cult practices to the settlement of the Chama River soon after 1740 as a buffer zone between the Rio Grande towns and the marauding Indian groups to the northwest (cf. R. Fisher, "Notes on the Relation of the Franciscans to the Penitentes," *El Palacio* 48, 1941, 263–71).

One or two remarks in conclusion will put this book and its present edition into better perspective than without them.

The original study began in 1936 under the influence at Yale of Henri Focillon's seminars on Medieval architecture. This was when American graduate students during the Depression were returning, like many expatriates, to New World topics in a temper best described by Archibald MacLeish in *New Found Land* (1930). New Mexico seen from New England was then and still is the best entry into deep colonial time as well as into American antiquity.

The mission churches compounded neolithic and baroque worlds in forms of mud and wood that expressed both ancestries with the least waste. A. V. Kidder's *Pecos*, unforgettable and indestructible, led the way into the Pueblo past, and Robert Ricard's '*Conquête Spirituelle*' *du Mexique* explained the Mendicant mission. New Mexico led me back to sixteenth-century churches in Mexico (published in 1948); to the colonial Quechua (1946); then forward to Spanish architecture of 1500–1800 (1959); and back again into ancient American art and architecture (1962). *The Shape of Time* (1962) arose in part from the consideration of minimal change in New Mexican colonial churches during three centuries.

Most recently, a return to the study of minimal resources and maximal expression during an era of poverty in Portugal is about to appear (*Portuguese Plain Architecture, 1526–1706*, Wesleyan Press, 1972). This reverts to the questions that underlie *The Religious Architecture of New Mexico*: the interaction of local and alien traditions in building activity under minimal economic conditions; the relation of frugality to expression; the pluralism of "style" at any time and place; the permanence of efficient forms; and their relation to art's perfection. The humanistic translation of social-scientific data has been another continuing preoccupation since the 1930s.

This corrected edition owes its publication in part to the efforts of Paul Horgan and D. W. Schwartz. Alden Hayes generously sent me his unpublished manuscript on Pecos. Its 1622 church now emerges as the "prime object" in seventeenth-century New Mexico.

George Kubler
New Haven
January 13, 1972

PREFACE TO FIRST EDITION

THE religious architecture of New Mexico has hitherto received attention chiefly from historians, whose admirable studies discuss the organization and influence of the Church throughout the province.[1] Many others have written about the antiquity of the churches, or about the romantic aspects of Spanish influence in this country.[2] The churches themselves have never been considered pertinent to the history of building.[3] It therefore appeared to me that the monuments might be analyzed and classified according to their architectural aspect alone.

The casual visitor to New Mexico is rarely aware of such an aspect. During part of the year, the plastered earth walls may be discolored and rain-furrowed (Fig. 57). Often the sagging timbers, the ill-made tin or shingle roofs, and the unpainted commercial trim compose an impression of rustic disrepair. Even the neatly kept churches may disappoint the tourist: they are neither vast nor richly decorated. But he always responds to the spectacle of Acoma, dominating the gigantic boulder which is its pedestal (Fig. 170), with the massive forms of a clean, simple style of building. From the railroad, moreover, as he travels by San Felipe, the tan bulk of the church rides like a battleship among a fleet of barges, its terraced silhouette profiled against the black basalt of the mesa that crowds the pueblo into the river. And at Laguna, whose buildings huddle on a bald shelf of rock, the whited church evokes the profiles of no other architecture in the world.

Coherent, organized architectural form characterizes these churches. The material is the soil itself piled high and thick, pierced by few windows, with a roof line that recalls the deck levels of ships at sea upon the desert (Fig. 79). The scale of these buildings dominates the urban profile; where the town buildings hug the landscape in low files, the churches stand forth in a scale that is neither human nor canonical, but military and hieratic. Inside, the treatment of light is theatrical: the nave is cool and dark, but at the sanctuary there prevails an intense daylight, focused and concentrated by vertical skylights installed at the difference of roof level between the nave and the sanctuary (Figs. 93–96).

A closer examination of the older monuments reveals their construction as an unusual feat of European adaptation to limited materials and aboriginal techniques. There existed the fundamental problem of roofing a considerable span. It was necessary to adapt a system of fenestration which depended upon arched and domed construction to the trabeated construction of the Pueblo Indians. There are a few indications that effects of false perspective or

1. Shea, 1855. Salpointe, 1898. Scholes, 1928, 1929, 1930, 1932, 1935, 1935a, 1937. Davis, 1857, 1869. Bloom, 1913, 1914, 1923, 1928, 1930, 1931, 1933, 1935. Wuthenau, 1935. Stallings, 1937. Twitchell, 1911, 1912, 1914, 1914a, 1916, 1917, 1917a, 1917b, 1919. Ocaranza, 1934.

2. Governor Prince's work on the churches (Prince, 1915) contains summary descriptions of the monuments,

occasional documentation, and important photographs, but tends generally to anecdote and guidebook directions. See also Hallenbeck, 1926; Forrest, 1929; Vierra, 1918.

3. Invaluable material for such studies has been made available in the measured drawings prepared and issued by the Historic American Buildings Survey.

spatial illusion may have been attempted. Since its formulation in the early seventeenth century, the architectural type has persisted, unchanged but for the progressive coarsening of its early refinement.

In the treatment of an architecture of such limited means, the need for a carefully documented chronology does not seem great. Beyond a certain point of analysis, however, some recourse to documentary materials and techniques of dating was inevitable. The sluggish rate of change over a period of three hundred years, obvious from the first moments of study, then demanded the precise statement of a chronological table. To place the monuments in that order was simple enough: the table nevertheless falls far short of precision (p. 114). Most of the churches of the seventeenth century have been destroyed, and later monuments have undergone frequent repair and remodeling. For the villagers to rebuild a sacristy, enlarge the windows, or alter the silhouette of a parapet was the matter of a few days' work, and more often than not, no record was made of such changes in the fabric. It has been possible to present a few older drawings and photographs, together with the written sources. The latter, with few exceptions, are well known to students, and the excuse for adducing them here is that they may be useful as a collection referring solely to the monuments.

The method of presentation is an old-fashioned one for this class of studies. The treatment of the elements of the style is distinct from the historical documentation of individual buildings. Thus the descriptive section of the work is generalizing and unhistorical, while the historical section lacks the detail of archaeological description. The uniformity of the buildings within the style seemed, however, to warrant this treatment, and an attempt has been made in the Conclusion to reconcile descriptive generalization with the chronological catalogue. Essentially, it is the older French archaeological method of appending a *statistique monumentale* to the descriptive work. Although this method leads to confusion in the study of swiftly changing styles, I hope that clarity and ease of consultation will result from its use with this material, where the movements of style are imperceptibly slow over long reaches of time.

Certain classes of buildings have been omitted entirely or in part. The seventeenth-century ruins on the Hopi reservation in northeastern Arizona are closely related in kind to those of New Mexico. The forthcoming report of the Jeddito Project of Peabody Museum at Awatovi will throw much light upon the mission area at that site.[4] Little has been said about the Penitente *morada* structures. Materials for the study of the cult are available in the State Museum of New Mexico and the Taylor Museum in Colorado Springs; its architectural style is closer to the domestic architecture of New Mexico than to the churches. The chronological catalogue makes no exhaustive mention of the many destroyed churches. Wherever possible, known features of such monuments are mentioned in the general discussion, but the chronological list contains mainly the edifices of which material remains or adequate docu-

4. Brew, 1939, pp. 108–110, indicates features at Awatovi which are unprecedented in New Mexico proper: "an entrance-way with two columns," and "two round towers," as well as "a private friar's choir to the right of the main altar." Further, the fabric was probably in use during the Rebellion, 1680–92. A short account of the Jeddito Project occurs in Fisher, 1937.

mentary notices exist. Future field work may, of course, augment this catalogue. Many modern churches, furthermore, receive no mention because of their conformity to types which are unrelated to the one under discussion.

I am grateful to Archbishop Gerken for his letter of introduction to the governors of the pueblos. Archbishop Gerken also extended his permission to examine the archives of the Archdiocese in Santa Fe. The Very Reverend Monsignor P. F. Mahoney, and Father Garcia, secretary to the Archbishop in 1935, were most generous with their time and help. Mr. W. S. Stallings, Jr., of the Laboratory of Anthropology, gave me his friendly permission to use dendrochronological datings from the churches. He also contributed much of his crowded time to the reading of the manuscript. Many of the photographs come from his scholarly collection.

Professor Henri Focillon gave his direction to the study at Yale: his method has contributed whatever clarity the work may offer. To Professor Marcel Aubert, at Yale, I am indebted for instruction and guidance. Mr. S. L. Faison, of Williams College, Mr. C. L. V. Meeks, of Yale, Mr. France V. Scholes, and Dr. Lansing B. Bloom were kind enough to read and improve the manuscript. For many photographs and communications I owe thanks to Mr. J. H. Toulouse, Jr., whose work at Abó was in progress during the writing; to Mr. John Gaw Meem, who gave me access to his valuable files in Santa Fe; to the Museum of the American Indian, Heye Foundation, New York City; to Mr. Paul Child; to the staff of the State Museum in Santa Fe; to Father Hartmann, who was curate at Isleta in 1935; and to Mr. E. G. Thomas. In its present form, the work was presented as a dissertation for the Degree of Doctor of Philosophy in Yale University.

Porfirio Montoya, Governor of Santa Ana in 1938, has been a good and helpful friend. Finally, the realization of this volume has been made possible through the efforts of the staff of the Taylor Museum, especially Mr. and Mrs. Mitchell Wilder, whose suggestions figure prominently throughout the following pages. Miss Olive Bradley, of the Taylor Museum, typed and clarified the text. Mrs. Wilder prepared several plans and the folding map. Many of the photographs were made for this book by Mr. Wilder, without whose friendly collaboration the text would be much less complete. The book has been designed by Mr. Carl Purington Rollins of the Yale University Press.

G. K.

New Haven, Connecticut
  April 30, 1940

CONTENTS

PART ONE
THE MISSIONARY ENTERPRISE

PART TWO
THE ARCHITECTURE

CONTENTS   xix

PART THREE
THE BUILDINGS

ILLUSTRATIONS

Numbers 1 to 42 are figures in the text; the succeeding numbers refer to collotype plates following the text.

PART ONE
THE MISSIONARY ENTERPRISE

CHAPTER I

THE FORMATIVE STAGE
1598–1680

I.

IN the southwestern United States, the civilization of English-speaking peoples lies thinly over the broken topography of a provincial Hispanic frontier. In the long, beautiful mountain valleys which terrace away from the banks of the upper Rio Grande, villages exist where English is an alien tongue, spoken by none of the inhabitants. Beneath this Latin-American frontier society, still caught in the atmosphere of a rural eighteenth century, there survives an autochthonous culture, tribally diverse, enjoying for the moment at least a political and social separatism that clashes with the enveloping ethnic groups. Centuries ago, the hybridization of this culture, or system of related cultures, was attempted; the process has never reached completion, and today the stratifications of occupancy, like certain geological formations, are clear both in plan and in section. The immediacy of raw contrasts is unparalleled: the stratification has no great chronological depth, but the projection of various time patterns upon the present is in good focus. Today, segments of neolithic, Counter Reformation, industrial feudalism, vagrant bourgeoisie are juxtaposed in a swaying pattern, maintained by the spaciousness of the land and the invisible guy wires of the federal structure. In this panorama of partial civilizations, softened for our eyes only by the flat, overlying tones of Anglo-Saxon, Protestant culture, New Mexico occupies a unique position.

Once no European knew or chose to know its limits, and the "Kingdom of New Mexico" extended northward without definition, embracing theoretical civilizations and uncounted riches.[1] In actuality, the Spanish colonization covered a large "cross-shaped" area,[2] following the drainage of the upper Rio Grande, and reaching out laterally to the eastern and western settlements of high indigenous culture (Fig. 1). The whole area was occupied by the Pueblo tribes, sedentary, agricultural people dwelling in permanent villages of stone or adobe. In 1540, when Coronado first visited New Mexico, the Pueblo Indians probably numbered between 20,000 and 30,000, living in some seventy settlements and divided in distinct linguistic groups. The missionary colonization began during the early years of the seventeenth century, principally along the Rio Grande between Taos and Senecu, eastward to the Galisteo basin, the Pecos valley, and the Salinas plains, westward as far as the Zuñi, and the Hopi towns of Arizona.

This spatial extension obeys a principle evident throughout the New World in the first

---

1. Alcedo, 1788, p. 183. "Confina por el S con las Provincias de Sinaloa, Nueva Viscaya y Nuevo Reyno de Leon; por el S y SE con la Florida; por el NE con el Canada o Nueva Francia; y por el O. NO. y SO con las Californias extendiendose por el N, cuyos limites se ignoran todavia." (Cited from Ayer, 1916, p. 211.)

2. Friar Juan de Prada, 1638, *apud* Maas, 1929, p. 20. Hackett, 1937, p. 107. The comparison to a cross is figurative. At all times, large unsettled gaps of desert interrupted any continuity, and the eastern frontier, by comparison with the western, ran but 30 to 40 miles east of the Rio Grande axis, and parallel with it (Fig. 1).

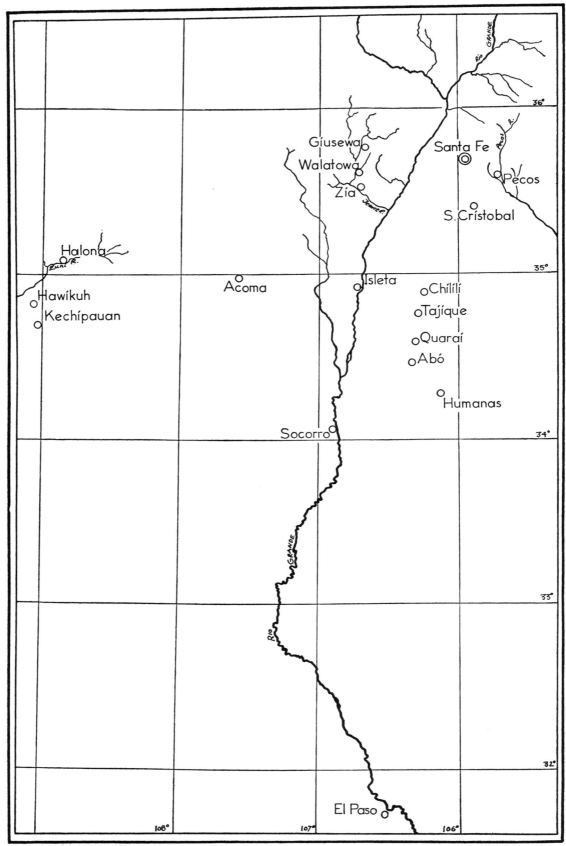

1. Seventeenth-century mission remains in New Mexico.

century following the generation of the Conquest: the allocation of permanent Hispanic administrative centers is predetermined by the already existing local urbanism. That is, two distribution charts, one showing late pre-Conquest cities of permanent monumental character, and the other showing early Spanish urban foundations, will coincide almost exactly, self-evidently because of the determinism set into motion by the presence or absence of an urbanized population and a trained supply of building labor. Later, of course, an improved technique of missionary colonization, such as that of Father Serra in California, and an advanced system for exploiting remote natural resources broke down this rule; in New Mexico, however, the significant fact is that a high local culture precipitated the colonization of the area a century and a half earlier than elsewhere in the southwestern United States, and that the technique of this colonization, especially in its architectural aspect, adhered to the "primitive" [3] era of the Church in Mexico. It is to be borne in mind that the portrait of New Mexico in the early colonial period has nothing in common with the colonial landscape in other southwestern states: chronological priority, ecological differences, and an authentically local tonality of colonial life distinguish it once and for all from southern Arizona, eastern Texas, and southern California in the eighteenth century.

2.

NEW MEXICO really possesses the earliest extensive European occupancy within the present boundaries of the United States. The historical antecedents of this primitive "Europeanization" are to be sought in Mexico proper. We are not concerned here with the definition of secular problems in the early history of New Mexico. The architecture which is the subject of this study was produced between the incoming churchmen and the resident natives; civil authorities had less than nothing to do with it. In a larger sense, furthermore, missionary history and colonial history are nearly identical at this period. Nothing about sixteenth- and early seventeenth-century Hispanic America can be understood without constant reference to the missionary activity responsible for the actual realization of the colonial *modus vivendi*.

Hence Ricard's thorough study of the "Golden Age" or "primitive" period of the Church in Mexico[4] partly illuminates the motivation of the colonization in the Pueblo area. To the Spanish invaders of the seventeenth century, the economic value of New Mexico was negligible. Its minerals were difficult to exploit, agriculture was limited, and commerce consisted in trivial barter. The only justification for its occupation was its character as a missionary area.[5] According to Ricard, the fundamental purpose of missionary activity is the foundation and organization of the Church: ideally its object is the development of a native clergy from which the bishops may ultimately be chosen. The founders and organizers of the early Church in Mexico were the Mendicant Orders, Franciscans, Dominicans, and Augustinians, who accomplished their work of spiritual conquest independently of episcopal authority. In this aspect, the "primitive" period of the American Church is exactly limited to the period 1523–72. The earliest systematic evangelizations began in Mexico in 1523. In 1572, the progressive secularization of the Indian communities was undertaken by the Jesuits, and the Metropolitan See of Mexico itself was held for the first time by a secular archbishop. This program forced the Mendicant Orders to withdraw from the ministry, either to their con-

---

3. Ricard, 1933, pp. viii–xi.   4. Ricard, 1933.   5. Scholes, 1935, p. 96.

ventual retreats, or to distant, unconverted countries. New Mexico was one of these, and the methods employed there by the friars were the same which had been used to convert and consolidate the congregations of Mexico proper.[6]

Thus we shall find, in the architectural expression of this displacement, not only the building forms of the sixteenth century, surviving because of their suitability to the program of incipient conversion, but also an increment of seventeenth-century forms. Both vocabularies will be seen to undergo transformations traceable to limited materials and the passive influence exercised upon construction by indigenous workmen. In other words, a recently discarded technique of colonization, a desolately poor countryside, and the passive resistance of a native race contributed to the formation of the style of architecture under discussion.

In New Mexico, as elsewhere in New Spain, missionary effort preceded the economic exploitation of the inhabitants by the civil authorities. The missionary effort, of course, came to constitute a form of exploitation in itself, but at the beginning, issues other than economic ones were involved, and Benavides no doubt speaks truly when he represents that the friars denied themselves food and clothing during the first campaigns of evangelization.[7] The religious body responsible for the conversion of the Pueblo Indians was the Order of the Friars of the Regular Observance of Saint Francis. Discounting the sporadic missionary efforts before 1607,[8] the extent and number of the conversions effected by 1626 was not inconsiderable. Zarate Salmerón,[9] using baptismal registers for his report written about 1629, states that 34,650 persons had been baptized, a number somewhat larger than the maximum estimated aboriginal population in 1540. Radiating at first from San Gabriel, and after 1609 from Santa Fe,[10] the friars took Christian teachings over an increasing area. By 1611, the Keres and Rio Grande Tiwa tribes had been indoctrinated, and in 1613, the Salinas tribes and Isleta were brought into the missionary program. A regular supply service from Mexico was established in 1617,[11] and Pecos, Taos, and the Jemez tribes were gradually won over. This supply service left Mexico City every four years,[12] and a royal grant to the friars from the Real Hacienda of Mexico varied around 60,000 pesos triennially.[13] The subsidy itself demonstrates that no immediate economic advantage motivated the evangelization. Ten years of unremitting labor lay behind these achievements. In short, the process of conversion, and of establishing the administrative machinery for an ambitious program, was by no means so rapid as it had been in the early years of the Mexican Church, a century earlier.[14]

3.

In a sense, the Franciscans were on trial, and New Mexico was their first major undertaking since the secularization of 1572. It was to their interest, therefore, to consolidate their holdings, especially when the truth concerning New Mexico's poor resources had become known.[15] Benavides gives a brief view of the actual methods used.[16] The care of the sick and poor in the pueblos entailed a reorganization of the tribal economy. Livestock, new crops, and European methods of cultivation were introduced. Scattered Indians were brought to live together in new settlements. The building of the church and priest's house was generally

6. Ricard, 1933, pp. viii–xi.
7. Ayer, 1916, p. 66.
8. Idem, p. 195.
9. Zarate Salmerón, 1899, p. 341.
10. Scholes, 1937, p. 21.
11. Scholes, 1930.
12. Scholes, 1937, p. 69.
13. Hackett, 1912, p. 147.
14. Ricard, 1933, p. 104.
15. Scholes, 1937, p. 19.
16. Ayer, 1916, pp. 66–68, 170–173.

undertaken by the single friar assigned to a district. Instruction was given in many different crafts, as well as in reading, writing, and music. The entire settlement, with all these activities, with its church and conventual buildings, was the *mission,* a term often misused to describe the religious edifices alone.

Elsewhere Benavides describes some aspects of the construction of the churches.[17] A peculiar, but not unique, situation existed at this time. The custom was for the women, boys, and girls to build walls. Men considered this a disgraceful occupation, and confined themselves to war, hunting, spinning, and weaving, although they took readily to carpentry and other crafts. Thus the fabric of the churches was the work principally of women, while the woodwork was evidently produced by men. In some ways, these conditions favored the friars. A building project had to be executed by the entire population, men, women, and children. That their participation was voluntary may be inferred from the fact that the work was often done at the suggestion of a lone man, or at most, two or three friars, numerically incapable of forcing labor from their charges. The paltry size of the garrison in Santa Fe,[18] and its remoteness from most of the missions, would have made coercion sporadic at best. In any case, total reliance on native labor was unavoidable, given the limitations not only of the European personnel but of the population at large. About fifty churches had been built by 1628,[19] under the direction of twenty-six friars, of whom only eight had been in the province since 1609,[20] and twelve of these arrived late in 1625.[21]

During the first decades of Spanish colonization in Mexico and South America, professional architects and engineers brought building knowledge to the new provinces.[22] Such was not the case in seventeenth-century New Mexico. No secular building experts, no engineers entered New Mexico among the early colonists. The friars were left to their own devices, with the result that each missionary established the program, evolved the design, and superintended the construction and decoration of the church at his post. The combined efforts of all the friars constitute a homogeneous style, marked by occasional variants and experiments. It would be of interest to determine the intellectual history of this style, but no pertinent record of the leading personalities or of group deliberations seems to have been made. Sketches, and detailed records of seventeenth-century building operations, with the exception of the passage cited from Benavides, are at present completely unknown. All that can be done is to examine the material equipment of the friars, and to relate the scanty biographies of individual friars with the churches attributed to them.

By the terms of a viceregal contract made in Mexico City in 1631, the King of Spain assumed the expenses of equipment and supplies for the religious establishment of New Mexico. The contract provided that there should be given each friar, the first time that he went to the province, a quantity of tools and materials for building his church. These included "for every friar, for building his church," ten axes, three adzes, three spits (spades),

17. Idem, p. 33.

18. Bandelier, 1890, p. 228. Usually 100 men, in the eighteenth century. The garrisons consisted of professional soldier-citizens, who held and farmed the land as *encomenderos*. Their military duty consisted in frontier-guard and escort duty for the friars. Scholes, 1930, p. 98.

The religious establishments provided for their use in Santa Fe have been studied by Wuthenau, 1935.

19. Ayer, 1916, p. 33. Zarate Salmerón, 1899, p. 341, gives 43 churches, in 1626.

20. Scholes, 1937, p. 20.

21. Idem, p. 97.

22. Noel and Torre Revello, 1934.

ten hoes, one medium-sized saw, one chisel, two augers, and one plane. A large latch for the church door, two small locks, a dozen hinges, some small latches, and 6,000 nails of various sizes were also included in the contract.[23] These provisions were decreed some years after the intense building activity reported by Benavides[24] and Zarate Salmerón,[25] and it is reasonable to assume that they represent no more meager equipment than that used in the 1620's. The only finished building materials that figure in this list are articles of small hardware. Everything else was to be manufactured on the spot, with the simple hand tools provided by the government. Pulley blocks and other hoisting devices, if they were used, were contrived by the ingenuity of the friars.

4.

LITTLE by little, then, a picture of the activity of the early Franciscans can be reconstructed. Aside from the task of diverting a massive population from its ancient beliefs, these men executed ambitious building projects for which they themselves were the architects, contractors, foremen, and building-supply agents. Most of them were highly educated men, and in some cases later became important figures in the administration of the Order. Nearly all of them were Europeans by birth.[26] Francisco de Velasco held the title of *lector iubilatus,* granted in the ultramontane branch of the Order to teachers of special distinction, whose preparation included three years of philosophical and twelve years of theological studies.[27] Tomás Manso, who later (1656) became Bishop of Nicaragua, was *procurador* of the province in the 1630's, and administered the mission supply service.[28] Roque de Figueredo, whom Hodge thinks responsible, with Agustin de Cuellar, for the building of churches among the Zuñi tribes,[29] was one of the *definitores* of the Province of the Holy Gospel in Mexico, a position involving doctrinal responsibilities.[30] Juan de Salas, whose name is associated with the building of Isleta,[31] may have been *provincial* of Jalisco and Michoacan between 1603 and 1607,[32] an office analogous to that of a territorial Governor. Unfortunately little is known about the education of the other men whose building activity was extensive, beyond that they usually attended the missionary college in the Convento of Saint Francis in Mexico City.[33]

Evidence exists, however, that Figueredo, for instance, was a person of considerable literacy, linguistic proficiency, and musical skill.[34] Another musician was Miguel de Guevara, mentioned in 1665 for his special skill at notation.[35] Friar Alonso Gil de Avila, who was posted at Senecu in 1676, had been a captain of cuirassiers in Flanders and Catalonia.[36] On the other hand, the many enemies of the friars among the civil population reported unfavorably upon their character. Typical is the abuse poured upon them by the infamous Mendizabal, who, while Governor in 1663, wrote that the friars were "sailors, artillery-men, and men of ill-repute, engaged in evil pursuits. . . . They served no novitiate, and were without religion, which they did not understand, but took orders only to avoid work and live with greater

23. Scholes, 1930, pp. 103–104.
24. Ayer, 1916, p. 33.
25. Zarate Salmerón, 1899, p. 341.
26. Bandelier, 1890, p. 228.
27. Scholes, 1930, p. 99. Holzapfel, 1909, pp. 569–570.
28. Scholes, 1937, p. 186.
29. Hodge, 1937, p. 96.

30. Holzapfel, 1909, p. 455.
31. Vetancurt, 1697, p. 99.
32. Ayer, 1916, p. 199.
33. Vetancurt, 1697, *passim.*
34. Hodge, 1937, pp. 78–91.
35. Hackett, 1937, p. 266.
36. Idem, p. 297.

liberty than in worldly pursuits." [37] Against such statements there is the reliable testimony of the missions and churches.

Nothing has been said about the architectural knowledge or training of the friars. If their status as men of education be admitted, it must follow that they were capable of acquiring the principles of construction. As Gillet[38] has pointed out in the case of the religious architecture of the sixteenth century in Mexico, the friars were self-trained architects, *artistes d'occasion,* working out their solutions in direct practice. But they occasionally had the benefit of Spanish workmen, quarry workers and stonemasons, to instruct the Indians in special techniques. Even then, design and the theory of construction were independently acquired. An illustrious case was that of Friar Francisco de Tembleque, who built the 45-kilometer aqueduct of Otumba in seventeen years. In New Mexico, the situation was generically similar. Certain architectural elements based partly upon native practice, and partly upon formal conventions inherited from Europe, were organized by nonprofessional designers into a coherent, practical system. The solution can have been worked out only during construction itself, by men of exceptional teaching and creative ability. Exactly who they were cannot now be determined among the poorly documented names: Alonso Peinado at Santa Fe and Chilili before 1617, Estevan de Perea at Sandia in 1609, Cristobal de Quiros at Zia, Ascencio de Zarate at Picuris, Martin de Arvide among the Jemez, Juan de Escalona at Santo Domingo before 1607, Alonso de Lugo at Jemez before 1601, Cristobal de Quiñones at San Felipe before 1609, Juan de Salas at Isleta in 1629, Geronimo de Zarate Salmerón among the Jemez before 1626, Antonio de Arteaga at Senecu in 1630, Francisco de Letrado and Diego de Santander at Humanas, Francisco de Acevedo at Abó, Tenabó, and Tabirá before 1659, Garcia de San Francisco y Zuñiga at Socorro and at El Paso in 1662, Juan Ramirez of Oaxaca at Acoma, Roque de Figueredo at Hawikuh, Francisco de Porras at Awatovi in 1629.

37. Idem, p. 225.   38. Gillet, 1929, p. 1030.

CHAPTER II

CIVIL CONFLICT. RECENT HISTORY

I.

INEXTRICABLY bound with this positive program of building and organization there figures a bizarre conflict between the ecclesiastical authorities and the civil government. The construction of churches and conventual buildings was a major concern of the friars. The ambitious scale of many projects necessitated taking large numbers of Indians from other work; once the mission was built, servants had to be provided for the clergy, and exempted from further tribute.[1] Although the civil authorities were instructed to aid missionary enterprise in every way, the expanding economy of the colonists, in stock raising and lands, was fundamentally at variance with that of the missionaries, who stood together, as independent of external episcopal authority as their predecessors had been in Mexico before 1572. Serious conflict soon embroiled the affairs of the province, as with the burning of the church at San Diego de los Jemez, about 1623, by Indians encouraged from the Governor's Palace in Santa Fe.[2] The governors not only sabotaged the missions, but themselves engaged in the crudest methods of expropriating and enslaving the native population, assisted by equally corrupt minor officials. Reconciliation between Church and State was impossible, and civil war was nearly precipitated in 1640, under the administration of Governor Rosas. The exact course of these events and the role played by the Inquisition after 1650 form the substance of Mr. Scholes's studies, and their recapitulation has no place here.[3] The effect upon missionary activity, however, was disastrous: early in the century, the Indians, realizing that the civil jurisdiction would not support and protect the religious establishments in which their only security was to be found, grew restless, and occasionally even abandoned the mission sites to return to their old villages, as among the Zuñi tribes in 1635.[4] To human disorders, others came: famine in 1670 and pestilence in 1671.[5] Along with these troubles went the catastrophic inroads made by Apache raiders upon the missionary settlements. Between 1672 and 1676, the populous frontier towns in the Salinas district, large by provincial standards, and provided with really magnificent stone churches, were depopulated once and for all.[6] The story is a tragic one: the garrison in Santa Fe was too poorly manned to send help, and the Custodian, Father Ayeta, was obliged to return the long road to Mexico City to get reinforcements. When he returned in 1676, with a detachment consisting of convicts, it was too late, and the work of two whole generations had perished.[7]

By 1680, the tension between Indians and Spaniards, who had long since forfeited their authority in the murderous squabbles among themselves, grew to such a pitch that after several preparatory attempts, the Indians revolted. Their underground conspiracy included the most powerful tribes and was conducted with great strategic skill. Several hundred Spaniards were killed and the rest abandoned the land, fleeing to El Paso, nearly four hundred miles south of Santa Fe.[8] The Indians retained their independence for twelve years, torn by

1. Scholes, 1937, p. 13.
2. Scholes, 1938, p. 68.
3. Scholes, 1937.
4. Idem, p. 108.
5. Scholes, 1930, p. 400.
6. Hackett, 1937, pp. 297–298.
7. Ibid.
8. Hackett, 1912.

discordant factions and unbalanced personalities. During this period, otherwise fascinating phenomena of cultural trauma and maladjustment may be detected through the scanty record; for our purposes, however, the mutilation and partial destruction of nearly all the churches needs to be reckoned with. In 1692, the Spaniards, under the command of General de Vargas, reconquered the province and settled it anew.[9] In 1696,[10] revolt broke out again in the missions, involving new damage to the churches.

2.

THE early years of the eighteenth century were relatively peaceful under the beneficent administration of Governor Cuervo y Valdez,[11] although the general affairs of the province soon resumed the pattern of raw disorder which had characterized the previous century. The records[12] are filled with accounts of renewed conflict between civil and religious authorities; the friars accused temporal officers of destructive interference, and the governors complained of the indolence and dissoluteness of the priests. About 1730, a long controversy broke out.[13] The Bishop of Durango, insisting upon his right to control ecclesiastic affairs in the remote province, brought serious charges against the friars. No decision was reached, but the number of missions and friars was reduced. In 1767, orders were issued to secularize the important establishments in Santa Fe, Santa Cruz, Albuquerque, and El Paso.[14] In the meanwhile, the Indians chafed under renewed oppression. Sporadic revolts occurred, subdued by deportation and massacre. In 1780–81, an epidemic of smallpox decimated the native population to such an extent that the government ordered the concentration of the surviving population into twenty missions, the remainder of the stations being abandoned.[15] The raids of nomad tribes increased in number and violence, and the Spanish military organization was unable to control their incursions. The remote cause was the dissolution of Spanish power in Europe. Nearer home, an effective factor was the continued isolation of the province from any important center of civilization. The only link with Mexico was the annual trade caravan which attended the January fair in Chihuahua, 700 miles away, over desert and mountainous country.[16] California and Missouri were even more remote, across unknown country, and trade with them was suppressed by the official policy forbidding all commerce other than that carried on with provinces to the south.[17] Finally, complete secularization of the missions was effected in 1834, against the protest of the friars.[18] Theoretically, the lands and resources of the missions were the property of the Indians, held in trust for them by the fathers. Secularization meant the return of mission property to the Indians, and their liberation from the control of the Order. In 1833, moreover, the Congress of Mexico had enacted laws curtailing the appropriations for the support of the churches and clergy.[19] The mission era was at an end, and the churches and conventual establishments rapidly fell into worse disrepair than since the Rebellion, although maintained here and there by small groups of the faithful.

9. Vargas, 1914a.

10. Twitchell, 1916.

11. Hackett, 1937, pp. 367–369.

12. Idem, pp. 438–459.

13. Bancroft, 1889, pp. 204–241.

14. Idem, p. 274. On earlier proposals for secularization, in 1750, see Hackett, 1937, pp. 450–451.

15. Hodge, 1907, p. 893, article "Missions."

16. Ayer, 1916, p. 236. Twitchell, 1925, pp. 157–158.

17. Bandelier, 1890, p. 227.

18. Bloom, 1914, pp. 359–360.

19. Salpointe, 1898, p. 165.

To be sure, some of these factors—conflict between the civil and ecclesiastical jurisdictions, nomad raids and ineffective protection, native insurrections, and virtual isolation from the central administration—were more disastrous in the seventeenth century than in the eighteenth.[20] But these were constant elements in Spanish colonial activity throughout the New World, and the differences are those of degree rather than kind. In New Mexico, a special consequence of the events of the eighteenth century was the gradual decay and suppression of the mission establishments, a process uninterrupted by that phase of enormous affluence which characterized the monastic economy in other parts of New Spain during the eighteenth century.

3.

THE most significant immediate aspect of the occupation of New Mexico in 1848 by American armed forces was a rapid increase of population. By 1860, the number of people resident in New Mexico had risen from 42,000 in 1822[21] to 80,567.[22] The increase was probably directly due to the long-drawn process of occupation, which found definitive expression in 1848, but had been progressing gradually since 1821 with the establishment of regular trade between New Mexico and Missouri.[23] The static population of the colonial period,[24] always much smaller than during the nineteenth century, had made the production of food an occupation absorbing most of the energies of the residents, and with the nineteenth-century immigration from the United States, larger numbers of people were released for other pursuits. The development of new industries and the exploitation of previously neglected resources immediately resulted. A certain amount of building, in the long-established style, was carried on during the early years of American occupation, but new tendencies were realized only after the arrival of Bishop Lamy in 1851,[25] when an extensive campaign of repairs and new building was initiated under the standard of French nineteenth-century taste. Parish priests arrived from France, and French architects were brought to New Mexico for the construction of the Cathedral in Santa Fe.[26] Beside these French influences, the Americans contributed relatively little to the style of the mid-nineteenth century. Fortunately, however, the military penetration produced a profusion of careful observations on the state of older monuments. This group of American army officers has perhaps no equivalent in the military history of the country. From Pike through Bourke, two generations of trained, observant travelers compiled journals and notes. Thus Abert, Simpson, Emory, Carleton, and Sitgreaves are often the only sources for much that has since been lost.

In general, the meeting of the two traditions, Catholic and Hispanic, Anglo-Saxon and Protestant, resulted in little violence, but the long-established frontier society of colonial times was slowly driven to the mountains or left behind in the dusty, moldering "old town" of the cities. It is a culture that figures less and less in the actual affairs of the State, but its permanent record survives in the earthen architecture of the Mexican villages and Indian pueblos.

20. Scholes, 1935a, pp. 195–196.
21. Bloom, 1913, p. 30.
22. Twitchell, 1912, p. 414, n. 340.
23. Sister Mary Loyola, 1939, pp. 42–43.
24. Hackett, 1937, pp. 25, 495, 500.

25. Twitchell, 1912, p. 331.
26. Twitchell, 1912, p. 344. The cornerstone of the Cathedral was laid on July 14, 1869. The architects were Antoine Mouly and his son Projectus, using a building stone quarried near Santa Fe.

PART TWO
THE ARCHITECTURE

CHAPTER I

EMPLACEMENT

1.

THE term *emplacement* is used here to signify the general problem of accommodating a proposed edifice, of which the design is already foreseen, to an existing architectural group, and to certain preconceptions concerning the proper location of religious buildings. Thus the question of the *distribution* of the churches in New Mexico depends upon some study of previous urban movements. The *location* of the buildings, with reference to specific Indian settlements, involves political and economic possibilities which it is necessary to explore. The variable factor of the *orientation* of the monuments, finally, evokes a few problems in the history of Christian architecture in Europe.

2.

Distribution. The character of Pueblo urbanism at the time of the Conquest, in the last years of the sixteenth century, is fundamental to an understanding of the missionary program and activity during subsequent periods. The culture takes its name from this urbanism, because the town concept and plan are an essential aspect of the life of the people. The pueblo itself[1] is a group of cellular community dwellings, built of stone or sun-dried clay, formed by the repeated addition of new chambers. Continuous party walls run throughout the structure in horizontal and vertical extension (Fig. 43). The plan generally includes open spaces between the "apartment houses" formed in this manner; esplanades between the long rows of buildings, as at Acoma (Fig. 44), and courts which may be completely enclosed or open on one or more sides, as at Quarai (Fig. 45). The genesis of these distinct types of plan, in rows, about courts, or block-shaped, is unknown. Each settlement appears to have been autonomous then as now, exercising a primitive agrarian collectivism, maintaining few relations with other settlements, and containing a highly organized social and ritual life.

Although large tracts of heavily forested land exist within the Pueblo area, chiefly on the slopes of the Rio Grande watershed, the greater part of the countryside is arid, thinly vegetated, and poorly watered. Near the streams, however, where the land is open and relatively flat, the soil is fertile, and with deep planting and careful cultivation, will bear the extensive corn crops that form the chief sustenance of the settlements. But likely sites for this type of agriculture often were never settled, and others seem to have been briefly occupied, then abandoned. Hence ecology alone will not explain the compact form, specialized structure, and erratic distribution of the pueblos.

A constant threat to this farming people was the nomadic hunting tribe, pressing in upon settled areas in search of the stored corn and other accumulations made by the sedentary people. Castañeda tells of such raids in 1540,[2] with the consequent depopulation of villages in

1. Brew, 1937, p. 133.   2. Winship, 1896, pp. 323, 324.

the Rio Grande district. The menace was also present in a more remote antiquity. Kidder[3] has shown that the shrinkage of the Pueblo culture area in archaeological history was probably due to nomadic influences that also determined the formation of large isolated urban communities, built for defensive occupation, but readily and frequently abandoned. The colonizing missionaries, then, found the Pueblo tribes still living in the shadow of their old enemy, maintaining a defensive society in relatively permanent urban establishments, such as Castaño de Sosa found in 1590,[4] provided with breastworks, and wooden bridges running from house to house across intersecting streets. But the town itself appears to have been a matter for little concern, according to our standards: durable as it was, it served as a transitory housing for the really permanent societal values. The history of the movements of the rebellious tribes after 1680 is most interesting in this connection; whole new towns were built after the expulsion of the Spaniards, as at Ashtialakwa[5] in the Jemez district, or at the village on the Red Mesa,[6] four leagues from Zia. The pre-Rebellion towns were still serviceable, but contaminated by alien occupancy, and the renewed attacks of nomads led to an apparent migratory attitude, for cultural and physical self-preservation.

Such was the situation faced by the early Spaniards. A sparsely populated, hostile, and economically unprofitable area lay before them. Its inhabitants knew and cared little about one another; there was no possibility of dominating a potent territorial chief and then using him to secure control over subordinate tribes. One by one the settlements had to be approached and subjected. Once the area had been brought under control, measures had to be taken to concentrate and stabilize its population. The execution of this aspect of the program devolved upon the friars. The *reducciones* were one of their achievements, and another was the application of an economic fixative to fluid populations, in the form of the mission establishments. The *reducción* provided security for previously scattered villages. Under Spanish direction it was a continuation of the prehistoric process of shrinkage and defensive concentration. The process is documented for the Jemez district,[7] where two preliminary campaigns of evangelization (1598–1601 and 1621–23) were abandoned for lack of adequate personnel. When the work was resumed in 1626,[8] the tribes had been scattered and decimated, but were successfully concentrated in two pueblos which henceforth flourished. On the other hand, it happened that the resettlements entailed the sacrifice of many crops for several seasons, with severe economic consequences, affecting particularly the relations between the missions and the civil government. But the mission establishment brought unquestioned advantages; occasionally, in frontier posts, such as San José at Giusewa (Fig. 118), a small garrison and the formidable church structure were provided for the protection of the neighborhood. Everywhere, domesticated animals, new crops and food plants, as well as the European utensils and techniques, accrued to Indians from their contact with the friars.

No *reducción* pueblo has been exhaustively studied for its plan, but it appears that a settlement such as that at Giusewa simply occupied previously extant dwellings,[9] and when new settlements were built for the *reducción*, as at San Diego de la Congregación de los Jemez in 1626, the indigenous plan and technique were used. We have no evidence that Hispanic town

3. Kidder, 1924, pp. 125-128.
4. Hull, 1916.
5. Reiter, 1938, p. 37.
6. Bandelier, 1892*a*, p. 195.

7. Bloom and Mitchell, 1938. Reiter, 1938. Scholes, 1938.
8. Ayer, 1916, p. 29.
9. Reiter, 1938, p. 88.

and house plans were imposed upon the settlements of Indians anywhere in the Pueblo area, although this had commonly been the practice of the Franciscans in Mexico during the six-teenth century, as at Acambaro, or Huejotzingo after 1529.[10] The situation in New Mexico provokes reflection: did the friars recognize the propriety of the planning habits of their charges; did the Indians reject alien methods; were the missionaries to New Mexico the intellectual inferiors of their predecessors in Mexico;[11] or was the necessary authority lacking in the relations between friars and Indians? The last seems unlikely, given the evidence of the churches. It is unrealistic to question the intelligence or training of the pioneer missionaries. The churches again refute the second hypothesis, although domestic building habits, once established, are tenacious. Probably the situation arises from mutual respect; the Indians accepting outside influences where these affected no traditional building form, and the friars in turn tolerating the age-old communal dwelling, quickly and easily constructed.

The concentration of the population reduced the need for a great number of missions; the modest personnel of the Franciscan enterprise naturally made any great number impossible. There remained, however, the vastness of the country itself, and its resources, which were placed to make major shifts of occupation impossible. Beyond a certain point, these condi-tions could not be trimmed or fitted to the friars' convenience. The actual distribution of the mission sites was therefore the resolution of a problem involving personnel, areal extent, and population density. Ricard,[12] in his studies of the Mexican aspect of this question as it existed in the sixteenth century, has proposed three classes of mission establishments: *missions d'occupation,* clustered together in a densely settled area; *missions de pénétration,* usually of impermanent character, in difficult outposts; and *missions de liaison,* providing links in a chain between the first two types and the center of administration. Of course, each type may be subject to historical change: the *mission de pénétration* characterizes the period of conquest in a local definition, but may later become *mission d'occupation,* and so on. These categories may be established for New Mexico, without special difficulty or the evocation of new types. The complicating factor is the rapidly shifting character of many establishments. A typical *mission d'occupation* was the principal *convento* of Saint Francis in Santa Fe, mentioned as a new structure in February, 1639;[13] others would be the group of establishments at San Ildefonso, Santa Clara, and San Juan de los Caballeros, above Santa Fe in the Rio Grande valley. Liaison institutions between these centers existed at Pojoaque, Tesuque, and Nambé, providing not only local services, but facilities for communication. A typical *mission de pénétration* was the sporadic, troubled evangelization among the Zuñis, initiated in 1629, abandoned in 1632, resumed about 1660, and abandoned again in 1672.[14] The missions in the Salinas district, however, not only were frontier outposts but also constituted a regional administrative unit before 1672. The mission at El Paso (Figs. 136, 177), dedicated in 1668,[15] was originally established for liaison purposes, but during the Rebellion it became the sole administrative center for the entire surviving Spanish population of New Mexico. The redistribution of these outposts, centers, and connective establishments in later periods might properly form the subject of a separate study.

10. Ricard, 1933, pp. 166–170.
11. Idem, p. 166.
12. Idem, pp. 97–98.
13. Hackett, 1937, pp. 54, 55, 61.
14. Hodge, 1937, pp. 94–97.
15. Scholes, 1929, p. 196.

3.

Location. It must become plain in the following chapters that the architecture of the mission establishments forms a defensive fabric (Fig. 88), with the massive construction, the high blank walls (Fig. 83), the spacious, unobstructed interiors, and the crenelated parapets of military architecture. How did this armed aspect fortify or weaken the settlement itself, what was the attitude of the Indians toward such structures, and for what purpose did the friars conceive them? These questions demand an examination of the location of the mission buildings with reference to the dwelling areas of the settlements. We have already noted the survival of the prehistoric Pueblo town plan and structural technique in the missionary era;

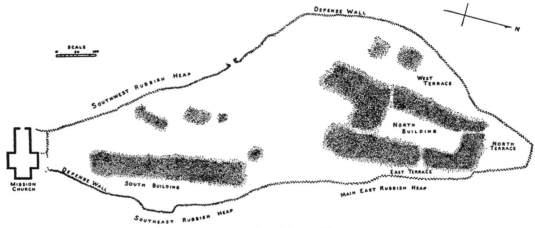

2. Pecos. Plan of the pueblo.

in all its modalities, the allocation of the church represents a compromise with that town plan. The obvious exception is in the Spanish settlement of Santa Fe (Fig. 46), founded in 1609,[16] which even today embodies the regulations issued for the laying out of new towns in New Spain by Philip II on July 3, 1572.[17] Santa Fe, of all Hispanic cities in the New World, is a paradigm of these ordinances; in it, the old parish church and conventual establishment, now replaced by the Cathedral, occupied an entire block, away from the plaza, according to Philip's ruling.[18]

In the Indian settlements, however, the concept of the communal dwelling and the concept of the Church are alien to one another, and the admission of the church to the indigenous layout was achieved by mutual concessions, determined on the spot, unsupported by historical precedent or bureaucratic afterthought. The Christian buildings appear to gravitate as closely as possible to the heart of the indigenous settlement. Several solutions characterize this process. The church buildings may be separated from the communal dwellings by an open space of some extent, as at Pecos (Fig. 2) or Acoma (Fig. 44). They may be peripheral to the village buildings, as at Giusewa, without an intervening sterile area. They may form an integral part of the village buildings, as at the exceptional site of San Felipe on the Mesa (Fig. 47). They may occupy a focal position within a plaza, surrounded on several sides by com-

16. Bloom, 1929a.   17. Nuttall, 1921.   18. Idem, p. 473.

munal dwellings, as at Zuñi (Fig. 43). Finally they may be intercalated among, but separate from, adjoining village buildings, as at Humanas (Fig. 48). The factors of resistance and prior conditioning are difficult to determine, but may be approached theoretically. It is too great a simplification to assume that the distance of the church from the center of the pueblo is in direct ratio to the resistance of the Indians. Still, the historical pattern seems partly to confirm such a hypothesis, in its broadest application. The isolated mission, distinct from the pueblo, occurs at Pecos, Acoma, and Hawikuh, churches built during the first generation of permanent mission activity. It is to be noted that both Pecos and Acoma, however, share a topographic unit with the pueblo; at San Estevan de Acoma, the church is on the rock, not below it, and at Pecos (Fig. 2), the church figures prominently at the south end of the long ridge occupied by the pueblo. The area between the two units has never been built up; it preserves the appearance of a neutral zone. An exactly analogous situation prevails at the modern pueblo of Santo Domingo, built anew on its present location after the flood of 1886. Santo Domingo is perhaps the most reactionary Indian group in the United States;[19] secretive, withdrawn from the surrounding civilization. The church, built in a pure seventeenth-century style, lies a few hundred yards from the edge of the pueblo (Fig. 190). It is an auxiliary structure, psychologically remote from the life of the village. Its seventeenth-century prototypes, however, surely involve a strategic consideration; but as with a corroded, long-disused knife, we can no longer tell which way this threat was intended to be effective. The pueblo dwellings formed an intricate rabbit warren; occupied by an enemy, they might have constituted a serious threat to any structure enclosed by them. Both types of enemy were probably envisaged here: enemies within and without the tribe. It seems reasonable, therefore, to regard the isolated type of mission structure as a deliberate choice made by the friars. Once at least, nevertheless, a seventeenth-century *convento* occupied the central position at the heart of the pueblo: Vetancurt[20] reports that San Diego de la Congregación de Jemez, because it was a frontier post, was arranged with the priest's house in the center of a plaza. Where the church itself was located is not given. In considering this question there must also be taken into account the considerable plant of the large seventeenth-century mission; livestock, orchards, produce gardens, and so forth, which all, for strategic reasons as well, required room not generally available within the pueblo. Such conditions prevailed only for the larger missions; at smaller establishments, such as Laguna, no major economic motive can be brought into play. Mutual mistrust, strategic considerations, and room for development, then, helped to determine the prevailing polar relationship between pueblo and church. It is surely the most common of all solutions, and may be noted also at Zia, Santa Ana, Santa Clara, Taos (Fig. 3), and San Ildefonso.

The cases in the seventeenth century, where the mission edifices are peripheral to the pueblo, will probably be augmented by careful studies in the Salinas area and among the Hopi towns. San José at Giusewa now offers the clearest example. The pueblo buildings share a party wall with the church,[21] which in turn dominates the approaches up and down the canyon at the edge of the village (Fig. 29). The short life of this mission perhaps demonstrates the weakness of the arrangement. At Quarai (Fig. 45) and Abó (Fig. 49), in the Salinas district, the church occupied an important part of the pueblo. The *convento* buildings sur-

19. White, 1935.   20. Vetancurt, 1697, p. 101.   21. Reiter, 1938.

rounded kivas,[22] or underground ceremonial chambers (Fig. 4), and it is to be noted that these frontier posts came to a disastrous end in 1674.[23]

Following the Reconquest of 1692, and during the relatively peaceful years of the eighteenth century, several solutions emerged which appear to reflect a loosening of the old defensive mechanisms, and a dissociation of the economic enterprise of the mission from its architectural expression. These are the various cases in which the mission may be included

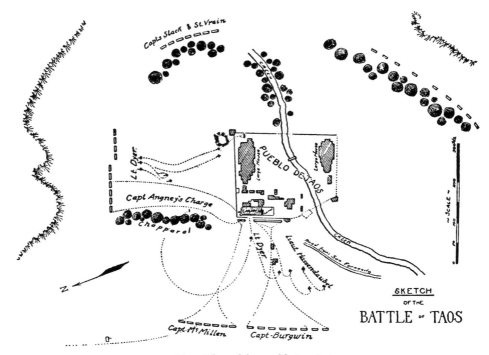

3. Taos. Plan of the pueblo in 1846.

continuously within the communal fabric, or centrally located in the plaza, or intercalated among the pueblo structures. Two interesting cases of an included church, coextensive with the pueblo dwellings, occur at Patokwa (Fig. 26), in the Jemez district, and at San Felipe on the Black Mesa (Fig. 47). Both pueblos and churches were built in 1694–95, perhaps to materialize the docile promises made to officers of the Reconquest, by rebels happy to renew their struggles against nomadic incursions under Spanish protection. Both sites are the realization of mutual if momentary concessions, for the towns on the mesas were traps for the missionaries, as in the instance of the murder of Friar Francisco de Jesus at Patokwa in 1696.[24]

22. Anonymous, 1936, p. 122. A structure which was perhaps a circular kiva figures in the *convento* at Abó. This information was kindly communicated by Joseph H. Toulouse, Jr., under whose direction the excavations were made in 1938–39 (Fig. 4).

23. Twitchell, 1917a, p. 501, notes that Quarai was a

walled city, like Pecos, and mentions a plan of this wall mapped by the School of American Archaeology. Bandelier (cited from Twitchell, ibid.), on the other hand, claimed that no defensive works existed at any of the pueblos of the Salinas district.

24. Bloom and Mitchell, 1938, pp. 105–107.

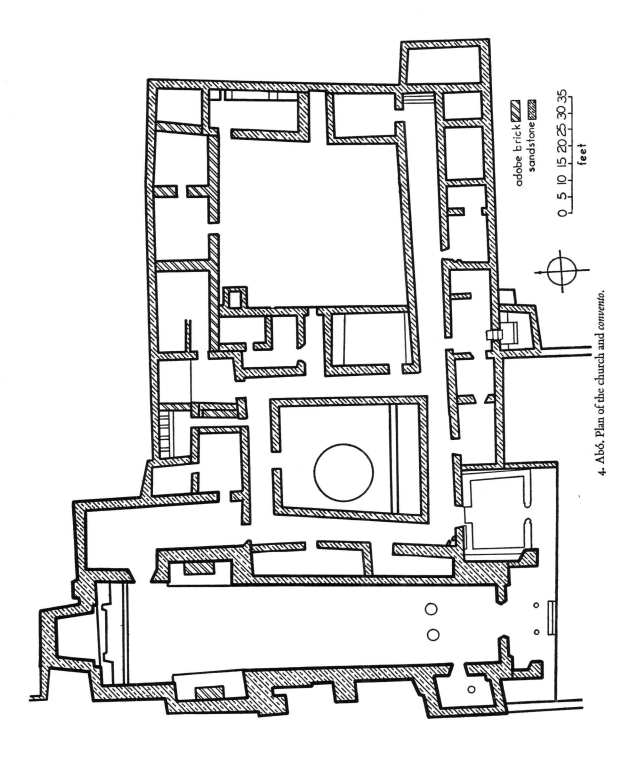

4. Abó, Plan of the church and *convento*.

adobe brick
sandstone

0 5 10 15 20 25 30 35
feet

With the centrally located mission structures of the full eighteenth century, however, the relationship was reversed, to favor a dominant religious establishment, rearing high above the surrounding roof terraces, with its farm buildings and corrals relegated to the outskirts of the pueblo. At Zuñi (Fig. 43), Walatowa, and Isleta, it is difficult to determine whether an existing plaza was appropriated for the purpose, or a plaza slowly grew up around the church. The point is immaterial, since in either case the relationship itself depends upon a local attitude of acceptance. The church, in these instances, has effectively become the focal point of the community plan. The churches, which are loosely intercalated among the dwellings, although they lack formal importance in the urban silhouette, are also completely accepted by the population. This arrangement, conformably to a historic pattern, occurs in pueblos of recent construction, such as Sandia, Tesuque, or the newer part of Taos pueblo.

It is worth noting, finally, that similar arrangements were observed in the Spanish settlements and in later Mexican villages. At La Bajada, for instance, the church, established in 1831,[25] lies some hundred feet away from the settlement. The motivation is of course different, and more casual, but the pattern itself is clear. By far the most frequent arrangement in Mexican towns is the central church location, at Cordova,

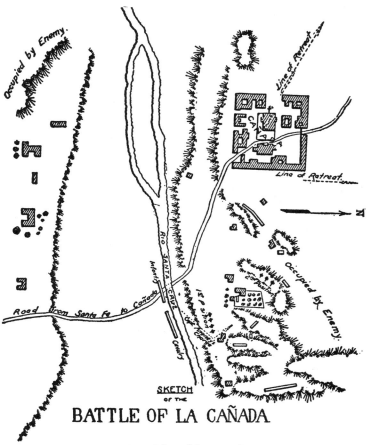

5. Santa Cruz. Plan of the town in 1846.

Cebolleta, Abiquiu, Santa Cruz (Fig. 5),[26] or Ranchos de Taos. Indeterminate relations often occur, as at Truchas or Peñasco. The bureaucratic regulation affecting the *parroquia* of Santa Fe may have found expression again in the present disposition at Socorro, while the destroyed Castrense of Santa Fe (Fig. 46), and the parish church of Trạmpas, both eighteenth-century foundations, exemplify respectively the included and intercalated types, again under quite different conditions than in the pueblos.

25. MS. license in Archives of the Archdiocese, Santa Fe.

26. Tamaron, 1937, p. 347, implies that in 1760 the settlement had not yet taken its present shape and plan. "La iglesia es algo grande pero con poco adorno, no hay forma de lugar [La Cañada]."

4.

Orientation. The traditional direction for churches, with the sanctuary at the eastern end, occurs in New Mexico only at Pecos (Fig. 2), at San Miguel, and the *parroquia* of Santa Fe (Fig. 46), at Tomé, and a few other sites. In Mexico proper, the Franciscans alone had observed the rule through the sixteenth century; after 1600, however, the churches faced in all directions depending upon factors of site and local preference.[27] In New Mexico, the façade usually looks east and the sanctuary faces west as at San Felipe, Santa Ana, or Zia. This arrangement may be considered standard, and it constitutes a reversal of traditional European practice. It is an exception when the churches are properly oriented, as in the examples just cited, and in fact, buildings are more likely to face south than west, as at Abó (Fig. 4), Quarai (Fig. 27), Giusewa (Fig. 29), the old church at Taos pueblo, and the smaller buildings at La Bajada or Las Colonias. Thus the façades look east, or south in some cases, rather than west, and this situation offers a problem to which the answer, again, is elusive.

It is theoretically possible, but not probable, that local, indigenous factors affected the choice of direction. These, if they existed, were soon absorbed in the tradition, for we find south or east the preferred directions in Hispanic as well as Indian villages. But a technical factor or limitation may be taken into account. The transverse clearstory window, which translates the function of the dome into a simple structural language (Figs. 93–96), renounces the light which enters the church from all directions. The transverse clearstory window admits light from one direction only, since it exists only as a difference of level between the nave and sanctuary roofs.[28] It is a vertical plane surface, not a curved one, such as the drum beneath a dome. Hence a direct light from the sun could strike the altar but once a day, and that time depended upon the direction in which the church faced. If the church faced east, the light of sunrise penetrated to the altar. A church facing west, however, would receive the sunset. And a church which faced south received a fairly bright light at all times of day, a mean average of the maximum and minimum intensities of direct daylight. Thus the choice of direction may have depended upon the local order of ceremonies. The mission routine seems to have favored early morning worship in the pueblos, and the churches therefore often faced east.[29] Elsewhere, services may have been conducted at various times of day; the churches were in fairly constant use, and it was desirable to secure an even lighting at the sanctuary during most of the day. Here it would have been natural for the churches to face south.[30] This heliotropism, if the term be allowed, may be the dominant consideration in the orientation of churches.

Occasionally the church faced north as with the private chapel at Giusewa,[31] or the destroyed Castrense of Santa Fe (Fig. 46), where the site allowed no other direction. In Christian church architecture, the north has usually been considered inauspicious, perhaps because of a medieval belief that the apocalyptic peoples of Gog and Magog would break in upon humanity at the Last Judgment from the north edge of the world disc. As late as the Council of Trent, the north was a forbidden direction excepting in special cases where no other solution was possible.[32]

27. Toussaint, 1927, pp. 17–19.

28. *Infra*, p. 48.

29. In the middle of the eighteenth century, prayers in the churches were held every morning at seven. Hackett, 1937, p. 368. Sunday Mass began at eight at San Diego

de los Jemez, in 1773, and at S. Agustin de la Isleta. Idem, p. 503.

30. In southern France, medieval churches often face south, to avoid the prevailing winds. Enlart, 1919, p. 14.

31. Dutton, 1938, p. 139.

32. Nissen, 1907, p. 247.

CHAPTER II

MATERIALS

I.

THE materials in which an architectural program is realized not only control the ultimate appearance of the structure, but also intervene in the processes of design, where they figure among the limits to which the projected structure must conform. The building materials of the colonial era in New Mexico are well known: adobe, stone, wood, an occasional window glazing of selenite or mica, and earth colors for the decoration of the walls. The extreme possibilities of these materials were of course never exploited to the limits of colonial technology. We shall note again the absence of arches and domes in the architecture of New Mexico, and adduce hypotheses to cover the negative phenomenon. Other negative aspects of the use of materials present themselves for consideration here. Why, for instance, in a land abundantly endowed with limestone and gypsum, was the use of lime mortar not developed until the late years of the nineteenth century?[1] Modern brickkilns supply New Mexico with serviceable fired bricks:[2] why was their use nearly totally avoided by colonial builders? Many varieties of splendid building stone are easily available in parts of New Mexico,[3] but an architecture of dressed stone rarely figures in the colonial repertory, and then only in a loose and casual technique with prehistoric antecedents. In one sense, the answer is obvious. Dressed stone, lime mortar, and fired bricks are more laborious to prepare than adobe, field stone, and wood. The former require a greater expenditure of either man power, or time, or both. Now, the Hispanic colonization of New Mexico never materially augmented the total population of the region. In 1660,[4] a census yielded somewhat more than 24,000 persons, including no more than 1,000 Europeans, or 4.3 per cent of the total. In 1679, the Indian population had dropped to 17,000;[5] the number of Spanish inhabitants had risen to approximately 2,800,[6] or 16 per cent, but the total population was 20 per cent less than in the previous decade. During the eighteenth century, the Indian population dropped alarmingly, from a relatively high figure following the Reconquest, to 17,500 in 1761.[7] Europeans numbered considerably less than 4,000 at this time,[8] and the total population still fell below that of 1660. A century later, however, the eighth United States Census of 1860 revealed a white population, exclusive of Indians, numbering 80,567,[9] and in 1900 the total population of New Mexico was 195,310.[10] The conclusion lies near that the persistence of adobe, field stone, and wood as colonial building materials was related to

1. Herrick and Johnson, 1900, p. 231, report that "a good supply of fresh burnt lime can be had from kilns near the city [Albuquerque]."

2. Idem, p. 232.

3. Idem, p. 231. In the Sandia mountains "is found an abundance of granite building rock. . . . Sandstone may be obtained in any quantity."

4. Bandelier, 1890, p. 121.

5. Hackett, 1937, p. 299.

6. Hackett, 1911, pp. 99–100.

7. Hackett, 1937, pp. 495, 500.

8. Idem, p. 496.

9. Twitchell, 1912, p. 414, n. 340.

10. Idem, p. 574, n. 484.

the dwindling population statistics. The maintenance of the simple frontier economy, against the inhospitality of the land itself, absorbed nearly all the available time and man power, with little left over for the technical improvement of such commodities as building materials.

It is difficult to measure the other factors that certainly contributed to the colonial reliance upon aboriginal materials, but they must at least be mentioned: the resistance of the Indians to alien influences; the low quality of the European settlers;[11] the provisional atmosphere of any outpost society.

2.

Adobe. An architecture of sun-dried mud bricks is common to most semiarid countries of the world, where the material has been used for building purposes since prehistoric times. In the southwestern states of this continent, the bricks are known as *adobes*.[12] The material is a clay soil, which is the result of the disintegration of rock, by various agencies of erosion, into colloidal particles. It accumulates at the surface of the ground and can be collected with little effort. In the Rio Grande drainage of New Mexico, adobe is by far the most common building material, for civil and religious architecture.

The methods of manufacture are nearly the same wherever the adobe brick is made. The clay is kneaded with the bare feet or with a hoe into an even paste. Straw or manure is worked in to act as a binder and prevent cracking during drying. The mud is quickly formed into bricks with a simple wooden mold (*adobero*). The brick dries a day or two on the ground, and can then be turned on edge without danger of losing its shape. Several days later the bricks are stacked in piles for the final drying.[13]

In a wall, the bricks are generally laid with mud mortar of the same consistency[14] as that of the original paste for the bricks (Fig. 54). The average brick in colonial times measured 10 x 18 x 5 inches and weighed fifty or sixty pounds. It usually represented the load which one man could handle. Modern adobes are smaller, 4 x 8 x 16 inches.[15]

In the Southwest, adobe is an eminently practical building material. Its stability, permanence, and insulation are well suited to the climatic conditions. Where the daily and seasonal fluctuations of the weather are great, an adobe building will maintain a relatively constant temperature. Under ideal conditions, adobe will withstand structural strains and weather erosion. Tests carried out at the University of New Mexico[16] have shown that a safe limit for the height of a wall made of good adobe and laterally supported is about 80 feet.[17] In the churches, however, the height of such walls never exceeds 35 feet. Similar tests have shown that under normal weathering conditions, walls built of a fair quality of clay will wear at the rate of one inch in twenty years.[18] Against these laboratory tests, nevertheless, the docu-

11. Scholes, 1935, pp. 99–104.

12. The word derives from an Egyptian hieroglyph for brick, through Arabic to the Spanish *adobar*, "to daub," or "to plaster." Hodge, 1907, p. 14.

13. Burnt adobe bricks were used in the seventeenth century to face the steps of the ruin at Giusewa. Bloom, 1923, p. 18. The use of burnt adobe bricks elsewhere is not known, until well after the American occupation. Modern bricks fired in New Mexico are discussed by Herrick and Johnson, 1900, pp. 232–234.

14. At Giusewa the mortar was made from the debris of older houses and contains fragments of pottery, obsidian, and charcoal. Hewett, 1906, p. 47. Likewise at Pecos, the mortar contains heterogeneous fragments. Bandelier, 1881, p. 43.

15. Herrick and Johnson, 1900, p. 231.

16. Eyre, 1935.

17. No specification for the thickness of such a wall is given.

18. Eyre, 1935.

mentation of the churches in New Mexico yields an extremely variable impression of the stable and durable properties of adobe construction. At one extreme, certain buildings were constantly in process of rebuilding and repair, as at Albuquerque (Figs. 181, 182), where the church built after 1706[19] had to be restored before the end of the century.[20] The church at Pecos pueblo (Fig. 55), abandoned in 1840,[21] threatened complete collapse before 1915.[22] At the other extreme, the adobe fabric of the church in the pueblo on the Black Mesa overlooking San Felipe (Fig. 56), abandoned before the close of the seventeenth century[23] and never reoccupied, still presents substantial remains, and might theoretically be rebuilt for use without radical expense. Likewise the churches at San Pascual and Socorro, abandoned in 1680, were landmarks along the Rio Grande as late as 1760.[24] San Miguel in Santa Fe, burned and pillaged in 1680, was substantially capable of re-use thirty years later.[25] Santa Rosa Abiquiu (Fig. 54), abandoned before 1767,[26] could be put to use today, with a new sanctuary and roof. The perishable element above all was the roof: at San Miguel in Santa Fe, the roof was under repair in 1710, in 1730, and again in 1760,[27] but the adobe fabric seems a relatively permanent construction.

These variations in the durability of adobe are perhaps to be attributed to local variations in the quality of clay and methods of manufacture. The processes of building wall, furthermore, may have been more or less careful in different districts. In any case, the historical life of the adobe structures reveals a temperamental, unpredictable building material, capable upon occasion of surprising resistance to weather and ruin, but generally deficient in durable surface qualities. The appearance of adobe after the wet season is that of furrowed, cracked disrepair (Fig. 57). These damages are everywhere repaired by the application of a smooth coat of whitewash, made from the gypsum rock and micaceous clay found in abundance throughout the region. In Mexican and Indian villages, plastering and whitewashing are done by the women of the village, who spread the material thickly over the wall, and smooth it with their hands or the fleece of a sheepskin. In prosperous and devout villages, exterior plastering is renewed annually after the rainy season. A wall may, in certain districts, on the other hand, go for fifty or sixty years without fresh surfacing, and suffer no irreparable damage, providing the erosion at ground level is not allowed to undermine the foundation.

3.

Stone. In most districts, building stone is easily available. West of Albuquerque, at Acoma and Laguna, varying sizes of field stone are laid up in adobe mortar. At Acoma (Fig. 58), the foundations and lower courses of the church façade are adobe brick faced with loosely laid field stone.[28] Several buttresses in the priest's house and the south bell tower are built of

19. Bloom, 1935, pp. 48–50. Hackett, 1937, p. 379.
20. Twitchell, 1914*a*, p. 351. Pereyro, 1808.
21. Bandelier, 1881, pp. 124–125.
22. Kidder, 1924, p. 15.
23. Bandelier, 1892, pp. 190–191.
24. Twitchell, 1916, p. 356.
25. Kubler, 1939*a*.
26. Twitchell, 1914, p. 162.
27. Kubler, 1939*a*.

28. See the measured drawings of the Historic American Buildings Survey, 36 NM 5, sheets 4, 6. These drawings may be obtained from the U.S. Department of the Interior; Office of National Parks, Buildings and Reservations; Branch of Plans and Design. The six churches which the Survey measured in New Mexico are at Acoma, Chimayo, Laguna, Ranchos de Taos, Santa Fe (San Miguel), and Talpa. Henceforth cited as H.A.B.S.

irregular stone throughout.[29] At Laguna likewise (Fig. 38) many walls of the church and dependent buildings are built of coarse stone laid in thick adobe mortar.[30]

Near the salt lakes of the Manzano region, southeast of Albuquerque, are several ruins built of sandstone. The stone was taken from stratified outcrops in the surrounding hills and prepared by fracture, probably with stone mauls. The courses were set in the usual adobe mortar. At Abó, the pieces are usually about two and one half inches thick, and generally not more than one foot in length (Fig. 59). Sandstone fragments are also used at the great ruin of Giusewa (Fig. 60), in Jemez canyon, as well as in the Zuñi district, at Kechipauan (Fig. 61), but the pieces are more irregularly shaped, and laid in extremely thick mortar. Walls built of this material range in color from blue-gray to dark red.[31]

The technique of these constructions departs very little from prehistoric methods of wall building in other parts of the Pueblo area. It is to be noted that a construction of stone laid up in sun-dried clay mortar hardly differs from one of adobe bricks. Permanent surface quality and durable mass may be greater in the former, but cohesion and flexibility will be no greater in one than the other.

The only case of a characteristically European stone-working technique occurs in the eighteenth-century church in Santa Fe, at the Castrense, or Madre Santissima de la Luz, which had the further distinction of being the only church held by secular clergy in the colonial era. The stone altarpiece of that church (Fig. 209), which now figures in the Church of Cristo Rey in Santa Fe, was carved in 1760 from white stone quarried near Santa Fe.[32] The joints and imperfections in the stone, however, appear to have been filled with stucco which then was carved to continue the design.[33]

4.

Wood. Benavides did not misrepresent when he said in 1630 that New Mexico possessed "marvelous highlands of every sort of timber,"[34] but he omitted to add that, to the Indians and the colonists of his day, the forests were remote, comparatively inaccessible to primitive lumbering methods, in the absence of suitable roads or navigable streams. Until late in the nineteenth century, the forest reserves of New Mexico were barely touched,[35] and sizable lumber was a relatively costly material, used in large quantities only for the churches and the houses and furniture of the wealthier colonists. Thus, in 1710, the wood for the rebuilding of San Miguel cost over 250 pesos, or the equivalent of three months' pay for the entire building crew of fifteen men.[36] A story also exists to the effect that the timbers for the church at Acoma were brought by the Indians from the San Mateo mountains, forty miles distant.[37]

29. H.A.B.S., 36 NM 5, sheet 16. The stone buildings and bell towers at Acoma are known to be recent repairs. Reuter, 1927.

30. H.A.B.S., 36 NM 3, sheets 3, 4.

31. The number of stone churches is limited: Quarai, Abó, Humanas, Giusewa, San Cristobal, and Kechipauan.

32. Wuthenau, 1935. Tamaron, 1937, p. 336. "Se había descubierto, ocho leguas de allí, una veta de piedra muy blanca, de donde se condujó la necesaria para un

retablo que llenase la tercera del altar mayor, que estaba ya casí labrado, el que después se concluyó y la iglesia." (1760.)

33. Communicated by Mr. John Gaw Meem, October, 1939.

34. Ayer, 1916, p. 32.

35. Jones, 1932, pp. 273–274.

36. Kubler, 1939a.

37. Sedgwick, 1927, pp. 37–38.

It therefore becomes of interest to know approximately how much lumber was used for temporary purposes in construction, such as scaffolds. The account of 1710 refers to wood used for scaffolds (*andamias*),[38] but their size and character are not given, and it seems likely that any waste of wood in this manner would have been avoided as much as possible by other expedients. The absence of arches and domes in the architecture of New Mexico further enabled the builders to economize on wood, since stagings and arch centers were not needed. Thus there is good reason to believe that wood was used mainly for permanent purposes, such as roofing, door and window trim, occasional floors, furniture, and stairways. In the roofs, however, beams of great size were sometimes used, as at Acoma, where a 42-foot beam has been found,[39] and at Abó, where the wall remains indicate that roof timbers may have been two feet square and more than 25 feet long (Fig. 63).

On the whole, wood was less laborious to procure and work than stone. Hence wood fulfills in New Mexico many of the functions ordinarily satisfied with stone in European architecture. The roofing technique, the moldings, and many elements of the church furniture are contrived of wood, so that the New Mexican church consists principally of perishable materials lacking the monumental stability and durability of its prototypes.

38. Kubler, 1939a.   39. Reuter, 1924.

CHAPTER III

PLAN

I.

ANTECEDENTS. The colonial churches of sixteenth-century Mexico (Figs. 6, 64) are characterized by the nearly uniform absence of the three-aisled plan which was usual in European religious architecture. In the cathedrals of Mexico, Puebla, or Oaxaca, built for the most part in the seventeenth century, the multiple-nave plan prevailed,[1] but in the vast majority of smaller monastic and parish churches, the complicated structural problems attendant upon the construction of lateral aisles were avoided. It is likely that military considerations may have played a part in the suppression of the aisle. That the churches were designed for military pur-poses we know from numerous sources. In 1531, for instance, Viceroy Mendoza re-quested that the projected cathedral at Puebla be built as a fortress;[2] at Etzatlan, in Jalisco, the church was built to protect the settlement against attacks from the neigh-boring mountains.[3] Now as Gillet[4] has pointed out, a functional identity exists between the Mexican fortress churches and the fortified churches of southwestern France in the Middle Ages, of which the most spectacular example is the Cathedral of Albi, with high, impregnable exterior surfaces offering no projections to the ene-my (Fig. 65). The plan of Albi, however, is exotic; the aisles become relatively small chapels without complicating the exterior outline of the plan. In other words, the aisles at Albi are vestigial, for strategic reasons. In sixteenth-century Mexico, the process is complete: in the interest of bland contours, offering the enemy no protection, the aisles are completely suppressed.[5] Similarly in New Mexico, the simple plan represents not only an avoidance of structural problems, but a military measure for the protection of the establishment. More important

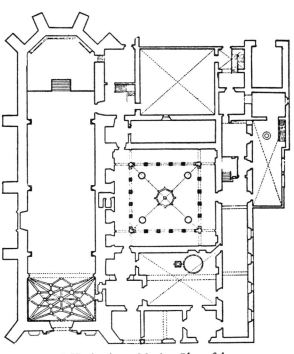

6. Huejotzingo, Mexico. Plan of the Franciscan establishment.

1. Toussaint, 1927, pp. 57–66.
2. Idem, p. 58.
3. Ricard, 1933, p. 198.
4. Gillet, 1929, p. 1026

5. Exceptions occur, even among smaller churches, as in the three-aisled basilical structure at Zacatlan, in the state of Puebla. Toussaint, 1927, p. 16.

still, a technical reason demanded this solution. The materials—loose stone and adobe bricks—were unsuitable to any dynamic structural extension. Had lateral aisles been added to the single nave of the existing churches, it would have become necessary to pierce arcades through the present lateral walls. To support the incumbent clearstory walls upon such arcades would have required pillars or supports which it was not practical to build of adobe brick.

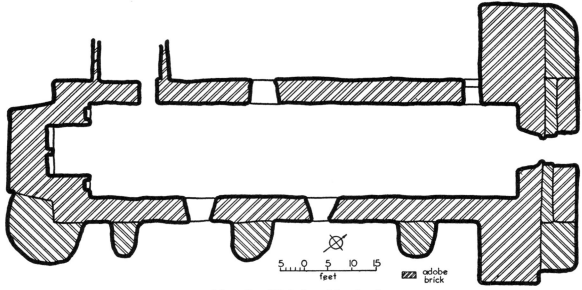

7. Isleta. Simplified plan of the church.

2.

Typology. The single-nave plan of New Mexico occurs with or without transepts. In cruciform plans, the chancel, or approach to the sanctuary, is always narrower than the nave. In noncruciform churches, two arrangements occur: (1) The chancel is narrower than the nave (Fig. 7); (2) The width of the chancel is equal to that of the nave (Fig. 8). In either case, the sanctuary is always a distinctly articulated element, and it constitutes the focal point of the plan. It may be rectangular (Fig. 7), trapezoidal (Fig. 4), or apsidal (Fig. 70).

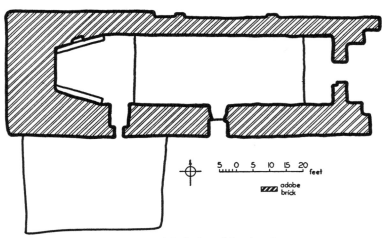

8. Zia. Simplified plan of the church.

The width of the nave and the width of the transept (across its own axis) are limited by the length of the roofing timbers available. Consequently an interior nave width of 33 or 34 feet is rarely exceeded.[6]

In the eighteenth century, chapels and altars subsidiary to the main altar are generally developed from the ends of the transepts, as at Santa Cruz (Fig. 9) and at Socorro (Fig. 33). Sometimes they fill the angles between transept and sanctuary, as at Tomé, and perhaps at Pecos (Fig. 66). The plan and disposition of other subsidiary rooms, such as sacristies, baptistries, and priests' houses, will be discussed under separate headings.

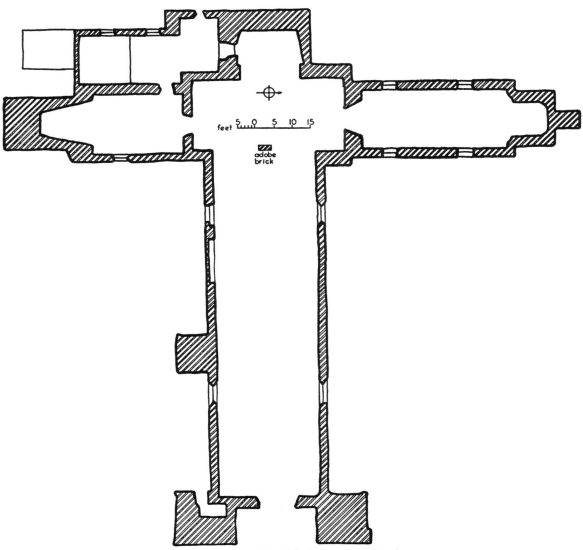

9. Santa Cruz. Simplified plan of the church.

6. The widest nave in New Mexico, excepting the Cathedral of 1869, is at San José de Giusewa, and measures 33 feet 10 inches from wall to wall. During the excavations of 1922, flat stones, widely spaced down the center of the nave, were found. Bloom, 1923, p. 17, suggests these were footing stones for á row of vertical supports relieving the load of the roof.

Attention may be called here to the close resemblances of Pecos and Quarai (Figs. 30, 27). The overall length and transept length are identical in both monuments.

In general, the fundamental variations upon the typical single-nave plan consist in the presence or absence of transepts, in various shapes of the sanctuary, and in the location of accessory rooms. It is a plan that undergoes few sudden transformations. The materials and the technique restrict its metamorphoses, although certain mutations, in the character and disposition of transepts, in the location of secondary rooms, may properly be treated later in the discussion.

3.

Irregularities.[7] Certain departures from symmetry, evident in the measured drawings, call for discussion. For example, a considerable difference in the thickness of the lateral walls (Fig. 8) occurs in a large number of churches. At Pecos the south nave wall is 5 feet 9 inches thick, whereas the north wall is 3 feet 9 inches thick (Fig. 30). At Acoma the south nave wall is 4 feet 9 inches thick and the north wall measures 7 feet 5 inches (Fig. 32). The west nave wall at Giusewa measures 6 feet 9 inches, but the east wall shows an average thickness of 7 feet 6 inches (Fig. 29). The east wall of the ruin at Quarai is 4 feet 9 inches thick, a foot or more thicker than the west wall of the nave (Fig. 27). Considerable differences in thickness were found in nearly every church measured, regardless of locality and size. The causes for such a widespread peculiarity of construction are probably technical. In the nearly complete absence of documents pertaining to early building technique in New Mexico, no more can be done than to review possibilities.

1. The irregularity may arise from the ignorance of the designers, or the labor, or both. This degree of ignorance must still be proved, nevertheless, and in any case, it is unlikely that amateur builders would erect walls with such painstaking disregard for symmetry and economy unless there were some necessary structural relationship between the thicker wall and another element of the building.

2. The buildings of the priest's house (*convento*) often abut the thicker wall of the nave (Fig. 67). The roofing timbers of the priest's house then rest in the nave wall,[8] which takes the added load of the adjacent roof. With unreliable materials the builders may therefore have increased the thickness of the burdened wall. The notion stands in need of additional data from other early buildings. At Santa Ana and San Felipe, where the location of the priests' houses is known, the inhabitants would not allow measurements to be taken.

3. The thicker wall may have been designed to counteract the weakening effects of fenestration. In the older churches, before the reconstructions of the nineteenth century, nave windows generally occurred in one wall only. For every case, however, in which the windows are in the thicker wall (Trampas, Fig. 25; Zia, Fig. 8), there is an instance of windows in the thin wall (Quarai, Fig. 27; Acoma, Fig. 32). Evidently no such structural necessity was in effect.

4. We do not know how the roof timbers were maneuvered into position, once the walls had been brought to the required height. This problem may bear upon the phenomenon of

7. These considerations might also be studied in the chapter pertaining to structure. They are legible, however, only upon the ground plans, and constitute elements of the design which properly belong in that stage of architectural composition where the plan is being developed in detail.

8. H.A.B.S., Acoma, 36 NM 5, sheet 11.

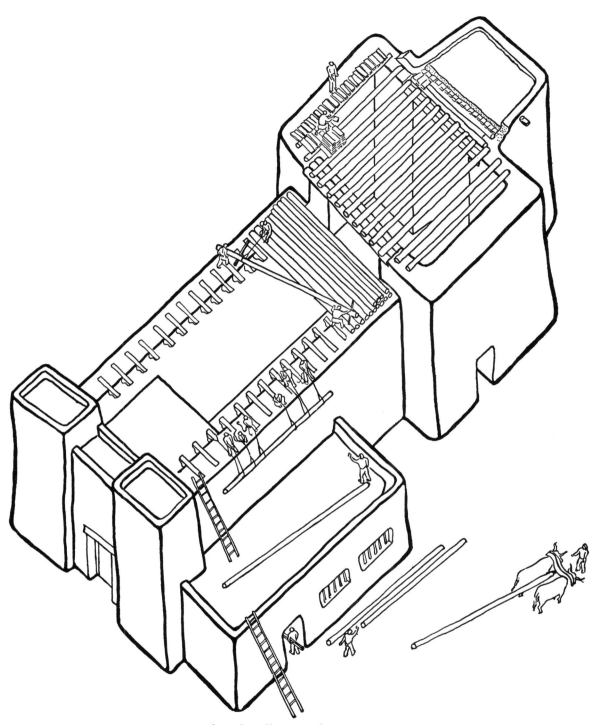

10. Hypothetical roof laying in the seventeenth century.

the thicker wall. Whatever the method, a fulcrum at some point above the intended roof level was needed. That hoisting cranes were contrived for this purpose seems unlikely. The time and labor expended in setting up a hoisting yard and in fashioning adequate pulley blocks would have been out of proportion both to the amount of work required from the crane and to the amount of work involved in the routine process of building more wall. A large number of men posted at roof level perhaps provided the fulcrum, but only one wall, of platform-like thickness, would have been needed to accommodate them (Fig. 10).

5. Aside from structural considerations, the thicker wall may be the result, in very few cases, of long-continued weathering. This would naturally apply only to adobe buildings, and could not be made to account for the thicker wall in sandstone buildings. Drainage from the flat roofs follows a lateral inclination (Fig. 11). It frequently happens that the pitch of a roof is downward from the thicker wall. It is possible, therefore, that both walls were originally of the same thickness, and that the difference of today is the result of years of concentrated erosion on one side of the building. It must not be forgotten, however, that the average rate of erosion removes but one inch of material in twenty years;[9] hardly enough to account for the three-foot difference observed in some monuments. To sum up, it is difficult to associate the thicker wall either with fenestration or with the added load of the adjacent priest's-house buildings. Weathering does not apply to the sandstone monuments, nor in adobe

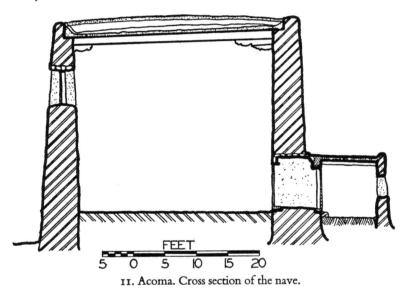

11. Acoma. Cross section of the nave.

structures can it account satisfactorily for the amount of difference observed. All things considered, the most plausible hypothesis for its genesis is that of the use of the thicker wall as a fulcrum for the hoisting crew.[10]

4.

SIMILARLY, attention may be called here to the imperfect parallelism between the nave walls, which tend to converge as they approach the sanctuary (Fig. 12). The discussion of the theoretical possibilities of this irregularity may be reserved for later.[11]

9. Eyre, 1935.

10. The English Dominican, Thomas Gage, traveling in Mexico in 1626, reported an example of the use of the walls for continuing the construction at Santo Domingo in Oaxaca. "The walls are of stone so broad that . . . I saw carts go upon them, with stone and other materials." Gage, 1928, p. 121.

11. *Infra*, p. 70.

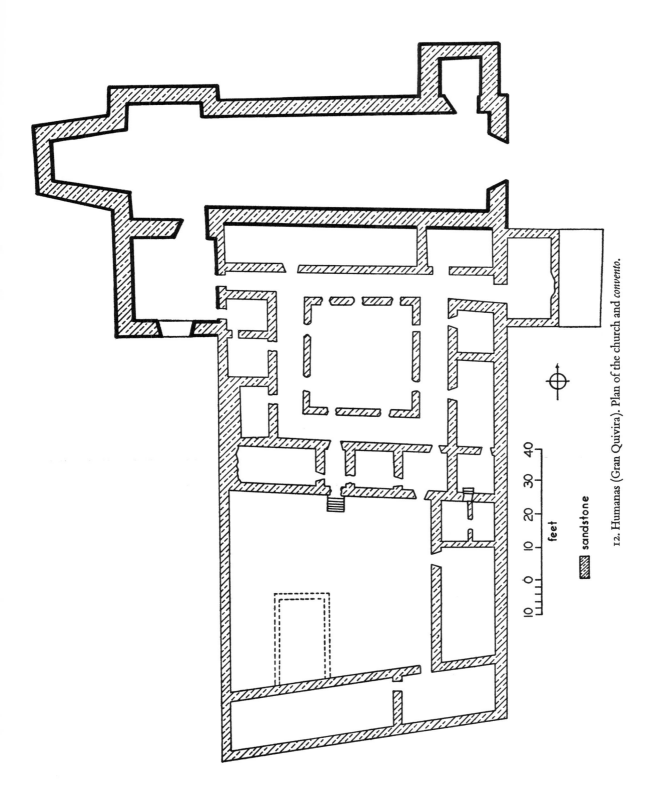

12. Humanas (Gran Quivira). Plan of the church and *convento*.

sandstone

feet

10   0   10   20   30   40

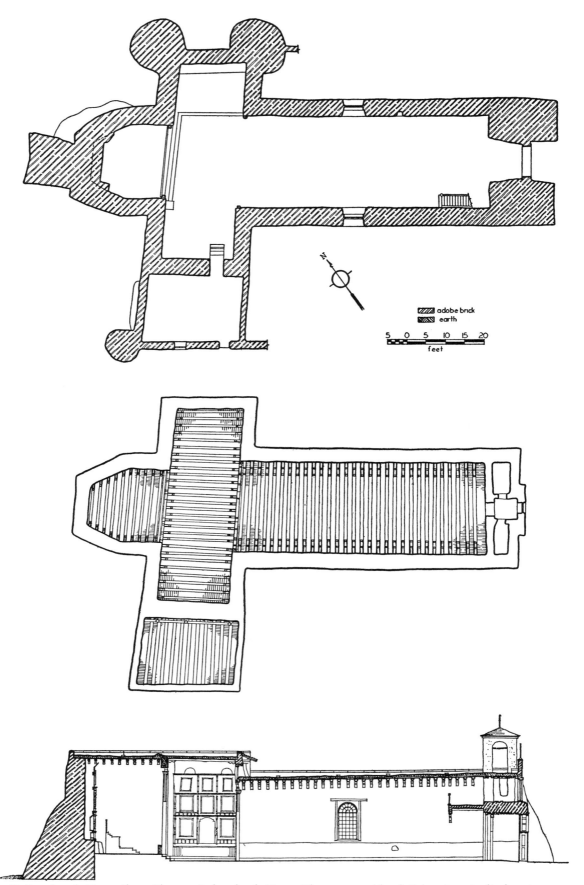

13. Ranchos de Taos. *Above:* Plan at window level. *Center:* Plan at ground level. *Below:* Longitudinal section.

5.

Deviation of Axis. The measured drawings reveal another consistent irregularity. The sanctuary is usually a polygonal recess of which the rear wall is narrower than the nave. But the axis of the nave is rarely continuous through the sanctuary.[12] The sanctuary develops from an axis of its own, with the result that, although the center of the chancel lies on the axis of the nave, one lateral wall of the sanctuary is shorter in length than the other, and its rear wall faces several degrees out of a plane parallel to that of the main façade, with which it should, according to conventional notions, be strictly parallel. Stated another way, the rear wall is rarely, if ever, at right angles to the longitudinal axis of the building (Fig. 13). At Laguna (Fig. 38), the angle is obtuse to the north by several degrees.[13] At Ranchos de Taos, a similar inclination turns the sanctuary southward a few degrees.[14] Medieval churches in Europe frequently show a similar multiplicity of axes. According to tradition and legend, this irregularity symbolized the drooping of the head of Christ upon the Cross.[15] It also has been maintained that the axis of the sanctuary indicated the point on the horizon at which the sun rose on the day of the dedication of the church to its patron saint.[16] Neither of these explanations is valid in New Mexico, for the deflection occurs in continuous-nave churches, that is to say, in churches of which the plan does not symbolize the Cross, and, on the other hand, in churches of which the sanctuaries do not look toward the rising sun. It is theoretically possible that the deflection constitutes one element in a system of perspective illusion. Discussion of this point will be resumed later.

12. H.A.B.S., 36 NM 7, sheet 2.
13. H.A.B.S., 36 NM 3, sheet 3.
14. H.A.B.S., 36 NM 7, sheet 2.
15. Lasteyrie, 1905, pp. 422–459, gives a thorough discussion of the alleged symbolism.

16. Carey, 1860, pp. 312–313; 1861, pp. 55–56. See the monumental treatment of this question in Nissen, 1906, 1907, 1910.

CHAPTER IV

STRUCTURE

I.

THE evidence of the buildings constitutes proof that two commonplace devices of European building found no use in New Mexico during the missionary era. The arch is almost nonexistent,[1] and the dome is completely lacking, but both forms may readily be built with the local materials. Why were they excluded from the architectural repertory of the mission buildings? It is to be recalled that, to this day, the Indians themselves never use either the arch or the dome. In dealing with these negative aspects of the structure, reference must be made to the passage already cited from Benavides,[2] pertaining to the participation of women in construction. Since Benavides, the roles have been reversed: the women now spin and weave, and the men build wall. But the women own the houses in the pueblos, and the ownership itself is perhaps a remnant from the time when building was the women's prerogative. Does this indifference to alien forms, so unlike the ready acceptance found in Mexico,[3] stem from the women? Or were the friars, pressed for time, reluctant to delay matters by giving instruction? This was not the case in Mexico, where time was also short.[4] It is likely that resistance was encountered in New Mexico, for in the more leisurely program of the eighteenth century, the arch and the dome still do not figure, and it seems reasonable to localize this resistance in the participation of women. The point cannot be proved by asserting that women are temperamentally more conservative, or indifferent to structural considerations: the evidence of the monuments and the known control of their construction by Indian women induce a correlation between the two, without reference to a priori considerations. Perhaps this correlation is to be expressed in terms of a traditional division of labor among men and women,[5] the men executing the carpentry and woodwork, as indicated by Benavides, and the women opposing any increase in their own share, such as the suppression of post and lintel construction through the introduction of domes and arches. Conversely, the manufacture of stagings and centers for the construction of arches involves a new kind of woodwork, and perhaps an increased amount, to be opposed by the men.

An avoidance of arched and domed construction also prevailed among the European population, as we know from the document pertaining to the rebuilding of San Miguel in Santa Fe in 1710.[6] Exclusive of the cook for the crew, the carpenter, and the workmen who furnished materials without regular employment, the construction crew consisted of four-

---

1. The lateral entrances to the sanctuary at Pecos, restored in 1915 (Fig. 101), and the arcade (Fig. 99) flanking the façade at Isleta (destroyed after 1881) are the only examples of any antiquity known to the writer.

2. Ayer, 1916, p. 33. Confirmed by Castañeda, 1904, p. 97.

3. Toussaint, 1927, p. 70.

4. Idem, pp. 59–71.

5. A division of construction labor between the sexes still occurs. At Zia in July, 1937, I observed the women of the pueblo refinishing the exterior walls of the church with adobe plaster mixed and carried by the men.

6. Kubler, 1939a.

teen men, including the foreman and the clerk. The laborers were all men, characterized as *peones,* or freemen who entered voluntary servitude in payment of debts. The actual time consumed in building about 11,000 cubic feet of wall, and placing over 200 timbers, lasted from March to September, 1710, a little over six months. This record is unique, for the time being, and yields a standard whereby to measure the probable length of similar building operations. The significant fact, however, is that we find Europeans adopting Indian technique *in toto,* confining technique to the lowest common denominator in the area. Note, however, that the labor was paid for, that the materials were produced elsewhere than on the site, and that scaffolds (*andamios*) were used in 1710. These factors compose a primitive industrial technique which was lacking in the pueblos, where labor was donated, and materials of all kinds, with very few exceptions, were contrived on the spot.

2.

Walls. Foundations for the walls, whether adobe or stone, are prepared with a minimum of effort. The usual practice is to dig a shallow trench, no wider than the intended wall, and fill it with courses of adobes, or stone slabs, or field stones (Fig. 17). The wall may also foot directly upon the ground, without foundations. As the courses of the wall rise, long timbers are occasionally introduced into the courses, parallel to the ground (Figs. 203, 153). The function of these timbers is to bind and stiffen the courses against the vertical cracks caused by settling.

The thickness of the older adobe walls is always greatest at the ground level. Thus at Acoma the south wall of the church is 30 inches thicker at the base than at the crest (Fig. 11).[7] The diminishing thickness of the walls of the older churches is characteristic, and it forms the pylon-like silhouette of the façade and lateral elevations.

The tendency to taper the thickness of a high wall is natural where the breaking strength of the material is unknown. In many cases, however, the pylon silhouette is partly caused by the formation of an erosion talus. Heavy seasonal rains and constant wind erosion tend to remove material from the upper portions of the walls and deposit it at the ground level, leaving the walls scarred by pockets and channels of varying depth (Fig. 69). The erosion talus has not yet formed about the walls of recently built churches. At Santa Clara (Fig. 70) and Llano Quemado, the walls rise vertically from the ground without taper. Recently built walls are uniformly thinner than those of older monuments. Where sandstone is used, the pylon-like silhouette is less evident than in adobe structures. The habit of tapering the ascent of the wall persists, although the taper is achieved by a number of slight setbacks, rarely more than a few inches at a time, as at Quarai (Frontispiece). The erosion talus is found here as well as in the adobe buildings, deposited by erosion from the clay mortar.

Sometimes the site affords one or more of the necessary walls. At Giusewa, the north wall of the sanctuary is partly formed by an excavation into the hillside at that point (Fig. 60). The rock was chipped and shaped to a vertical plane, then built up with masonry. The chapel at Humanas likewise uses an excavation into the rocky slope as a sanctuary (Fig. 31).

In general, the principles of construction are elementary, and the walls usually maintain stability by their mass alone, with one exception, at Abó, in the Salinas district, east of Albu-

7. Reuter, 1926.

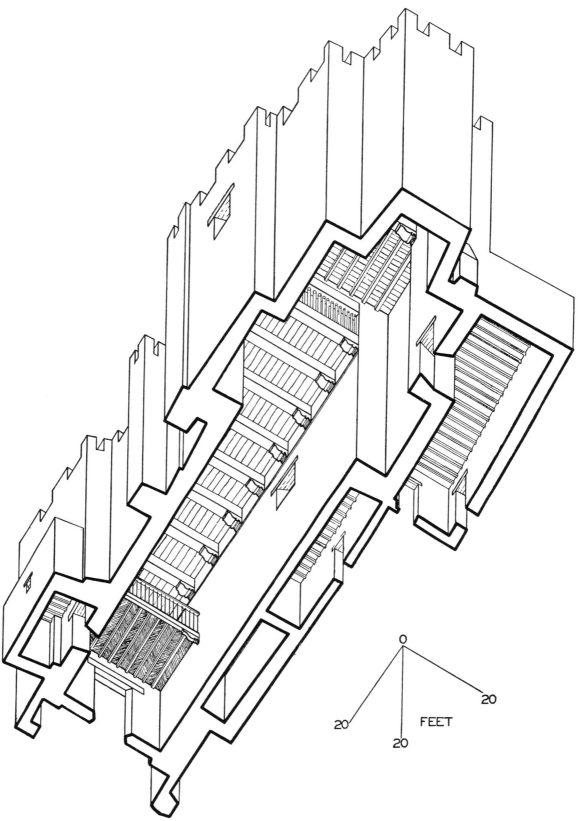

14. Abó. Reconstruction of the church. Isometric.

querque. Built about 1646,[8] the structure comprises massive buttress elements which support a relatively thin curtain wall between them (Fig. 14). A certain economy of material results, and the dynamic principle of construction is the opposite of that in which the wall stands by virtue of its mass alone. The significance of this lone experiment at Abó is considerable. Attributed to Friar Francisco de Acevedo,[9] the monument may be filiated with the structural tradition of the Middle Ages in Europe, through the Mexican survivals of the rib vault and buttressed fabric, in the sixteenth century.[10]

3.

Floors. The relationship between floor levels and building grades indicates that the ground was usually prepared before construction. In a number of churches, it is evident that the present floor level lies several feet below the apparent building grade. Much of this difference is produced by high erosion batters. Occasionally it is caused by excavation before building. At Chimayo, the building grade falls away under the sanctuary, and the nave floor was dug from the hillside to a depth of two or three feet at the main façade (Fig. 15). At Giusewa the

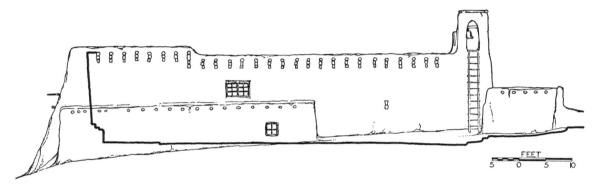

15. Chimayo. Elevation and schematic section of the church.

sanctuary steps and altar tables were carved in part from the rock of the hillside (Fig. 60). In some cases the floor level is higher than the building grade. At Acoma, the floor is an adobe platform four feet high, resting on the bedrock building grade (Fig. 11).

The floor itself, in nave, choir loft, and sanctuary, is usually of packed earth or adobe clay. An ash fill occurred between floors at Giusewa.[11] At Quarai the floor was paved with red sandstone flags (Fig. 68) measuring about 24 inches by 18 inches.[12] Traces of flagstone floors were also found at Humanas, and Abó.[13] At Trampas the floor is made of hand-hewn slabs of wood set in rough frames (Fig. 71). The slabs measure five feet by two feet. In churches still in use, the bare adobe floors, or hand-hewn wooden floors, have rarely survived (Fig. 72). In the late nineteenth century, modern floors of scrap lumber in uneven widths (Fig.178) were laid on sleepers over the original floor.[14]

8. *Infra,* p. 90.

9. Vetancurt, 1697, p. 81.

10. Toussaint, 1935.

11. *Infra,* p. 83.

12. Ely, 1935.

13. Communicated by Joseph H. Toulouse, Jr.

14. At Socorro, the new floor is 18 inches higher than the original packed clay.

Steps between the nave and sanctuary, or transept and sanctuary, at the chancel, were carved or built from the clay of the floor (Fig. 16). The treads were faced with wood (Hawikuh), or rarely with burnt bricks (Giusewa).

Bodies were frequently interred under the nave or sanctuary floor. During the excavations at Quarai, forty-one skeletons were removed from the nave alone.[15] When the *parroquia* of Santa Fe was torn down in 1870, many bones were found under the floor.[16] The practice of burying bodies within the churches continued well into the nineteenth century and was discontinued only after repeated orders from the ecclesiastical authorities of the district.[17]

Floors are not level. Generally they slope up toward the sanctuary from the entrance (Fig. 16), as much as two feet in eighty. In some cases they slope downward to the sanctuary. In the majority of cases observed, however, the inclination is upward to the sanctuary. Where modern lumber floors have been added it is not known in which direction the floor originally sloped.

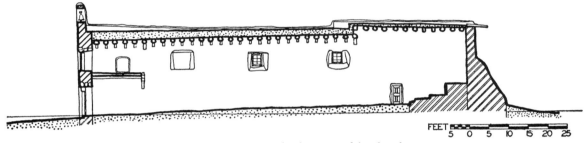

16. Laguna. Longitudinal section of the church.

4.

Roofs. Investigation of the methods of roofing used in older churches is hindered by a number of conditions. The monuments known with some certainty to date from the first half of the seventeenth century, at Quarai, Abó, Pecos, and Giusewa, have all been unroofed in the course of time. Direct evidence is lacking for several details of construction, although it is evident from the ruins that the methods used were very similar in principle to those of later periods.

Many of the existing roofs have suffered such embellishments and alterations during the last forty or fifty years that little of their original character can be determined. Frequently the beamed ceilings have been concealed by another ceiling of ornamental stamped tin. Ironically, the carved timbers and corbels from fallen or rebuilt churches now command fancy prices in the antique market.[18] Over the flat roof, a gabled tin or shingle roof has generally been added (Fig. 81), for protection from leakage. In some localities,[19] however, the Society for the Restoration and Preservation of New Mexico Churches has worked since 1924

15. Ely, 1935.

16. Twitchell, 1919, p. 152.

17. Terrasas, 1821.

18. The Harvey Company acquired the beams from the old church at San Juan for its inn, El Ortiz, at Lamy.

Anonymous, 1914, p. 335. Mrs. Gerald Cassidy, of Santa Fe, owns the eighteenth-century beams from Nambé, which have been reused in her house on Canyon Road, Santa Fe (Fig. 110).

19. Zia, Laguna, Acoma, Santa Ana, Trampas.

to restore and strengthen the fabric of the monuments without departing any farther than necessary from the original appearance. The Society has replaced rotted beams and spalls wherever possible. At Acoma, the entire roof (Fig. 11) was covered with a concrete slab.[20]

In spite of alterations and restoration of many kinds, the methods of building changed very little. With a few roofs in their original condition, it is possible without chance of great error to apply findings derived from them to virtually all other monuments of the same class, regardless of the time at which they were originally built. Thus W. W. H. Davis, writing in 1857, described methods of roofing used then which are current today as they have been since long before the Conquest.[21] Davis writes: "The roof is flat, with a slight parapet running around it . . . and the water which collects upon it is carried off by means of wooden spouts that extend into the street, and which look not unlike the guns of a small fortress looking through the embrasures. The only wood used about the roof is the sleepers and the boards laid across them to hold the earth. . . . They cover the sleepers with a foot or eighteen inches of dirt, which they pack down, and then besmear it with a top coating of mud to make it water-proof. . . . Sometimes a single roof will weigh several tons. . . . When a roof begins to leak, it is repaired by putting a few sacks of dirt upon it." [22]

The sleepers to which Davis referred are the long transverse timbers (*vigas*) upon which the roof is supported. The timbers usually rest on wooden corbels. Beneath the corbelled table there is often a decorated wooden bed molding of carved poles laid end to end and projecting slightly at the inner surface of the wall (Fig. 73).[23] The molding not only is ornamental, but also serves to bind and strengthen the courses at the level of direct loading from the roof.[24]

Corbels and beams are set more or less closely according to the size of the space to be roofed. In narrow churches, the spacing amounts to about 18 inches (Fig. 158); in the larger monuments (Fig. 73) it varies between 3 feet and 3 feet 6 inches from center to center. At Abó, an exceptional case, the spacing in the nave was seven feet between beams, and the timbers were of extraordinary size, over two feet square, resting on corbels of similar dimensions (Fig. 14), spanning a nave 24 feet 10 inches wide.[25]

The exceptional span (33 feet) at Giusewa, extreme for New Mexico, was perhaps supported by a medial row of wooden supports down the center of the nave. Exact information on the baselike stones for such supports, uncovered during the excavations of 1922, is not available.[26] The case, if properly reconstructed, is unique, and leads to the inference that roofing timbers, under the heavy load of the dirt roof, were inefficient beyond an actual span of more than about thirty feet. The beams are generally round, occasionally squared (Socorro, San Juan timbers now at El Ortiz in Lamy). Squared beams are often adorned

20. Riley, 1925, p. 3.

21. Mindeleff, 1891, pp. 148–151.

22. Davis, 1857, p. 164.

23. San Miguel (Santa Fe), Socorro, Humanas, etc. See H.A.B.S., 36 NM 1, sheet 13.

24. This is sometimes imitated in cut adobe and plaster (Fig. 113). The ornamental treatment represents the

Franciscan cord, symbol of resistance to temptation, widely used in Franciscan art. Mâle, 1932, p. 480. Major Carleton observed such a molding ("entablature") under the choir loft at Humanas. 1855, p. 307.

25. Communicated by Joseph H. Toulouse, Jr.

26. Bloom, 1923, p. 17.

either with a stop chamfer (Fig. 74) or with varieties of floral and geometrical ornament on three faces (Fig. 75).[27]

From center to center, at right angles to the beams, is laid a system of retaining boards or spalls (Fig. 76). Over this surface, packed adobe earth or loose dirt is packed at least six inches deep. The retaining boards are generally rough-hewn planks (Sebogeta), sometimes painted with geometrical ornament (Fig. 76). Another common type of roofing between beams consists of cedar twigs (*savinos*) laid closely together, in a herringbone pattern (Fig. 73), or perpendicular to the principal timbers (El Paso, Laguna, Acoma).

At Giusewa, Laguna, and Acoma a matting of plant fiber is laid between the *savinos* and the coating of adobe earth. The fiber hardens to a rocklike substance and forms an excellent waterproofing material. At Giusewa, fragments of roofing lodged in the walls showed that a bed of brush and splinter lay between the *savinos* and the dirt mass of the roof (Fig. 77).

On the exterior, in adobe buildings, both *vigas* and corbels frequently project beyond the walls, sometimes as far as two or three feet (Fig. 78). In the sandstone structures the roof timbers were often bedded to the end in the body of the wall.

These methods of roofing are customary for virtually all chambers, regardless of size, from the nave and sanctuary to the rooms of the priest's house and the diminutive ceilings over the lantern of a bell tower, or the constrained width of an enclosed stairway, as at Acoma.

A parapet usually rises over the nave and sanctuary, above the dirt of the roof and in continuation of the walls, at least a few inches, and sometimes as much as several feet. The parapet serves as a windbreak, to preserve the loose materials of the roof. It also serves to direct the flow of collected rain water to the wooden drainpipes. The parapet was generally crenelated, according to the evidence of pictures and documents of the nineteenth century (Fig. 182). The crenelations have mostly disappeared, although at Acoma the south wall parapet is still interrupted, crenelationwise (Fig. 58), at several points.[28] At Zia (Fig. 79), the north parapet is interrupted several times.[29] In these instances, the crenelations are little more than passages for the wooden drainpipes. In older photographs, however, the breaks in the parapet were numerous enough to be called crenelations.[30] There is a notable resemblance to the battlemented parapets of the fortress-churches of the sixteenth century in Mexico (Fig. 80).[31]

The drainpipes are fed by the inclination of the entire roof to one side or the other (Fig. 17). This inclination varies from four inches to over a foot, depending on the width of the roof to be drained. The lateral wall in which the windows occur is the most susceptible to damage from rain water. Rain water pouring down the wall can wash away the courses of bricks above the window lintels and cause the collapse of the affected portions (Fig. 54). Consequently the downward pitch of the roof is generally away from the window side of the building (Fig. 17). Since it is desirable to prevent drainage waters from eroding the lower

27. The Moorish-Andalusian ancestry of certain of these forms is striking. For instance, the *zapatas* (Fig. 111) of the priest's house at San Ildefonso (now destroyed) are identical with the *modillon à copeaux* of the Mozarabic builders. It is tempting to see a remote derivative of the Moorish *artesonado* ceilings in the New Mexican roofs, with their herringbone pattern of *savinos* painted in areas of contrasting color (Fig. 73).

28. At Abó, the walls were crenelated. Carleton, 1855, p. 300.

29. From old photographs it is evident that this parapet is a recent addition (Fig. 167).

30. Wittick photographs of Albuquerque (Fig. 182), San Miguel, Santa Fe (Fig. 152), and the North Chapel of the Cathedral, Santa Fe.

31. Atl, 1927, p. 73.

roofs of the priest's house, the nave roof generally slopes away from the wall against which the lower buildings abut. A close relationship consequently exists between the location of the adjacent buildings and the fenestration of the nave (Fig. 17). The notable exception is at Acoma, where the priest's house is north, and the nave windows are south (Fig. 11). Elsewhere, however, the priest's house and the nave windows are on the same side of the nave (Fig. 114).

The roof is subject not only to a lateral inclination, but also to a longitudinal pitch. Measurements show that this pitch averages one foot in one hundred feet. The pitch is more frequently from the façade down toward the sanctuary than in the opposite direction. This feature, with its theoretical relationship to other irregularities, will be resumed later in the discussion.[32]

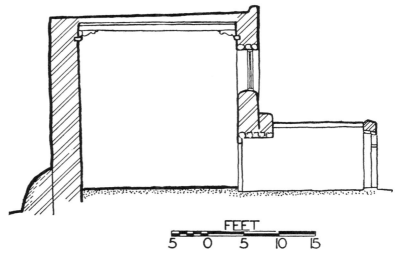

17. Santa Fe. Cross section of the nave, San Miguel.

5.

Buttressing. The numerous heavy wall buttresses which surround the flanks of many of the churches undoubtedly answer certain structural needs. On the other hand, the number and size of the buttresses at Chimayo (Fig. 22), Santa Ana (Fig. 82), Ranchos de Taos (Fig. 83), and Isleta (Fig. 84), for instance, soften and amplify the silhouette of the buildings. The function of buttressing could be satisfied with less material in more commonplace shapes; actually the buttressing seems to satisfy certain formal rather than structural needs. The notable exception is the ruin at Abó (Fig. 14), where the buttresses served a dynamic, actively supporting function, analogous to that of the wall buttress in medieval Christian architecture. Between the widespread elements, a relatively light curtain wall was erected, instead of the usual massive fabric, of which the buttressing remains inarticulated, as at Humanas (Fig. 85).

Elsewhere, the need for buttressing arises from obvious causes. (1) Undercutting of the walls at ground level by water erosion, most likely to occur at points from which the ground level drops away. Projecting corners are vulnerable, particularly at the rear wall of the sanctuary. At the ruins near Abiquiu (Fig. 86) and at Pecos (Fig. 156), the lateral sanctuary walls have remained standing, while the rear wall has collapsed, falling outside the building. Such undercutting may generally be laid to the casual, inadequate character of the foundations and base courses. A common remedy is the addition of continuous horizontal wall buttresses, resembling benches (Cochiti). The principle is to erect a suitable erosion guard around the matrix of an already existing wall.[33] The truncated façade buttresses at

32. *Infra,* p. 69.

33. At Humanas, Quarai (Fig. 154), and Juarez City (Fig. 177), the foundations are wider than the wall and the wall itself rises with occasional setbacks of an inch or two.

Picuris, or Isleta (Fig. 87), serve this purpose as well as that of lending emphasis by bulk. (2) The unforeseen and ill-distributed thrusts from the gabled tin roofs of the nineteenth century tend to crack the walls. When this happens, wall buttresses become necessary between the windows (Fig. 84) and at reëntrant corners, such as those formed between the nave and transept walls.[34] If, on the other hand, a church has escaped the burden of a gabled roof and the lower courses of its walls have been kept in repair, there is no need for buttressing. At Acoma, a church of considerable age and great size, no buttressing has been necessary, with the exception of one corner of the priest's house which rests on a slope falling away from the walls (Fig. 88).

6.

Fenestration. In most monuments, the number of windows was fewer before the restorations of the late nineteenth century. In the nave, openings were small and high. One such window was often enough (Fig. 72); more than three were exceptional. The nave windows occurred in only one wall,[35] leaving the opposite wall an unbroken surface. Through the façade wall there was generally a window lighting the choir loft, over the main entrance (Fig. 89). Windows were pierced in the sanctuary walls under exceptional circumstances, and usually only in the late nineteenth century (Fig. 91). High lateral windows occurred frequently in either one or both arms of the transept (Fig. 90). Three or four windows altogether was average lateral fenestration: two in the nave, perhaps one in the transept, and one in the choir loft.

Such economy of fenestration was convenient for several reasons; to temper the brilliant light of outdoors and to maintain the insulating property of the materials in hot weather and cold. The high, small window in a tapering wall, furthermore, imposes less strain on the fabric than a tall, wide window. Considerations of military defense may also have reduced the number of vulnerable openings.

The methods of window construction were simple (Fig. 18). Originally, the openings of the older churches were wider than high. Given the thickness of the walls, considerable reveals were necessary. These were splayed either to the inside (Isleta, Fig. 7) or to the outside (Quarai, Fig. 27), or both to the inside and the outside (Ranchos de Taos, Fig. 13). Outer sills were splayed downward (Quarai); inner sills were also splayed downward, to the interior. In adobe monuments, the reveals were sometimes extremely irregular, the shape at the wall surface tending to a rude ellipse rather than conforming to the rectangle of the glazing (Fig. 16). In sandstone monuments the reveals show finished workmanship (Fig. 92). The opening is occasionally framed inside and out with carved or painted woodwork (Talpa chapel).

34. A third effective but minor cause for buttressing arises when the walls have been weakened by cutting deep niches into the thickness of the walls. These niches are often of considerable size and are used for altars and shrines. Vetancurt, 1697, p. 102, describes Pecos as having walls so thick that services could be held in their recesses ("concavidades"). Such a recess is still used as a Holy Sepulcher in the south wall of the nave at Santa Cruz (Fig. 112).

35. Exception: Pecos. The drawings in Bandelier, 1881, p. 41, show two nave windows, in opposite walls, near the crossing, and a third window in the south transept. The church was burned, however, during the Rebellion of 1680, and it is possible that one or more of these windows are later additions.

Two types of window construction occur:[36] one displaying conventional European frames and sashes, and the other a gridiron frame of upright spindles. The gridiron windows are earlier than the sash windows (Fig. 186).[37] Common to both is a lintel construction of rough-hewn planks or logs (Fig. 18). The frames and sashes often have handmade mortise-and-tenon joints set with wooden pins. The closely set vertical spindles of the gridiron windows are grooved to hold the glazing material (Fig. 18).

When and where panes of glass were not available, the gridiron windows were used. Between the spindles, sheets of mica or talc were set. No windows glazed in this fashion have survived, although many were in evidence in the middle of the nineteenth century.[38]

Since the American occupation of the territory, the churches still in use have suffered great changes in the number, size, and location of openings. The custom of the remodelers has been to increase by two or three times the size of already existing openings, usually bringing their sills closer to the ground, as in the south wall at Zia (Fig. 167). Complementary open-

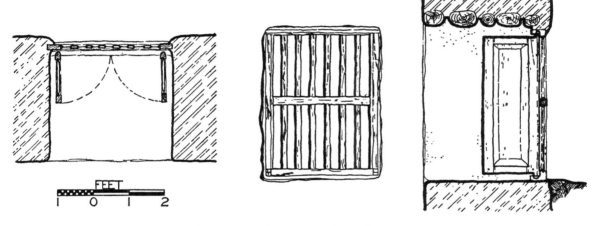

18. Chimayo. Window construction in the Santuario.

ings are often pierced (Fig. 9) through the opposite nave wall.[39] The openings have often been recut, in pointed neo-Gothic shapes, as at Cebolleta, Santa Cruz, and Ranchos de Taos (Fig. 123). New openings have been pierced in the transept. At Socorro, a new chapel was added to the north transept. Openings in the sanctuary, however superfluous and unnecessary, as will be shown below, have been pierced through one or both of its walls at Santa Cruz (Fig. 91) and Acoma. The rectangular opening of the façade has sometimes been altered to an oculus. In other cases, already existing openings, necessary for the balance of the lighting system, have been walled up; for instance, the clearstory windows at Socorro (Fig. 94) and Santa Cruz.

36. For detailed and measured drawings, see H.A.B.S., Chimayo 36 NM 9, sheet 20; Acoma 36 NM 5, sheet 25; Laguna 36 NM 3, sheets 11, 15; Talpa 36 NM 10, sheet 11.

37. Herrick and Johnson, 1900, p. 230, report that the sashes used in their time were shipped from Chicago.

38. Mindeleff, 1891, p. 196.

39. An inventory made at Santa Cruz in 1821 described the church as having two windows. Terrasas, 1821. Today Santa Cruz has four windows in the nave alone (Fig. 9).

The handmade frames and sashes have been replaced with cheap millwork and factory-made glass at Ranchos, Isleta, and San Felipe. The sills and jambs have been paneled with old railroad sidings and cheap lath at Laguna (Fig. 129). The carved and painted woodwork surrounding the openings has been stripped away for mill-sawn facings of whitewashed two-by-fours at Santa Cruz.

Without overhead lighting, the system of lateral fenestration is inadequate. We have seen that the sanctuary should have no lateral windows. If some other means of lighting is not provided for the sanctuary, this part of the structure remains an obscure wall recess (Figs. 97–98). Actually, however, light enters the sanctuary from an overhead window formed by the difference in roof level between the nave and the sanctuary (Figs. 93–96). The roof of the sanctuary is several feet higher than the nave roof. Between the last beam of the nave roof and the first beam of the sanctuary roof, a gap occurs which may be called the *transverse clerestory light* (Figs. 93–96). It is generally equal to the width of the nave, and its height is equal to the difference in roof level.[40]

Where transepts occur, as at Ranchos de Taos (Fig. 13), the difference in roof level may exist between the nave and transept only (the roof of the sanctuary having the same height as the transept). In other cases, the transept roof may be higher than both nave and sanctuary roofs (Quarai, Fig. 68). In the latter case, the space between transept and sanctuary roofs was probably filled in.

7.

Doorways. Doorways generally are rectangular openings. The lintel is made up of several rough-hewn timbers lying side by side (Fig. 11). Arched openings have never been common in New Mexico, although adobe lends itself fairly well to such construction, as in California, where roundheaded bays and windows of many descriptions are common. Few early examples in New Mexico have survived: the arched doorways leading from the sanctuary of Pecos, and the arcade which flanked the façade of Isleta till about 1880 (Fig. 99).[41] At Pecos the voussoir construction, rebuilt in 1915, is skillfully executed (Fig. 101). At Santa Cruz, the stone arches in the towers were probably not built before the nineteenth century (Fig. 102). The limited use of arches has already been discussed (p. 38).

The main entrance to the church is generally splayed at an angle of forty-five degrees to the inside (Fig. 100). The doors, except for a rabbeted meeting of wall and jambs, are flush with the façade. Doorways which lead from the sanctuary to the adjoining sacristy are frequently tunnellike perforations (Fig. 8) through the thickness of the sanctuary wall (Santa Cruz, Ranchos de Taos, Santa Ana). Doorways from the nave to the baptistry are usually wide and low, hung with two-valved doors (Laguna), which are usually more ornately carved than any other secondary doors in the church (Fig. 103). Certain external doorways leading into the buildings of the priest's house (Fig. 109) are of irregular shape (Laguna, Acoma), recalling the modern practice of fitting an adjacent window and door into one frame, without support or wall between. In New Mexico and Arizona such doorways are found in the prehistoric cliff ruins (Canyon de Chelly) as well as in modern Zuñi villages.[42]

40. For details of construction, see the following drawings: H.A.B.S., Ranchos de Taos, 36 NM 7, sheet 20; San Miguel 36 NM 1, sheet 6.

41. There may be an analogy here to the open chapels flanking Mexican churches, *infra,* p. 73ff.

42. Mindeleff, 1891, p. 190.

The shape may have grown from the aboriginal practice of blocking up a doorway when it was not in use, and later only partially reopening it.[43] Occasionally another prehistoric practice survives in the doorways of the Spanish churches: certain thresholds are not flush with the floor, as in Europe, but are raised as much as a foot above the floor. These windowlike doorways (Fig. 104) are common in ancient pueblos, for avoiding drafts.[44]

The doors themselves are paneled in frames with wooden pegs to hold the tenons in place. One vertical member of the frame is provided at both ends with solid round pins which fit into cuplike sockets in the lintel and sill (Fig. 105).[45] All doors were originally hung in this fashion, whether the lintel was of stone (Humanas) or of wood. Mindeleff supposed that this method of hanging doors was imported by the Mormons in the middle of the nineteenth century,[46] but the doors of the churches in New Mexico are much earlier and of Spanish manufacture.

Many of the doors were originally carved with some form of ornament. Usually they were simply paneled (Fig. 105); occasionally the panels took a heraldic or floral decoration in deep relief (Figs. 107, 108); elsewhere an openwork of carved wooden spindles (Fig. 103) was substituted for the panels. Many old doors have vanished into the antique trade, others have been destroyed,[47] and most of the doors seen in churches today are mill-made articles with inexpensive hardware (Fig. 200).

8.

Staircases and Ladders. The ladder is by far the most common means of ascent (Fig. 15) in the indigenous domestic architecture of the Indians, although where stone is abundant, the natives built rude stairs from one level to another of their many-storied dwellings.[48] Likewise in religious architecture: in small churches the ascent to the roof is commonly by means of a ladder (Zia, Laguna). In larger buildings, stairs were either of stone or of wood, depending on the material at hand.

The staircases at Acoma are characteristic. The ascent to the choir loft of the church is through the north wall of the church, and into the choir loft through a now disused doorway (Fig. 67). At Acoma the wooden treads are modern, but their size and number probably correspond to the original stairs, since the stair well remains the same. There are sixteen risers, each 9 and 3/5 inches high, with treads 7 inches deep. The staircase is 2 feet 10 inches wide, lighted by small windows in the north and west walls of the stair well.[49] Other exterior ascents to the choir loft, at Santa Ana, Laguna, and Isleta, are by straight, open-air staircases.

---

43. Mindeleff, 1891, p. 183. Evidences of this habit were found in the church at Quarai. See also Hammond and Rey, 1929, p. 74. "The doors are shaped like a *tau* so as to allow only one person to go through."

44. Mindeleff, 1891, p. 186.

45. For detailed drawings of the construction see H.A.B.S., Acoma 36 NM 5, sheet 25; Talpa 36 NM 10, sheet 9; Laguna 36 NM 3, sheet 14. Such doors are timeless: the treasury of Atreus in Mycenae was provided with them about 1450 B.C. The pivots are the *scapi cardinales* of Roman construction, and large, heavy doors in

modern building are still provided with them. At Abó, iron hinge sockets have recently been discovered in the sill of the principal doorway. Toulouse, 1938, pp. 106–107.

46. Mindeleff, 1891, p. 184.

47. At Ranchos de Taos the main entrance was originally a square doorway, but has recently been changed to a pointed arch. See H.A.B.S., 36 NM 7, sheet 26.

48. Mindeleff, 1891, pp. 160–162.

49. H.A.B.S., 36 NM 5, sheet 20.

A similar arrangement may originally have been in use at Giusewa. The custom is common in the later Franciscan architecture of California, where outside staircases mount not only to the choir loft but also to the pulpit.[50]

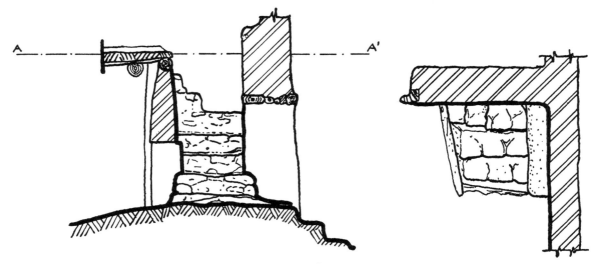

19. Acoma. Detail of the *convento* stair.

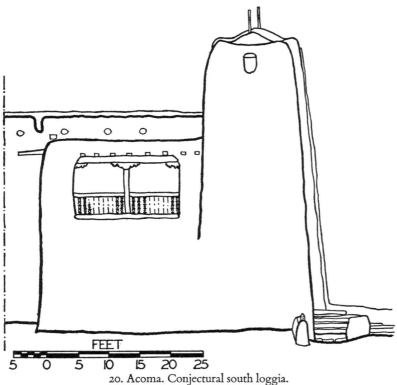

20. Acoma. Conjectural south loggia.

In the north wing of the priest's house at Acoma, ascent to the second floor is by an adobe staircase of peculiar construction (Fig. 19). Whether by lack of foresight, or through later remodeling, the stair well is too small to accommodate the number of steps necessary. Consequently, the stairs rise normally for four risers: the fifth tread, however, is broken into several more risers across its width, thus constituting a flight in itself, at right angles to the other four steps. The treads are faced with slabs of stone.[51]

Such staircases are difficult to maintain. Whether the treads are faced with boards

50. San Gabriel Arcangel. This custom has its antecedents in Mexican architecture.

51. Mindeleff, 1891, p. 162, shows a similar flight of steps at Zuñi.

(Quarai sanctuary), with bricks (Giusewa), or stone slabs (Acoma), the stairs eventually settle and break out of shape. Most old staircases or steps have consequently been replaced with modern wooden constructions.

In certain large churches, access to the belfry is by a winding staircase (Fig. 106) ingeniously fitted into a circular shaft at the core of the tower (Acoma, Albuquerque, Santa Cruz).

At Giusewa (Fig. 60), the sockets which carried the timbers of the winding stairs may be seen in the octagonal tower rising above the sanctuary. The timbers themselves have recently been restored. At Albuquerque, in spite of the many restorations the church has suffered, the winding stairs still exist in the east tower. At Acoma, the winding stairs begin about twenty feet above ground level. Access to the shaft is now provided by a ladder, although originally an inside flight of stairs may have led through a conjectural baptistry and second-floor loggia to the base of the caracole (Fig. 20).[52]

52. H.A.B.S., 36 NM 5, sheets 20, 30.

CHAPTER V

MASS

I.

AN architectural mass differs from a sculptural mass in that the building encloses spaces which constitute its internal mass, or volume. The historical treatment of architecture is therefore incomplete without some systematic treatment of this double aspect of the mass of a building or group of buildings. For architectural masses are subject to the processes of change as surely as any of the subsidiary details of the building. Reference has been made more than once to the stylistic predecessors of the religious architecture of New Mexico, to those fortress-churches of the sixteenth century in Mexico, and it becomes important to demonstrate the visible changes that overtake the model in its transplanted form. The Mexican fortress-church is characterized by the presence of numerous wall buttresses, countering the thrust of the rib vaults within, and establishing a ponderous rhythm along the flanks of the building (Figs. 64, 80). In New Mexico, except at Abó, this rhythm is suppressed; the thick walls themselves usurp the function of the buttresses. In Mexico again, the monastic churches of the sixteenth century are distinguished by a fairly extensive lateral fenestration, and by a lateral doorway opening upon the nave (Fig. 64). Considered together, these apertures lighten the appearance of the structure, break its mass, and open it to the outside world. The number and size of such openings in New Mexico, however, is cut to an irreducible minimum; the windows are rarely more than two or three, in the original state (Fig. 58), and the auxiliary entrance to the nave is usually suppressed. The consequence of these shifts of accent is to reduce external mass to the status of geometric abstraction, to a block-shaped solid (Fig. 21) which appeals strongly to the formal imagination of many living artists (Fig. 83).

Because of the relative abundance of fenestration in Mexico, the roof level is continuous (Fig. 64). The aesthetic and practical need for overhead illumination had not yet been evoked. In New Mexico, a century later, both new needs were satisfied by the invention of the transverse clearstory window, with the resultant break in the roof level. This stepped roof level (Fig. 79) constitutes a rich variant upon the occasional monotony of mass and silhouette to be observed in the sixteenth-century churches. The structure is articulated; new interior relationships affect the exterior massing, and the raised sanctuary dominates the entire effect, with the wide, low window introduced at the difference of roof level. An analogous shift in massing is to be noted in the introduction of the transept. This element, conspicuously absent from the monastic architecture of Mexico, adds supplementary masses to the block of the nave and sanctuary, enriching the play of light and shadow over the surfaces, and leading the eye from mass to mass (Frontispiece).

The churches of New Mexico, then, mutate away from their sixteenth-century models in clearly defined directions. The secondary projections, apertures, and rhythms are suppressed in favor of monolithic planes (Fig. 83). The balanced regularity of the Mexican profile is abandoned in favor of a terraced silhouette, subordinated to the dominant mass of the sanctuary (Fig. 79). The frequent introduction of the transept, furthermore, enhances the solid geometry of the clear, simple massing.

2.

The Façade. The chronological uncertainties described elsewhere grow particularly confusing in the classification of façades. Endless remodelings complicate the question. At Santa Cruz, an elaborate parapet crowned the façade (Fig. 115) before the imposition of the new gabled roof, about 1886. At Isleta, the original plain façade (Fig. 99) has been augmented by buttresses, a balcony, and a gabled roof. In such cases the pictorial documentation of remodelings does not antedate 1846.

There is evidence, however, that a balcony spanning the façade occurred in some churches of the seventeenth century. Emory's drawing of the ruin at Pecos, made in 1846,[1] shows such a balcony recessed between flanking towers (Fig. 116). Access to it appears to have been through a window in the façade, giving on the choir loft. At Giusewa a deep break runs across the façade some feet above the door (Fig. 118). Timbers may once have lain in this break, to form the roof of a balcony recessed into the center of the façade.

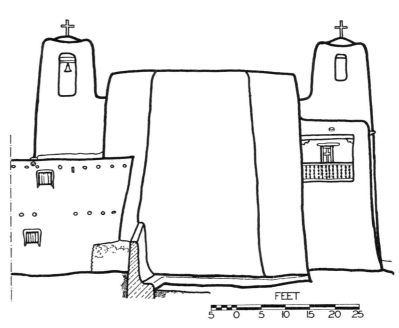

21. Acoma. The sanctuary restored to its probable seventeenth-century condition.

Among monuments surviving today, three distinct types of façade may be distinguished. Such a classification has no reference to possible chronology. It is based on the presence or absence of certain architectural elements.

1. *The plain end wall.* The only openings are the doorway and choir-loft window (Fig. 114). There is generally an ornamental parapet and a belfry arcade for one or more bells. This is by far the most common type of façade. It is found throughout the Rio Grande district, in both Indian and Mexican villages, as well as in towns.

2. *The façade with flanking towers.* The towers may be more or less clearly articulated from the plane of the façade. In Abert's drawing of the *parroquia* of Santa Fe (Fig. 117), made in 1846,[2] the shafts of the towers are extensions of the plane of the façade itself. At Santa Cruz they emerge prominently from the façade, rising as individual masses from the ground level

1. Emory, 1848, p. 30.   2. Abert, 1848, unnumbered plate.

to the belfry (Fig. 120).[3] Various modifications of the towered façade occur. The towers may be relatively slender units defining the corners of the façade, as at Trampas (Fig. 119). In some cases they appear as mere projections of the lateral walls, defining the recess in which balcony and door occur, as at Cochiti (Fig. 121) or at Santo Domingo (Fig. 190). Some towers resemble large buttresses inclined to the façade. At Ranchos de Taos (Fig. 123) their projection at the ground level is considerable; in rising they approach the façade. At the parapet their projection is absorbed by the façade. Truncated buttresses, resembling abbreviated towers, are often used to accent the façade. They add bulk to the lower courses of the elevation, as at Picuris (Fig. 87), Arroyo Hondo,[4] or at Isleta.[5]

3. *The balconied façade.* The balcony is formed by the projection of the choir-loft timbers, the recessing of the façade behind the plane of flanking towers or buttresses, and the overhang of the nave roof beyond the plane of the façade. Sometimes the balcony is formed by the slight overhang of choir-loft timbers and roofing materials (Fig. 122). In such cases the balcony is not recessed and the façade itself is unbroken. The usual choir-loft window gives access to the balcony from the interior. The ornamental parapet occurs less frequently than on the plain end-wall façades. A belfry arcade is usual. The balcony may have been used for ceremonies before an outdoor congregation.[6] Apart from ritual purposes, its value in a shadeless country is obvious. Precedent for the balcony exists in Mexican religious architecture (Fig. 139).[7] In the provinces of northern Spain, furthermore, such balconies are common in domestic architecture.[8] Their construction is similar to that of the New Mexican balconies, and the resemblance in some cases extends to the minor details of decoration.[9]

Of these three types of façades, the plain end-wall façade occurs most frequently, in large and small towns, as well as in Mexican and Indian villages. The balconied façade is generally found in Indian villages. The façade with flanking towers but no balcony usually occurs in Mexican towns, although the church at Acoma presents this type (Fig. 88).

On façades which have not suffered the addition of a tin roof, some form of ornamental parapet is common. Often, as at Laguna, the bells are hung in openings pierced through the central motive of the parapet (Fig. 114). The derivation of the ornamental parapet is clearly Hispanic. Models for its generous curved or angular forms occur in the religious ornament of the colonial period in Mexico.

Certain atypical façades occur. In a few cases, a rudimentary narthex forms the approach to the church. The best example is at Chimayo (Figs. 22, 124), where a range of buildings one room high abuts the façade, forming a vestibule flanked by two chambers. There is evidence that this may have been the case at Giusewa. Kern's drawing (1849) shows sections of wall

---

3. Where the towers have a hollow core, at Trampas, Ranchos de Taos, Albuquerque, Acoma, or the destroyed church at Tesuque (Fig. 140), access is generally either from the choir loft or the balcony. At Santa Cruz, however, the bell tower may be entered at ground level. Vetancurt, 1697, p. 102, mentions six towers at Pecos, presumably defining the arms of the transept as well as the façade. The ruins at Abó show that transept towers may have existed there (Fig. 63).

4. Illustrated by Prince, 1915, opposite p. 259.

5. At Isleta these buttresses were added late in the nineteenth century (Fig. 84).

6. *Infra,* p. 75.

7. Secretaria de educación publica, 1933, Plates 35, 36, 38, 42. Ayres, 1926, Plate 35. *Infra,* p. 75.

8. Bernard, 1928, Plates 45–48.

9. Bernard, 1928.

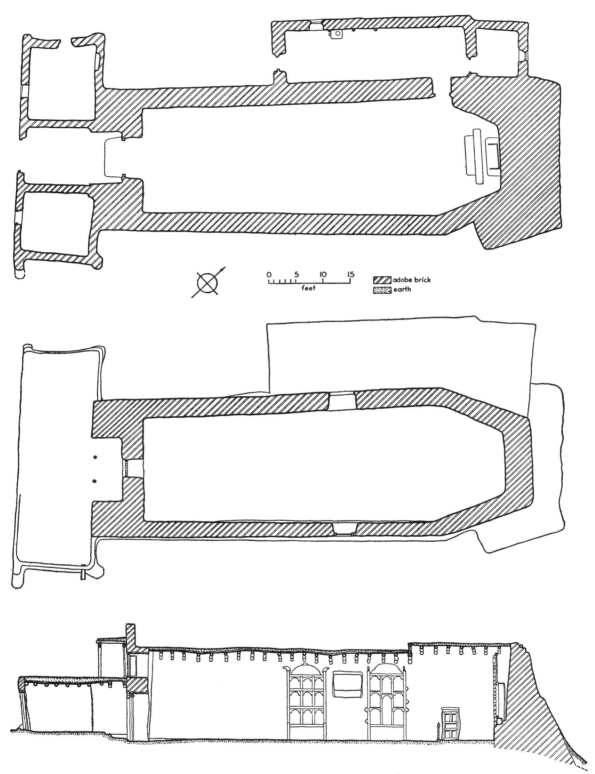

22. Chimayo. The Santuario. *Above:* Plan at ground level. *Center:* Plan at window level. *Below:* Longitudinal section.

defining one end of such a disposition at the façade (Fig. 125).[10] Excavations conducted by the University of New Mexico in 1936 revealed a baptistry at this point (Fig. 29).[11] At Talpa (Fig. 42) and at Truchas, the doorway is deeply recessed into a façade which offers no other breaks (Fig. 126). At Cochiti, a narthex, added after 1880, presents a triple arcade to the courtyard. Exceptional also is the entrance through the base of a well-developed tower at the church of San Miguel in Santa Fe (Fig. 127).[12] The façade of Santa Ana (Fig. 128), as it appeared some years ago, was broken by three deep balconies or bays, formed by prominent buttress projections; the central bay was wider than its neighbors and crowned with two tower belfries. Whether this façade has always been unique it is impossible to say.

3.

The Nave. An architectural volume is the space enclosed or indicated by floor, walls, and roof, and as such constitutes the internal mass of the structure. It not only affords shelter, but may be treated to induce constraint, well-being, restlessness, calm, awe, or oppression in the occupants.[13] The architect may manipulate the dimensions, angles, lighting, textures, or the voids and solids, to secure these effects. The character of the manipulations will of course be affected by the quality of materials, the methods of construction, and the programmatic size of the intended structure. In New Mexico, these conditions are already known: the width of any church is limited by the size of available roof timbers, its height may not exceed the limits of reasonably economical adobe construction, and its length is consequently derived from the size of the congregation to be accommodated. The typical volume is continuous: apart from transept and sanctuary, no subsidiary volumes, such as aisles or lateral chapels, interrupt the flow of space in the nave (Fig. 72).

A manipulation for the sake of design is evident in the fact that the height of the walls usually approximates the width of the nave (Isleta, Fig. 178; Quarai, Fig. 68; Ranchos de Taos, Fig. 184; Santa Cruz). Adobe walls, properly constructed, can theoretically rise to a height of eighty feet,[14] twice the length of the best roof timbers. At the other extreme of possibility, a room need be no higher than its tallest occupant, as in the Indian dwellings. In their choice of a point midway between these limits, the seventeenth-century builders obeyed the simple need to enclose an adequate amount of air. More important, the Catholic ritual requires a monumental development in space to enhance the word, the gesture, and their musical accompaniments. In this respect, the soaring volumes of medieval architecture, like wafers of space set on edge, are foreign to the aesthetic of the seventeenth century, charac-

---

10. Simpson, 1852, p. 20.

11. Dutton, 1938, p. 139.

12. This tower fell in 1872, and was not repaired until 1887. See Forrest, 1929, p. 42. It is not known for how long prior to 1872 the tower had been standing, although the Urrutia map (Fig. 46), made during the second half of the eighteenth century, shows San Miguel in plan, with an unmistakable harmonic façade. The Huntington Library manuscript, moreover, refers to the construction of *torres,* plural, in 1710. Kubler, 1939a, p. 12.

13. The volume is therefore an element of design long neglected by the historians and critics of architecture.

Instead, discussion has centered about the "good" or "bad" proportions of a room. Proportion is a metrical relationship that excludes several of the above-mentioned manipulations of volume. The degree to which architects may be concerned with the treatment of volumes is, of course, subject to historical change. The temple builders of Greek antiquity were concerned more with the character of the enclosing walls than with the enclosed space; in Christian religious architecture, the interior volume has always determined the form of the enveloping walls.

14. *Supra,* p. 25.

teristically manifested in European architecture by the continuous volume, in which the height approximates the width on a plan of relatively modest length (Fig. 23). The volume chosen, therefore, by the early friar-priests of New Mexico[15] corresponds to the preference in volumes observable in the architecture of the seventeenth century in Europe and Mexico.

4.

The Choir Loft. A national peculiarity of Spanish religious architecture is the separation of the choir and the sanctuary.[16] In the religious architecture of the Middle Ages in other countries, notably France, the term "choir" became a synonym for sanctuary, and, in fact, generally replaced the latter.[17] In Spain, however, the choir was relegated to other parts of the church, notably to a tribune usually reserved in France for the organ, spanning the nave at the façade. The development of this tribune, or choir loft, in many late Gothic monastic churches of Spain[18] attains much formal importance. Not only does the tribune itself afford room for large companies of musicians, but below the tribune an entrance chamber is formed, with a low ceiling, constituting a sort of anteroom. In Europe the arrangement had a long and illustrious life. From its magnificent formulation in the basilica of the Escorial, where the choir loft became a mezzanine church for the use of the court, it was developed at Versailles, Dresden, Naples, and Barcelona into the typical court chapel of the great palaces, with two levels, the lower one for the common people, the upper for the use of the royal family and their attendants.

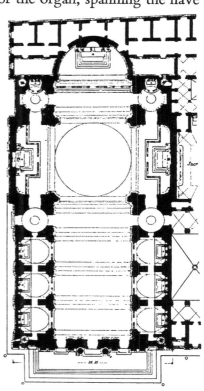

23. Rome. Plan of Il Gesú (1568–75).

Now this choir loft, spanning the nave at the façade, played an important part in the Mexican churches of the sixteenth century,[19] where it was used in exactly the same way as in contemporary Spain. From Mexico, it passed with the Franciscans to New Mexico, undergoing translation, along with other imported elements, into the terms of post-and-lintel construction.

Thus, in 1668, Nuestra Señora de Guadalupe at El Paso (Juarez City) had "a handsome

15. The height is roughly equivalent to the width, in many cases: it tends to be less than the width in the nineteenth century (Chimayo, Fig. 187). Worth noting are the unusual proportions of the church at Patokwa (Fig. 26). The nave is 25 feet wide, for a total interior length of 58 feet 9 inches. Can it have been planned to lengthen the church at some later date?

16. Weise, 1933, p. 65, has studied the significance of this dislocation in another aspect; that of the choir en-

closure located in the middle of the nave of the Spanish cathedrals.

17. Viollet-le-Duc, 1854, pp. 226–227.

18. Good examples, illustrated in another context, figure in Weise, 1933, pp. 39 (Alcanadre), 47 (San Marcos, Leon), 55 (San Jeronimo el real, Madrid), 57 (San Estevan, Salamanca).

19. Atl, 1927, *passim.* Toussaint, 1927, *passim.*

choir-loft, so spacious that the services of fifty clerics and of the Mansito choir-boys could easily be celebrated there."[20] Nearly every church was thus provided with its choir loft, varying in size with the population of the settlement. Usually it is a deep gallery as wide as the nave, facing the sanctuary (Figs. 129–132).[21] The floor of the choir loft stands 6 to 12 feet above the nave. Its depth is rarely more than half the width of the nave. The loft is always lighted from a window in the center of the façade. Access to the loft is supplied either by a door giving directly into the loft from the second-story rooms or from the roof of the adjacent priest's house (Laguna), or, internally, from the nave by a ladder or staircase (Cordova).

The gallery is supported by the end and lateral walls of the nave. At the desired height, a cross timber carries joists of which the opposite ends are embedded in the end wall (or project to support the balcony of the façade). Between the joists are laid *savinos,* or spalls. Over these a layer of packed adobe clay is spread, as on the roofs (Fig. 16).

The cross timber frequently rests on carved or painted corbels. The beam itself may be squared, carved, and painted. The joist ends are sometimes carved as brackets in the usual scroll form (Fig. 132). The exposed sides of the spalls or *savinos* are often painted in contrasting areas of color with geometrical designs (Fig. 76). A balustrade with carved balusters[22] spans the width of the loft.

In the wider naves, the cross timber may be shored up by one or more vertical timbers with carved bracket capitals (Fig. 130).[23]

Occasionally the clay flooring has been replaced by a light modern floor of one-inch lumber in uneven widths.[24] In some cases the entire choir loft has been torn out, as at Chimayo, where, however, the cross-timber butts are still visible on the exterior (Fig. 15). With the disappearance of the priest's house, or its partial destruction, the doorways giving directly into the choir loft at its own level have been blocked up (as at Acoma, Isleta, Laguna, Santa Ana).

5.

The Transept. The characteristic architectural form of the seventeenth and eighteenth centuries in Mexico is the parish church, provided with a transept and a dome at the crossing (Fig. 133). It is impossible to determine, from the evidence of the Mexican churches alone,

20. Scholes, 1929, p. 198. There was musical activity in the province long before 1668. Benavides reported in 1630 that three Masses were sung daily in Santa Fe, also that an organ had been installed by Friar Cristobal de Quiñones as early as 1609. Ayer, 1916, p. 198. In 1664, it is recorded that there was an organ, or a choir "with many musical instruments," in 18 of the 28 churches then existing in the province. There were also numerous schools to train the Indians in singing and instrument playing. Spell, 1927, p. 27. Dr. ten Broeck witnessed a charming performance at Laguna in 1851 on Christmas day. "Just over the entrance door there was a small gallery and no sooner had the Mexican commenced his rosary, than there issued from this a sound like the warbling of a multitude of birds . . . thru the whole house, bounding from side to side, echoing from the very rafters—fine, tiny warblings, and deep-toned, thrilling sounds. The note of the wood-thrush, and the trillings of the canary were particularly distinct. What could it mean? I determined to find out, and having worked my way up into the gallery, I there found fifteen or twenty small boys lying prone upon the floor, each with a small basin two-thirds full of water in front of him, and one or more short reeds, perforated and split in a peculiar manner. Placing one end in the water, and blowing through the water, they imitated the notes of different birds most wonderfully." Schoolcraft, 1854, pp. 72–74. Compare a sensitive account of the music in the church at Isleta in 1881 by Bourke, in Bloom, 1938, p. 197.

whether one of these two elements gave rise to the other. Both are nonexistent in the repertory of the sixteenth century, at least in this specific relation. It might seem that the addition of the transept necessitated a more extensive lighting system, such as that provided by the dome. Conversely, it might also appear that the wish to augment the fenestration by means of the dome would have engendered the spatial extension of the transept. The answer to this delicate question is to be found in contemporary European experiments. The religious architecture of Europe was dominated for two centuries by a Jesuit edifice in Rome, the Gesù, designed by Vignola and built between 1568 and 1577. The peculiarity of this structure is the concentrated, self-sufficient character of the sanctuary and its immediate surroundings (Fig. 23). This unity is secured by means of the transept and the crossing dome. The nave itself undergoes unification: the aisles are reduced to modest lateral chapels, and the projections of the nave elevations are minimized. The Gesù plan affords great compactness; the volume of the building is continuous, uninterrupted by secondary spatial values. Now Weise[25] has demonstrated, following Dehio-Bezold[26] and Mâle,[27] that this Gesù type was directly dependent upon certain prior experiments in the monastic churches of Spain,[28] where the coordination of sanctuary, transept, nave, and overhead lighting had been effected before the middle of the sixteenth century. Thus the domed parish church of the seventeenth century in Mexico[29] constitutes not only a remote sphere of the baroque influence emanating from the Gesù, but also a resumption of Spanish peninsular experiments, following the medievalizing phase represented by the fortress-church. In this context, the centralized sanctuary, achieved by transepts in conjunction with the dome, forms an American phase of the Counter Reformation architecture initiated by the Gesù.

The frequent use of the transept in New Mexico, at Humanas, Quarai, or Abó, is therefore to be understood in the same way, as a spatial device used in conjunction with overhead lighting, to emphasize and unify the vicinity of the sanctuary. But, as Gillet has noted,[30] the dome in Mexico acquired independent value: local factors conditioned its extravagant use, even without the transept, and similar instances are to be mentioned in New Mexico, as at Zia or Laguna, where overhead lighting was installed, but without the characteristic accompanying feature of the transept.

21. Joists and cross timbers embedded in the walls of the south transept at Pecos indicate that a gallery once spanned the transept there. Joist holes also occur in the surviving west transept of Abó. At Tomé, each arm of the transept is furnished with a gallery of recent construction. In all probability, the purpose of these auxiliary galleries was to increase the capacity of the edifice.

22. For identical baluster types in the loggias of village houses in northern Spain see Bernard, 1928, Plate 56 (Anso).

23. Major Carleton's description of the now-vanished choir loft at Humanas (Gran Quivira) is detailed enough to be quoted extensively. "The width of the nave is twenty-seven feet. . . . A gallery extended along the body of the cathedral for the first twenty-four feet. Some of the beams which sustained it, and the remains of two of the pillars, that stood along under the end of it which was nearest to the altar, are still here; the beams in a tolerably good state of preservation—the pillars very much decayed; they are of pine wood, and are very elaborately carved." 1855, p. 307.

24. At Cebolleta, only the packed adobe has been removed, leaving the original spalls directly under foot.

25. Weise, 1933, pp. 31–60.

26. Dehio and Bezold, 1901, p. 478.

27. Mâle, 1927, pp. 155–159.

28. The most notable example is the former monastery of St. Francis at Medina de Rioseco, in the province of Valladolid, founded and built about 1520–30. Weise, 1933, pp. 52–60.

29. Atl, 1924.

30. Gillet, 1929, p. 1037.

Certain factors condition and limit the appearance of the transept in New Mexico. It depends for light upon the transverse clearstory window, which is accordingly installed at the difference in roof level between the nave and transept, rather than between the transept and sanctuary. The reason for this is obvious: the transept would be a mere extension of the dark nave if it did not share a common source of light with the sanctuary. The transept, however, is not totally deprived of lateral fenestration. At Pecos (Fig. 90) and Quarai, for instance, the end walls of the transepts contain windows, placed high, beneath the corbel course. Their light, however, is minimal, for were it more intense, the sanctuary would be obscured behind the cross lighting from these sources. Actually this has happened in certain cases where the clearstory window has been suppressed and the transept windows enlarged, as at El Paso (Juarez City). But it is a principle of baroque style to coalesce the spatial units of the transepts and sanctuary by means of light, so that the source of illumination (transverse clearstory window) never occurs at the sanctuary, but always at the transept. Other consequences were derived from this principle. The transept arms must always be subordinate to the main axis formed through the nave and sanctuary. They may expand only at the expense of this axial unity, and in so doing they tend to destroy the focus of the space design. Another factor limiting the transept is the roofing technique. The postulate of spatial unity determines the length, and the roof timbers restrict its width to that of the nave. The roofing technique, however, simultaneously promotes and destroys the spatial unity. In the limitation of their width, nave and cross vessel are commensurable, but the direction of the timbers in nave and transept must be at right angles to one another (Fig. 14), producing an important variation in the plastic value of the roof as a whole. This variation, while contributing to the optical effect, marks the transept as an autonomous member, distinct from the sanctuary. Historically, nevertheless, many variant solutions exist within these theoretical limits. At one extreme, there is the transept which is conceived as an incident of minor significance, as at the large church of Humanas (Fig. 12), where the total transept length exceeds the width of the nave by a few feet. At the other extreme, we find the transept realized as a cross vessel of independent spatial character. At Ranchos de Taos (Fig. 13), the transepts constitute a separate church at right angles to the nave: the north arm contains an altar in a kind of sanctuary formed with steps and other furniture. The south arm is deep enough to serve as a nave for this church within a church. Between these extremes, other solutions are found. At Pecos (Fig. 156) and Abó (Fig. 4), the transept arms are relatively shallow, but they contained galleries, like choir lofts, of which the exact use is uncertain. Elsewhere, at Quarai (Fig. 27) or Trampas (Fig. 25), the transept arms served as chapels, each with its altar and chapel furniture. At Abó, the solution is unique (Fig. 4). The nave is a rectangular enclosure, with an appended sanctuary, of which the chancel width is less than that of the nave. In this arrangement itself there is nothing remarkable. But the lateral walls of the nave are interrupted by the arms of a shallow transept, located not at the end of the nave, but at some distance from the sanctuary. In terms of the massing the effect here is to multiply the points of interest subordinate to the sanctuary. Several corners are secured: the transept corner (salient), the nave corner (reëntrant), and the sanctuary corner (salient). This composition of salient and retiring angles, six in all at the sanctuary, effectively drives sanctuary, transept, and part of the nave together into a spatial unity in which the "vibration" from angle to angle must have been impressive. The general character of this effect may be estimated from the photograph of the north end of the church at Quarai (Fig. 68), where the number of angles falls short, but where the visual effect is legible.

At Socorro and Santa Cruz (Fig. 9), as well as the old *parroquia* of Santa Fe, another treatment of the transept is found. In these churches, the cross vessel nearly attains independent status, and its external length is even further developed by the addition of extra chapels. These do not affect the interior length of the transept, although they shut off the cross lighting otherwise available through windows in the end walls. The process here seems to be one of slow accretion rather than of a single, fluent campaign of building. A programmatic need for further chapels presumably dictates the expansion, rather than a principle of design.

6.

The Sanctuary. As I have just indicated, the treatment of the sanctuary was the critical point of seventeenth-century design. In the Gesù, the union of a basilical and a central plan in one structure (Fig. 23) established a relationship between nave and sanctuary that had never before been realized with such clarity of purpose. A theatrical polarity prevailed: the nave, simplified and restrained, served as an audience hall for the dramatic set at the sanctuary, with its intense overhead lighting, and the imposing convergent volumes of the transept arms. In New Mexico, the sanctuary is the object of various devices intended to emphasize its importance, unify its effect, and accent its autonomy.

It is always a clearly articulated member of the structure.[31] Seen from outside, the greater height of its roof distinguishes it from the nave and other members of the edifice (Figs. 79, 84). Several devices are used to emphasize its interior character. Overhead lighting is its principal distinction (Figs. 137, 138). In churches of cruciform plan, as well as in certain continuous-nave churches (Cochiti; Isleta, Fig. 178; Truchas), its frame, the chancel, is always narrower than the nave (Fig. 138). In both cruciform and continuous-nave churches, the chancel (Fig. 136) may be accented with pilasters (San Miguel in Santa Fe, Fig. 151), or special treatments of the chancel beam, such as ornate carving (Fig. 71) or oversize timbers (Laguna), extra corbeling (Fig. 204), diagonal struts to the sanctuary walls (Ranchos de Taos, Fig. 185), or an arched treatment in wood (Fig. 136). The floor level of the sanctuary is invariably some steps higher than the floor level of the nave or transepts.[32]

Altar steps and altar tables in the sanctuary are often built of the same material as the walls (Zia, Fig. 98; Acoma; Giusewa). Niches and recesses for keeping liturgical instruments are sometimes hollowed from the walls (Zia, Cordova). Thus the sanctuary presents not only a homogeneous spatial effect, but also the unity of a structure of which the materials are homogeneous, and as if carved into the forms of architecture.

---

31. Contrast the Franciscan practice in California in the eighteenth century, where the sanctuary is the end wall of the nave, without other distinction in structure.

32. One riser at Chimayo; seven at Hawikuh.

CHAPTER VI

OPTICAL EFFECTS. THE TREATMENT OF LIGHT

1.

IT is intended here to treat those aspects of the architecture that incorporate the relations of the building with light. The distribution of lights and shadows over the exterior elevations; the stratifications of light and shadow that exist within a complex of highly organized moldings; and the remaining large-scale treatments of light—these are the subjects usually treated under this heading. For the plan, the structure, and the massing do not exhaust the organization of an architecture; they merely establish its rational and spatial articulation. Without a consideration of light, of the fashion in which light is made to model the building and is itself deflected and qualified, the aesthetic values of architecture defy treatment.

Structural necessities are often made to conform to some preconceived treatment of the light, and the plan itself may reveal an intention to deal with light as a source of visual gratification. The massing, furthermore, may often conform to a controlling principle in the treatment of light. Thus it often becomes necessary, at a certain stage of the study, to reconsider the plan, structure, and massing in terms of light. But beyond these categories, the building's relation to light is revealed in the system of plastic and mural decorations of the structure.

2.

Plastic Decoration. Adobe brick, in its intermediate position between hard stone and plastic material, lacks both the cohesion of stone and the elasticity of properly fictile materials. It cannot be made to withstand the considerable crushing and breaking strength of stone, nor can it assume the nervous, taut forms of concrete or of the clay used for ceramic decoration. It is unfired dirt, cohering only because of a limited clay content; a friable, porous material conducive to few plastic effects. Thus, wall built of adobe will always preserve the mural values of pure masonry, tending to the appearance, perhaps, of monolithic construction, but never allowing the exploitation of the material to the point of the destruction of the mural values, as with stone treated by the stylistic precepts of certain periods. We have already examined the structural limitations of the material: the plastic limitations are their corollary. The structural limitations of adobe affect even the stone constructions of the Salinas area and elsewhere: a masonry held together by an armature of sun-dried adobe clay cannot much exceed either the structural or plastic limits of adobe itself.

The architectural forms of European building, which have always been dependent upon the use of stone, undergo translation or suppression in New Mexico. Moldings, for instance, are either entirely absent, as at San José de Chama (Fig. 72), or else they are realized in wood (Fig. 158). Elements of the church furniture may occasionally be manufactured in adobe, as baptismal fonts (Fig. 146) and altar tables, but a complex system of base or wall moldings is lacking. There is no need for them, since such moldings spring from the presence of many columnar supports and the vertical and horizontal divisions of a complex and dynamic elevation. Such forms, however, when they occur, are translated into wood. The bed moldings underneath the corbel courses of the roof, and upon which the corbels rest, are wooden poles carved usually with a rope motive derived from the Franciscan cord symbolizing the vow of chastity (Fig. 73). But the wooden rope moldings of New Mexico serve more than a plastic purpose; they seem also to strengthen the wall courses at the point of greatest load. Points of programmatic interest, such as the chancel, usually take a decoration of wooden elements, since adobe cannot adopt these arched and crocketed forms. These wooden chancel beams and arches also serve a trussing function.

The vaulted and domed forms of roofing in European construction, as we have also seen, are converted into post-and-lintel construction in New Mexico. Here the structural postulates automatically present plastic values; the rhythm of parallel roof beams, supported upon corbels, down the length of the nave and at right angles over the transept, presents a plastic value which may be emphasized by various means. Square and round beams, with a vocabulary of carved decoration; corbels of some variety of silhouette (Fig. 24), usually recalling the brackets of classical antiquity; or even, upon occasion, the *modillon à copeaux* of Mozarabic corbeled ornament; and the actual ceiling materials, laid across the roof timbers in patterns of varying character, picked out with paint—all these compose an overhead decoration that is not merely structural, but rhythmic and plastic as well.

But this vocabulary of plastic forms is small; the roof timbers are either square or round; the corbels nearly all follow a basic and simple type, with minor variations of detail;[1] the bed moldings are always the Franciscan cord. On the timber surfaces, the patterns are simple floral compositions, relieved by compartmentation, occasional inscriptions, frets, and meanders. The balustrades of the façade balconies, choir lofts, and altar rails follow a few abstract types, almost never in the round, but as fretwork silhouettes cut from boards (Fig. 113).

In the terms of exterior decoration, however, adobe is occasionally made to serve the purposes of plastic decoration. The crenelations, occasionally of fanciful shapes, as on the church at Albuquerque (Fig. 182) some years ago, may be adobe elements. The façade elements housing the bells often assume relatively elaborate profiles, as at Laguna (Fig. 114), or in the turret elements housing the bells at Acoma (Fig. 67) and at Cordova. On the whole, however, the vocabulary of plastic decorative effects is relegated to wood, within which, however, the builders of New Mexico realized very few of the possibilities. The intricate *artesonado* work of the Moorish carpenters, as at Tlaxcala in Mexico, was never exploited in New Mexico. An extensive sculpture in wood, in the full round, for purposes of church decoration, also never came to fruition, although the numerous *bulto* figures, images of the saints, carved in the full round, might appear to offer the exception. These, nevertheless, preserve a rigid quality determined by the original shape of the block of wood, and it is difficult, in the terms of architectural decoration, to discover an extensive vocabulary of plastic effects in New Mexico other than that of the ceilings and balustrades, together with an

1. The corbels which adorn the ceiling vary in bulk, silhouette, and detail from monument to monument. These variants appear to occur in no orderly evolution. In the same district, highly finished examples appear simultaneously with specimens of inferior workmanship (cf. Chimayo, Fig. 187, and Cordova, Fig. 113). The affluence of the community may explain the particular quality of execution, but the time at which the work was done seems to account for little.

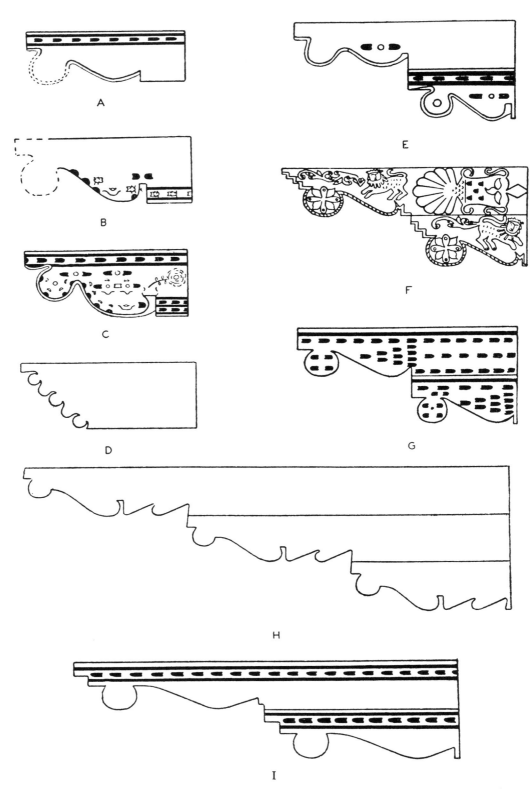

24. Various corbels from New Mexico. A. Pecos, early eighteenth century. B. Pecos, early eighteenth century. C. San Miguel, Santa Fe, 1710. D. San Ildefonso portal (destroyed), eighteenth century. E. The parish church, Santa Fe, north transept. F. Privately owned. G. Santa Fe, church of La Guadalupe. H. Santa Clara, chancel, early eighteenth century. I. San Juan (now at El Ortiz, Lamy).

occasional bed molding running directly underneath the corbel course. Wooden doors, pulpits, retables, and occasional floors complete the translation of the forms of masonry into the plastic values of another material.

3.

Painted Decoration. A technique of mural painting existed in prehistoric New Mexico. Villagra, who described New Mexico in 1598,[2] refers repeatedly to the mural painting of the Indian houses at various sites. The recent discovery (1935) of such murals in the square kiva at Kuaua confirms the literary evidence for their existence. The designs, on 17 of the 85 coats of plaster in one chamber, represented masked dancers, painted in black, white, blue-green, yellow, and red.[3] The tradition for a mural decoration of figural character was therefore available to the missionary builders of the seventeenth century.

A trace of seventeenth-century mural decoration was discovered in 1922 in the ruined edifice at Giusewa in the Jemez canyon. The illustrated fragment,[4] which has been preserved only in photographs and drawings, represents a fleur-de-lis pattern,[5] painted on plaster (Fig. 141). The draftsmanship is firm and bold, striving to recompose the conventional lily pattern into the asymmetrical, dislocated forms of Keresan ceramic design. From the fragment, there may be inferred the presence of mural decoration in other churches of the seventeenth century.

Extensive areas of painted wall occur in several churches built or repaired during the eighteenth century. The most complete example is at Laguna, where the church decoration was recorded by the Historic American Buildings Survey in 1934. Similar decorations, though less extensive, occur at Acoma. The style of the murals at Laguna evokes problems of some complexity. Bishop Tamaron, who visited Laguna in 1760,[6] implied that the church decoration was poor, a condition that cannot be identified with the present decoration of the building (Fig. 142). Sometime between 1760 and 1846, when Abert[7] noted the church, the existing mural decoration was probably painted. Its style, however, is in no sense that of the eighteenth century elsewhere in the Spanish world. Rather does it evoke the ornamental vocabulary of the seventeenth century, consisting of heavy painted scrolls, painted Salomonic columns, and floral arabesques which have their closest analogies in the church decorations of the seventeenth century in Mexico, as at the Rosario chapel at Santo Domingo in Puebla. Associated with the elements of this decoration are numerous motives from Pueblo iconography: cornstalks, terraced motives, sun, rain, and thunder symbols disposed along the nave walls. Similar decorations occur at Acoma (Fig. 171) and Zia (Fig. 143). Elsewhere, dados painted in monochrome, without design, follow the lower courses of the nave walls,

2. Villagra, 1933.

3. Hewett, 1938a. Compare Brew, 1939, Plate IX, for prehistoric murals uncovered at Awatovi.

4. Bloom, 1923. Brew, 1937, p. 112, reports twenty-one painted layers on the church walls at Awatovi, "consisting of geometric and floral motifs . . . sometimes arranged as . . . decorated tiles."

5. The advocacy of this church has recently been corrected from San Diego de los Jemez to San José. A common attribute of Saint Joseph, in Christian iconography, is the lily signifying his chastity and the miracle of the flowering wand. Verneuil, n.d., p. 101. Kuenstle, 1926, p. 606.

6. Tamaron, 1937, p. 350.

7. Abert, 1848, p. 53. The back of the altar bears this inscription: "Se pinto este coral y se yso à costa del alcalde mallor Dn Jose Manuel Aragon este año de 780." H.A.B.S., 36 NM 3, sheet 1.

as at Cordova (Fig. 183). Exterior mural decorations are rare, although not completely unknown. At Zia and San Felipe, the façade walls have occasionally been adorned with painted horses, flanking the doorway, executed as silhouette figures with some interior detail. At Zia, such horses were painted on the inner nave walls in 1937 (Fig. 143).

In most churches, painted decoration is restricted to the wooden portions of the buildings, principally to the ceilings and balustrades. The sections of roof timbers from Pecos, preserved in the Laboratory of Anthropology in Santa Fe, show traces of red and blue paint. At El Rito, a nineteenth-century church, the ceiling is polychromed with earth colors (Fig. 75). The soffit of the choir loft at Trampas (Fig. 76) bears many small designs in color, representing animals, humans, and objects in a simple style. The herringbone ceiling laid across the roof timbers at Laguna is painted in areas of contrasting color that carry the diagonal patterns. Railings and balusters are often painted, as on the façade of the new church at Santo Domingo.

On the whole it would appear that adobe construction, with its impermanent surface, discouraged the development of an extensive mural tradition, although the wall masses predicated by the structure offered ideal areas for painted decoration. Given the need to replaster every few seasons, both in and out, painters were not drawn to the development of extensive wall designs. The exception is at Laguna, or Acoma, where painted form survives the fugitive surface, because of an evident and intense local participation in this mode of decoration. The optical effect at Laguna (Fig. 142) is that of walls which vanish behind their decoration: the figures hang in an obscure space, seemingly independent of their support. In the sanctuary at Laguna, the painting replaces the stone carvings of the Mexican or European prototype. The case is unique, and cannot be regarded as typical for New Mexico. Rather does the detailed study of such mural painting belong in a separate work treating of the painting and sculpture of colonial New Mexico. Within the frame of architecture, the proper and usual locus for painted decoration was upon the wooden elements of the structure.

4.

Illumination. Where the system of lateral fenestration is supplemented by a transverse, overhead clearstory light, the church interior is divided into two areas of different intensities of light (Fig. 98). The prevailing obscurity of the nave is relieved by the light of one or two, perhaps three, diminutive and inaccessible windows in one wall. No cross lighting occurs: the unbroken expanse of the opposite wall lies in shadow. At the end of the tunnel, however, brilliant light envelops the painted reredos and altar furniture (Fig. 138). The eye is unable to resist the directional force of this contrasted system of lighting: the attention is immediately drawn, as in a theater, to the sanctuary.[8] Lateral windows alone in the sanctuary do not fulfill this purpose. The direction and intensity of laterally admitted light are the same as in the nave (Fig. 91), while the overhead light, which enters by an opening concealed from the congregation, strikes at another angle and with a different intensity.

Overhead illumination, when properly controlled, may be regarded as a means for the

8. Lieut. J. W. Abert attended a Mass at noon in the *parroquia* of Santa Fe in 1846 (now destroyed): his description of the source of light can apply only to a clearstory window. "From a high window a flood of crimson light, tinged by the curtain as it passed through, poured down upon the altar." 1848, p. 39.

concentration of attention on a given spot. Its architectural possibilities were commonly exploited during the seventeenth century in Europe.[9] For dramatic effects by the emphasis possible from controlled lighting, the dome, rising high above the structure on a drum pierced with numerous openings, was the most important instrument.

The heightened intensity and directional quality of such overhead illumination were indispensable elements in the formal vocabulary of the seventeenth century in Mexico. Every Mexican church of any importance was roofed with domes and the largest, most amply fenestrated dome always surmounted the transept crossing (Fig. 133).[10] The amount of lateral fenestration in the Mexican churches was, however, very limited, consisting again in the familiar system of few, small, inaccessibly placed openings. Here is the probable genesis of the system of lighting used in the churches of the upper Rio Grande. With untrustworthy materials, and laborers reluctant to use arched or domed construction, the friar-priests, whose architectural knowledge had been acquired in Spain or Mexico, found the most practical solution to their lighting problem in the ingenious transverse clearstory window. It gave the desired quality of light in the sanctuary without entailing the structural difficulties of the dome.

The question arises whether or not the transverse clearstory light was invented in New Mexico. No example elsewhere has come to my attention, unless it is the doubtful structure figured in a drawing of uncertain date, used by the historian Beaumont late in the eighteenth century. The drawing represents Bishop Quiroga's entry into Michoacan in the second quarter of the sixteenth century. At the right side of the drawing, a church is shown (Fig. 144) with an unmistakable clearstory window formed by the difference of roof level.[11]

Today, after a long period of alterations, nearly all the older churches of New Mexico have lost the transverse clearstory window, a critical location for destructive leaks. In many other cases, Santa Cruz, Socorro, San Miguel, when the flat roof was covered over with a gable of tin or shingle, the window no longer received any light and it was only natural to close the blind gap.[12] By suppressing the clearstory light, however, the remodelers have tampered with the most characteristic feature of the structure; without it, many New Mexican churches are virtually indistinguishable from adobe buildings the world over.[13]

9. Cf. Wölfflin's classic postulate concerning the function of the dome in baroque architecture: "Der Hauptzweck der Kuppel aber ist, jene Ströme des Lichtes von oben in die Kirche zu leiten, die für den weihevollen Charakter des Raumes so wesentlich sind. Im Gegensatz zu der überirdischen Helle wird das Langhaus verhältnismässig dunkel gehalten. . . . Der Barock rechnet mit dem Licht als einem Stimmungsfaktor." (The chief purpose of the dome is to direct that light, which is essential to the consecrated character of the space, from above into the church. In contrast to the supernatural brilliance, the nave is kept relatively dark. . . . The baroque accounts light as a factor with which to produce mood.) Wölfflin, 1926, p. 122.

10. Xochimilco has the earliest fully developed dome (1590) in Mexico, according to Atl, 1924, pp. 6–7.

11. Toussaint, 1937, p. 14, believes these are eighteenth-century drawings, with Indians "vestidos a la romana."

12. A noteworthy exception occurs at Isleta, where the clearstory window takes borrowed light from openings left for that purpose in the new gabled roof. Otherwise, the gabled roofs have done great damage. Not only do they disguise the stepped silhouette of the church, and render useless the clearstory window, but their weight has often caused the walls to falter and crumble. Santa Cruz, Isleta, and others have been partial victims of the gabled roof, while Nambé collapsed after the addition some years ago.

13. According to a local tradition, related by Porfirio Montoya, the native sacristan at Santa Ana, a small hole four inches in diameter once existed in the roof of the nave. It had a ritual significance, of which I was unable to discover the nature. In the Wittick photograph (1881) of the interior of Acoma, a similar hole is visible.

Measured Irregularities of Walls, Roofs, Floors

A. Convergence of nave walls toward sanctuary, at ground level:
    CORDOVA. Width of nave at façade . . . . 17′ 5″
            Width of nave at chancel . . . . 14′ 10″
    QUARAI. Width of nave at façade . . . . 27′ 5″
           Width of nave at chancel . . . . 27′ 2″
    GIUSEWA. Width of nave at façade . . . . 33′ 10″
          Width of nave at chancel . . . . 33′ 6″
    PATOKWA. Width of nave at façade . . . . 25′ 6″±
          Width of nave at chancel . . . . 24′ 5″
    RANCHOS DE TAOS (H.A.B.S.). Width of nave at façade . . . . 25′ 3″
                  Width of nave at chancel . . . . 24′ 6″
    HUMANAS. Width of nave at façade . . . . 30′ 1″
         Width of nave at chancel . . . . 27′ 2″

B. Expansion of width of nave, approaching sanctuary:
    CHIMAYO (H.A.B.S.). Width of nave at façade . . . . 19′ 10″
              Width of nave at chancel . . . . 22′ 5″
    ISLETA. Width of nave at façade . . . . 24′ 7″
        Width of nave at chancel . . . . 25′ 4″
    LAGUNA (H.A.B.S.). Width of nave at façade . . . . 18′ 10″
            Width of nave at chancel . . . . 19′ 10″
    HUMANAS (Chapel). Width of nave at façade . . . . 27′ 9″
            Width of nave at chancel . . . . 28′ 8″
    ABÓ. Width of nave at façade . . . . 24′ —
       Width of nave at chancel . . . . 26′ —

C. Rise of floor from entrance toward sanctuary:
    ACOMA (H.A.B.S.). Length of nave . . . . 90′ —
          Height of floor at chancel . . . . 2′ —
    LAGUNA (H.A.B.S.). Length of nave . . . . 80′ —
           Height of floor at chancel . . . . 2′ —

D. Drop of floor from entrance toward sanctuary:
    RANCHOS DE TAOS (H.A.B.S.). Length of nave . . . . 78′ —
               Drop of floor at chancel . . . . — 7½″

E. Drop of roof from entrance toward sanctuary:
    TALPA CHAPEL (H.A.B.S.). Length of roof . . . . 25′ 7″
             Drop of roof . . . . — 1½″
    RANCHOS DE TAOS (H.A.B.S.). Length of roof . . . . 64′ —
             Drop of roof . . . . — 5″

F. Rise of roof from entrance toward sanctuary:
    SAN MIGUEL (Santa Fe) (H.A.B.S.). Length of roof . . . . 50′ —
                Rise of roof . . . . — 5″
    ACOMA (H.A.B.S.). Length of roof . . . . 104′ 8″
         Rise of roof . . . . 1′ 8″
    LAGUNA (H.A.B.S.). Length of roof . . . . 85′ 5″
           Rise of roof . . . . — 10″

5.

Perspective Illusion. Another aspect of the treatment of volumes in the churches of New Mexico deserves attention. Certain irregularities of construction occur which may be attributed to unskilled building methods. It is clear, however, that the early builders possessed the knowledge and skill to lay out a plan of mathematical regularity, and to erect walls uniformly parallel, as at Acoma (Fig. 32), or perhaps Pecos (Fig. 30). When the irregularities mentioned in this discussion appear, they do so with a frequency and an occasional uniformity that excite curiosity.

The lateral walls of the nave are generally not parallel to one another. Thus at Quarai (Fig. 27), Humanas (Fig. 12), and Giusewa (Fig. 29) the width of the nave is greater near the entrance than at the altar end of the nave. The walls converge three to four inches as they approach the sanctuary. This amount seems slight when distributed over a nave 60 feet long, as at Quarai, or 80 feet at Giusewa, but it is an irregularity sufficient to deceive the eye under certain circumstances.[14] At Abó, on the contrary, the walls (Fig. 4) diverge toward the sanctuary, two feet in eighty.[15]

Unfortunately, the roofing of the seventeenth-century monuments, excepting El Paso (Fig. 73), has long since vanished, so that it cannot be established whether any longitudinal deflection from the horizontal was to be observed at the roof level. In later, more intact edifices, such deflections are measurable. At Ranchos de Taos the roof drops from the entrance toward the sanctuary five inches in 64 feet, but at Laguna it rises ten inches in 85 feet 5 inches (Fig. 16). These are again small amounts but they are sufficient to deceive or mislead the eye, in a certain context.

At the floor level, similar irregularities occur: at Laguna, the rise from the entrance toward the sanctuary is two feet over a length of 80 feet (Fig. 16).

In an arbitrary and theoretical union of these irregularities, the walls, floor, and roof all converge as they approach the sanctuary. A cross section through the nave at the end nearest the sanctuary would reveal an area materially less than that enclosed by a similar section taken near the entrance. The effect should be one of perspective illusion, deceiving the eye as to the actual length of the nave.[16] The reason for this is that the projection of parallel lines upon the retina appears to be convergent and foreshortened. The mind therefore believes that certain actually convergent lines are not only parallel but actually longer than reality. Thus the objective reality of convergent lines may be converted into the subjective illusion of parallel and longer lines. The illusion will prevail, however, only when the *actual* convergence is not perceived as such.

The case, however, for or against intentional optical refinements in New Mexico is diffi-

14. Elsewhere the lateral walls converge toward the sanctuary with much greater rapidity: at Cordova (Fig. 35) the nave is 52 feet long and the walls are 2 feet 7 inches closer at the chancel than at the entrance (Fig. 35). At Ranchos de Taos (Fig. 13) the amount of convergence is 9 inches in 70 feet. At Humanas the walls converge from 30 feet 1 inch to 27 feet 2 inches in 85 feet (Fig. 12). Acoma (Fig. 32), as far as we know, is, in the main, a seventeenth-century edifice (*infra,* p. 92), contemporaneous with the great church at Humanas, and the church at Quarai, where irregularities are evident. The nave walls at Pecos (Fig. 30) are also parallel, possibly the result of the concrete foundations laid down in 1915. Kidder, 1924.

15. Communicated by Joseph H. Toulouse, Jr.

16. Goodyear, 1896, 1896a.

cult to prove. In several monuments, the distance between lateral walls increases toward the sanctuary (Abó, Fig. 4; Chimayo, Fig. 22); occasionally the floor is level (Acoma) or the roof bears upward from the entrance (Laguna, Fig. 16). The unrestored monuments of the seventeenth century, San Cristobal, Quarai, Kechipauan, Hawikuh, Humanas, Abó, Giusewa, are in ruinous condition, and exact data on roofing and floor levels are not now available. Elsewhere an untold number of unrecorded repairs and remodelings makes it difficult to establish with certainty the original measurements of churches still in use (Socorro, Halona, Zia, Acoma, San Miguel). In some cases it is more than likely that careless or clumsy building was involved. Finally, deformation through settling of the walls is always possible.

The fact remains that at Humanas (Fig. 12), Quarai (Fig. 27), and Giusewa (Fig. 29), the lateral walls converge toward the sanctuary. This evidence is important because the structures were built of stone and abandoned before the revolt of 1680; hence they were subject to few remodelings. It is possible that optical refinements were part of the seventeenth-century formula for the building of churches, and that later generations of repairs were carried out in ignorance of such refinements, just as the reconstructions of the nineteenth century ignored the original system of fenestration. In replacing a rotted roof, for instance, the villagers would have forgotten the artful purpose of the inclination they were leveling or reversing. If the repairs were ignorantly executed, so also must the imitation of older models have degenerated during the eighteenth and nineteenth centuries.

Another irregularity or departure from symmetry consists in the deflection of the axis of the sanctuary from that of the nave (Fig. 13). The phenomenon occurs frequently in European medieval religious architecture, where it has occasionally been construed as an optical refinement designed to make the interior appear larger than it really is.[17] Here, again, objections on the ground of careless building may be raised, but in the measured drawings of the Historic American Buildings Survey the phenomenon occurs with provocative regularity.

17. Ibid. Porter, 1909, p. 142. Nissen, 1906, 1907, 1910.

CHAPTER VII
SECONDARY CONSTRUCTIONS

I.

BAPTISTRIES AND SACRISTIES. From the point of view of construction no difference exists between the baptistry and the sacristy. It often happens that one room serves both purposes, as at Chimayo and Abeytas. Where two rooms exist, one for each purpose, they are located at opposite ends of the building, and they are entered from opposite sides of the nave (Fig. 25).[1] Sixteenth-century Mexican precedent supports this arrangement, as at Yuriria, in the state of Guanajuato. In New Mexico, the sacristy is entered from near the altar, either directly from the sanctuary, or through one of the transepts.[2] The sacristy is invariably a modest room of which the function is indicated only by

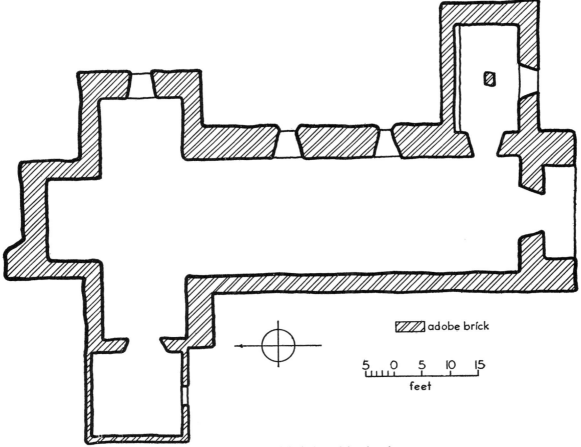

adobe brick

5 0 5 10 15
feet

25. Trampas. Simplified plan of the church.

1. Ricard, 1933, p. 206.

2. At N. S. de Guadalupe, El Paso (now Juarez City), the official report of the dedication in 1668 described these rooms in the following terms: "The baptistry has its door under the choir-loft, and is fifteen feet long and of the same width. The sacristy has its door at the transept." Scholes, 1929, p. 198.

location and furniture (Fig. 145). In it figure a cupboard, a small altar, a rack for liturgical instruments, and occasionally a fireplace.

The baptistry, when it is a room distinct from the rest of the church, is entered from the nave by relatively elaborate bivalve doors (Fig. 103), hand-hewn, with carved spindles and hand-wrought ironwork (Trampas, Laguna). It is square, low, and modestly lighted by one or two small windows. In some instances a baptismal font built of adobe rises from the center of the earthen floor (Fig. 146).

2.

Priests' Houses. The Spanish term, *convento,* describes those subsidiary buildings in which the friar-priests and lay brothers lived.[3] English-speaking authors have, almost without exception, translated *convento* by the English words "monastery" or "convent." Today the usage of "convent" implies a religious retreat for women, while "monastery" bears the connotation of a self-sufficient retreat for meditation and prayer. Today, neither of these terms, in its current usage, is applicable to the missionary establishments under discussion. To be sure, the Spanish term *convento* is itself loosely applied to the New Mexican missions. In the Franciscan Order, a distinction was originally drawn between *loca conventualia* (or *conventus* proper), where at least twelve or thirteen brothers resided, and *loca non conventualia,* with no more than four

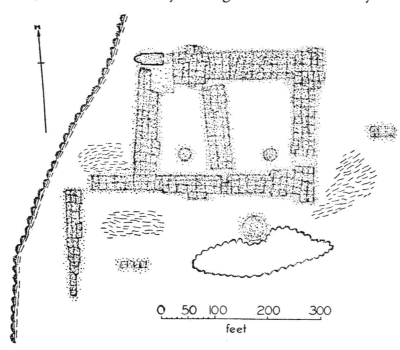

26. Patokwa. Plan of the pueblo and church.

brothers. Even smaller settlements were known as *eremitoria.*[4] It became general practice, nevertheless, in the Order at large, to refer to any domicile of friars by the name *convento.* An English term is needed which will be general enough to equal *convento,* while avoiding the restrictive meanings of "convent" or "monastery." The term "rectory," al-

---

3. An alternative for *convento* occurs in Vetancurt, 1697, who speaks of a *morada* (dwelling) *para religioso.* Brew, 1939, uses "friary," which has the connotation of *retreat,* as does *monastery.*

4. Holzapfel, 1909, p. 197. Cuevas, 1922, p. 160, indicates, however, that the practice among the Friars Minor in Mexico during the sixteenth century was to designate the houses that harbored two to four friars as *doctrinas.* The head of a *doctrina* was called *Presidente* in official language, but *doctrinero* in common usage. Actually, the term *convento* was almost always used in Mexico, both officially and unofficially, to refer to these smaller establishments.

though burdened with Anglican connotations, is suitable, as well as "priest's house," which is clumsy, but closest to the intended sense of *convento.*

In New Mexico, in the seventeenth century, the *conventos* were inhabited by one friar and in exceptionally large pueblos, such as Acoma and Giusewa, by two.[5] It was later claimed that the *convento* of Acoma could accommodate twenty resident friars, but no indication was given that the population of the *convento* was actually so great.[6] In 1754, however, a letter by Father Trigo[7] enumerates the typical mission outfit. The persons employed in the service of the establishment varied between six and twelve, usually including a bell ringer, a cook, two or three sacristans, a porter, two boys for the service of the friars' cells, two or three women to grind corn, and occasionally a gardener. These were of course all Indians, and a few of them lived in the *convento* itself.

Occasional descriptions of the *convento* exist. At Nuestra Señora de Guadalupe of El Paso (Juarez City) the *convento* comprised "a good porter's lodge, a spacious court and seven chambers, one with a rear chamber and little office, two with rear chambers, and three, like the rest, spacious, well lighted, and nicely finished off in wood. In addition to these there is a little hall *de profundis,* a refectory with an office . . . a kitchen, and closets . . . everything is furnished with doors, windows and keys."[8] An inventory taken at Santa Cruz in 1798[9] enumerated various living rooms, storerooms, workrooms, a corral, and gardens.[10] The residential character of these buildings is striking; there is no mention of chapter room, residence for the *guardian,* or parlor.

The location of the priest's house with relation to the church varies little. If the axis of the church lies east and west, the priest's house abuts against the south wall of the church (exception: Acoma, Fig. 32). If the church faces south, as at Quarai (Fig. 27) and Giusewa (Fig. 29), the priest's house is east of the church. Only one case is known in which the priest's house lies west of a church facing south, at Abó (Fig. 4), where the western court complemented an eastern one.[11]

The priest's house generally encloses a square court, or *claustro,* which is called the "cloister" by English-speaking writers. Such courts, or patios, are characteristic of Spanish and Mexican domestic architecture and usually contain gardens. At Acoma, by exception, the court is surrounded by a covered walk (Fig. 147). A few small windows open out from the walk into the court.[12]

The buildings of the priest's house are usually one story high, although at Acoma, Laguna, and Isleta[13] at least one side of the court was originally two stories high.

3.

Open Chapels. Motolinia, writing within twenty years after the conquest of Mexico, as an

5. Scholes, 1929, pp. 45, 58.

6. Morfi, 1932, p. 104.

7. Hackett, 1937, pp. 459–468.

8. Adapted from the translation by Scholes, 1929, p. 199.

9. Imbentario, 1798.

10. Terrasas, 1821.

11. Communicated by Joseph H. Toulouse, Jr.

12. At Quarai the recent excavations have revealed a stone-lined depression in the center of the court (Fig. 150). Certain features support the hypothesis that this was a pre-Spanish underground ceremonial chamber preserved by the friars to illustrate the victory of the Church over pagan customs. Anonymous, 1936, p. 122.

13. San Antonio de la Isleta, a seventeenth-century foundation, had two-storied conventual buildings ("claustros altos y bajos"). Vetancurt, 1697, p. 99.

eyewitness to the earliest evangelization of the Mexican highlands, says that the courtyards of the churches "are very large, because the faithful cannot be accommodated in the church, and there is a chapel in the courtyard where everyone may attend mass on Sundays and feast-days. The churches are used on weekdays."[14] Motolinia doubtless refers to the *atrio,* a walled enclosure of large size, located in front of the church. It is a ubiquitous element of New World religious architecture, commonly used as a burial ground, and in some cases as a fortified retreat.[15] In sixteenth-century Mexico and Yucatan, however, the *atrio* is distinguished by the presence of the chapel mentioned by Motolinia, for the celebration of the mass

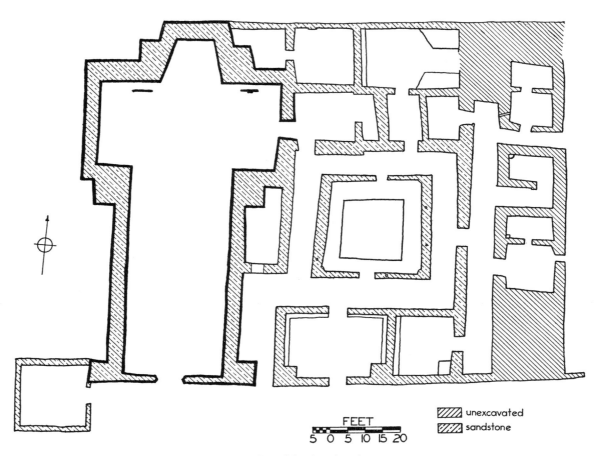

27. Quarai. Plan of the church and *convento.*

before large outdoor congregations. As Ricard has pointed out, the evangelization of Mexico was not progressive, but massive.[16] The enormous numbers of worshipers, and the necessity for administering the sacraments from a properly constituted sanctuary, led to the invention of accessory chapels,[17] opening generously upon the *atrio.* Liturgically, this open chapel is the

14. Motolinia, 1858, pp. 92–93.
15. Ricard, 1933, p. 199.
16. Ibid.

17. Other opinions are cited by Garcia Granados, 1935, p. 4.

most original contribution made by the Church in America. The concept of outdoor worship violates the theory of the mystic body of the Church, enclosing the communicants within its actual substance. Determined by necessity as the form certainly was, one nevertheless may assume that it was partly conditioned by remote recollections of Moslem congregations, assembled in vast open courtyards facing the *mihrab,* which gave the direction of Mecca. The problem and the solution are identical in both cases; whether independently invented or filiated by influence, the Mexican *atrio* follows the expulsion of the Moors from Granada by a scant forty years, and at the Capilla Real in Cholula,[18] or the vanished *atrio* chapel of San José de los Naturales in Mexico,[19] the immediacy of Moslem influences upon form and decoration is unquestionable.

The survival of the *atrio* chapel in New Mexico constitutes an important element in the displaced activity of the Franciscan Order. At Santa Ana, and in the destroyed establishment of San Ildefonso, there occur structures that can reasonably be interpreted as open chapels.[20] At San Ildefonso (Fig. 111) the structure abutted the church at right angles to the façade. Three large bays, formed by two wooden supports with elaborate capitals, opened upon the original *atrio,* giving a free view of the interior of the chamber, about one-third as deep as it was long. The system was exactly analogous to that of Tlamaco (Fig. 134) in the State of Hidalgo, Garcia's Type 1*b*,[21] and like the latter, the structure appears to have had no direct communication with the church itself, but constituted an auxiliary church, with one entire lateral wall omitted, like the sectional buildings in Italian *trecento* painting, where visual obstacles are graphically suppressed.

The *atrio* of Santa Ana presents a similar structure, facing the court along its north wall (Fig. 148). Of much smaller size than at San Ildefonso, the chapel here opens freely into the walled court, recalling the disposition in the Franciscan establishment at Calimaya in Mexico (Fig. 135).[22]

At Santo Domingo and Isleta, more problematic forms existed. At Santo Domingo, before 1886, a smaller church abutted the main structure, parallel to it, and provided with a large doorway and the conventional façade window (Fig. 149). Here the question arises: was an open chapel intended, or did one structure precede the other? Likewise at Isleta (Fig. 99), the purpose of the arcade flanking the façade on the north side, about 1881, is unclear.

The balconied façades, however, which have already been discussed,[23] may be associated with another open-chapel solution very common in Mexico. Garcia Granados has described this type:[24] the Mass is celebrated in a balcony chapel situated over the main entrance to the church. Access to the balcony is through the choir loft. Mexican examples (Fig. 139) at Real del Monte, Tepecoacuilco, and Tlacochahuaya are well known,[25] and their functional identity with the numerous balconied façades of New Mexico is a possibility not to be over-

18. Gillet, 1929, pp. 1029–1030.

19. Toussaint, 1927, p. 22.

20. In 1773 the catechumens gathered every morning at sunrise for prayers in the *atrio* at Jemez and Isleta. Hackett, 1937, pp. 502–504.

21. Garcia Granados, 1935, Plate IV.

22. Idem, Plate VIII.

23. *Supra,* p. 54.

24. Garcia Granados, 1935, p. 11.

25. Garcia Granados (ibid.) cites an interesting reflex of the balcony chapel in Spain, in the case of a Mass celebrated in the choir of the Escorial, attended by the army, congregated in the outdoor Patio de los Reyes. It is possible, however, that the custom had twelfth-century precedent in the balconied façades of Romanesque architecture.

looked, although we lack specific texts to prove that the New Mexican balconies were properly constituted sanctuaries for the celebration of the Mass.

All the possible instances of the open chapel, in any of its forms, in New Mexico, occur in fabrics which date, for the most part, from the eighteenth century, and their existence postulates local precedents in the seventeenth century. Thus the view of Pecos (Fig. 116) published by Emory[26] shows a balconied façade, of which, however, the date of construction is uncertain. Although the *atrio* boundaries in the Salinas district and at San José de Giusewa have not been exactly determined, there may have been a façade balcony at the last-named site in the seventeenth century (Fig. 118). Inferentially, at any rate, we must reckon with numerous possible seventeenth-century examples in New Mexico, for there is reason to believe that the open chapel in Mexico proper was restricted to the sixteenth century, and that its purpose had been forgotten by the middle of the seventeenth.[27] Thus, if very few or no open chapels were built in Mexico in the seventeenth century, then the form must have continued on the periphery of missionary activity, where conditions were analogous to those of the primitive evangelization. Garcia Granados believes that the open chapel was unknown outside Mexico, unless perhaps in Guatemala;[28] the examples from New Mexico, however, expand the distribution and prolong the life of this American form.

26. Emory, 1848, opposite p. 7.

27. Toussaint, 1927, p. 25, gives the open chapel at Tlalmanalco, built about 1600, as the last dated example in Mexico. In Oaxaca, at Cuilapam, the open chapel had been walled up before 1644, when Burgoa noted the structure, without appearing to realize its original purpose. Ricard, 1933, p. 202.

28. Garcia Granados, 1935, p. 15.

PART THREE
THE BUILDINGS

CHAPTER I
PRE-REBELLION MONUMENTS
1600–1680
1. The Capital

A HERMITA DE SAN MIGUEL, in Santa Fe, is mentioned in 1628. Scholes[1] believes this to be the church which was built during Benavides' term of office as Custodian. Scholes states further that it was used as the parish church, and then as an infirmary, until its destruction in 1640.[2] San Miguel, at any rate, was in active use again before 1680, for we learn that the church was burned by the rebels in August of that year.[3] A recently published document pertaining to the rebuilding of San Miguel in 1710[4] yields valuable information of general significance, permitting one to reconstruct the amount of damage done to the stone and adobe structures by the rebels after 1680, and to estimate the amount of labor necessary to recondition the burned shell. At San Miguel, in 1692, General de Vargas ordered the walls roofed and whitewashed, but the work was not carried out until 1710, when the Ensign, Agustin Flores de Vergara, collected the necessary funds, and hired a crew of fifteen men. Only 21,100 adobes were used in this campaign of reconstruction, a number with which but 15 feet of wall were built in addition to the already standing walls, seven feet high. A new roof was built with beams donated and purchased for the purpose, and by 1711, the church was again in use. An inscription on the choir-loft cross timber records the event: "El Señor Marquez de la Peñuela Hizo esta fabrica el aiferes Rl Dn Agn flos Vergara su criado Año de 1710."[5] All the elements of a situation we shall find repeated at Acoma, Halona, and Zia, are present here: the burning in 1680; General de Vargas' report that the walls are still standing in 1692; and the subsequent repair of the gutted but usable shell in the early years of the eighteenth century (Fig. 28).

According to the record of 1710, San Miguel was rebuilt with "towers," and the Urrutia map (Fig. 46) of Santa Fe, made late in the eighteenth century, shows San Miguel with two harmonic façade towers, represented in plan. Exactly when these were replaced with the present single façade tower is uncertain, although a campaign of rebuilding was carried out in 1830, according to Prince,[6] when the squared timbers of the roof were replaced with round beams. The single façade tower may have been built at that time. It is possible that still another renewal of the roof timbers occurred about 1730. A round, carved beam, said to come from under the floor of San Miguel, and now in the possession of J. W. Young of Santa Fe, has yielded a tree-ring date at 1730.[7] In 1760, again, the roof was being repaired.[8] Sometime before 1805, a citizen of Santa Fe, Antonio José Ortiz, repaired or rebuilt the sanctuary at his

1. Scholes, 1937, p. 150.

2. In a letter of September 10, 1644, the friars state that Governor Rosas "hizo echar en el suelo la enfermeria de S. Miguel." *Archivo General de las Indias. Patronato* 247, *exped.* 7. Communicated by Mr. Scholes.

3. Hackett, 1911, p. 140.

4. Kubler, 1939a.

5. H.A.B.S., 36 NM 1, sheet 12.

6. Prince, 1915, p. 93.

7. Stallings, 1937.

8. Tamaron, 1937, p. 336.

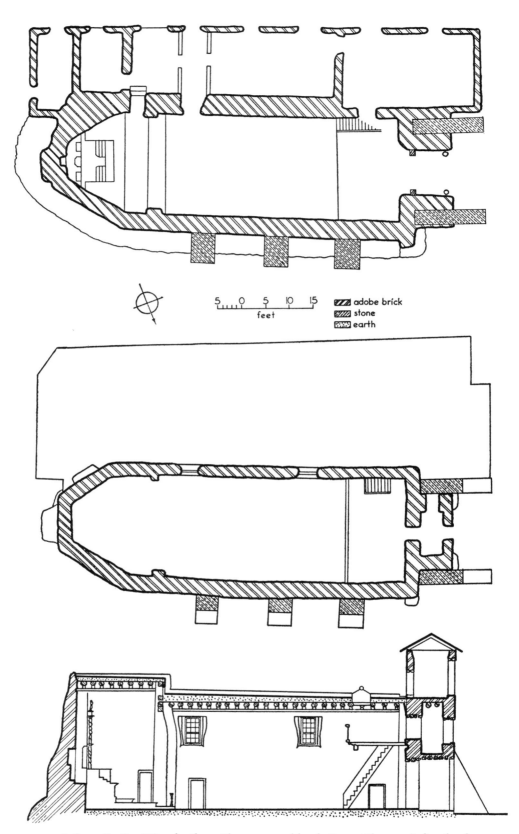

5   0   5   10   15
feet

▨ adobe brick
▧ stone
▦ earth

28. Santa Fe. San Miguel. *Above:* Plan at ground level. *Center:* Plan at window level.
Below: Longitudinal section.

own expense.[9] Other repairs may have been carried out in 1853, when Bishop Lamy installed an altar stone in San Miguel. This altar stone now resides in the vaults of the Archdiocese, following its removal a few years ago by the late Archbishop Daeger.[10]

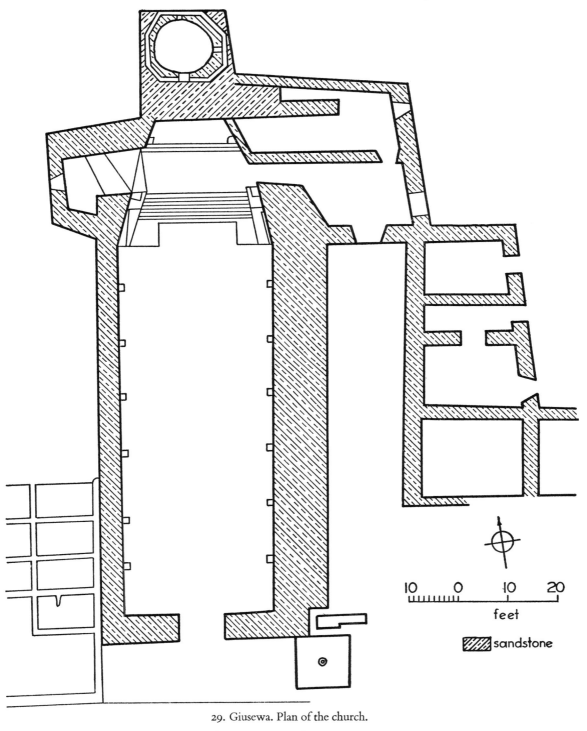

29. Giusewa. Plan of the church.

9. Sena, 1938, p. 356.   10. Anonymous, 1937b, p. 104.

2. THE JEMEZ DISTRICT

San José, Giusewa. At least since Bandelier,[11] the great church ruin at Giusewa (Fig. 29) has erroneously been known as San Diego de la Congregación de los Jemez. In 1935, following Benavides, I sought to prove that the correct designation for the church at Giusewa is San José. The two versions of the *Memorial*[12] not only agree but complement one another on this point. It appears that Benavides ordered the scattered Jemez tribes to be concentrated shortly after 1625, in two settlements, named San Diego and San José. At San José, there already existed "una muy suntuosa, y curiosa Iglesia, y Convento," in the pueblo founded after 1621[13] by Geronimo de Zarate Salmerón. Benavides expressly states that San José was the principal pueblo of the Jemez.[14] The other pueblo, San Diego, was a *reducción* established before Benavides' time, and after having been burned, it was founded anew in 1626 or 1628 by Martin de Arvide,[15] and thereafter thrived as one of the best establishments in the province, with an "iglesia muy buena."

The critical points here are that San José was the more splendid of the two establishments, and that it was built before Benavides assigned Martin de Arvide to the Jemez in 1626 or 1628. Now not only does Giusewa possess the most important church ruin in the Jemez district, but it is probable that this church was either finished or under construction in 1626. So much has been indicated by the dendrochronological studies of Stallings, showing that certain wall timbers were probably cut within two years of 1625.[16] Therefore, Giusewa cannot be San Diego, which was not rebuilt until 1626 or later, "otra vez de nuevo todo aquel pueblo con mas de 300 casas y su iglesia."[17]

Other sources made it difficult to associate Giusewa with San Diego. Vetancurt says the *convento* of "San Diego de los Hemes" stood in the center of a square ("y por estar en frontera de enemigos tenian en medio de una plaza el Convento").[18] Clearly the *convento* of Giusewa never stood in the center of the plaza of the pueblo. Hewett says of Giusewa that "the eastern houses of the pueblo nearly touch the western walls of the church,"[19] while to

---

11. Bandelier, 1892a, p. 207. Lamy merely calls it the "Hot Springs church ruin" in 1874, p. 25. Reagan, 1917, p. 31, identified the ruin as San Juan. Loew, 1876, p. 211, calls it the ruin at Ojos Calientes.

12. (a) *Memorial Qve Fray Ivan De Santander De La Orden de san Francisco, Comissario General de Indias, presenta a la Magestad Catolica del Rey don Felipe qvarto nuestro Señor. Hecho Por El Padre Fray Alonso de Benauides Comissario del Santo Oficio, y Custodio que ha sido de las Prouincias, y conuersiones del Nueuo-Mexico. . . . En Madrid en la Imprenta Real. Año M. DC. XXX.* This edition is reproduced in facsimile in *The Memorial of Fray Alonso de Benavides 1630,* translated by Mrs. Edward E. Ayer, annotated by Frederick Webb Hodge and Charles Fletcher Lummis. Chicago, 1916. (Cited here as Ayer, 1916.)

(b) *Memorial a la sanctitad de Vrbano 8 nro señor acerca de las conuersiones del Nuevo Mexico hechas en el feliss° tpo del gouierno de su pontificado y presentado a su s^d por el P^e fr. Alonso de Benauides de la orden de nro P^e San Francisco, cust° de las dichas converciones en 12 de febrero del año de 1634.* Archivio de Propaganda Fide, Rome. Scritture riferite nella Congregazione generali. Vol. 259. A photostatic copy exists in the Huntington Library, San Marino, California.

The relevant passages from both versions are quoted by Scholes, 1938, pp. 66–68.

13. Scholes, 1938, pp. 64–65.

14. Benavides, 1634, paragraph 34.

15. Benavides (ibid.) gives 1628. See Scholes, 1938, p. 70.

16. See Appendix; also Stallings, 1937, p. 5.

17. Benavides, 1634, paragraph 34.

18. Vetancurt, 1697, p. 101.

19. Hewett, 1906, p. 48. Pueblo and church are actually contiguous (Fig. 29).

the north of the church rises a steep acclivity, and to the south "the lower end of the church and the walled enclosure extend down to the border of the arroyo."[20]

In 1696, the murder of Friar Francisco Casañas de Jesus was committed by an Indian from the pueblo "on the *Mesa* of San Diego de Gemes."[21] It subsequently appears that the pueblo is the one in which Friar Francisco was murdered, at the church door.[22] Giusewa, however, lies near the river on a small tributary of San Diego canyon.

Espinosa[23] relates that Friar Juan de Jesus died the death of a martyr in 1680, "in the pueblo of San Diego de los Hemes," his church and *convento* ablaze with flames ("ardiendo en llamas"). All the timbers found at Giusewa were untouched by fire, and their tree-ring date precludes the possibility of their having been built in during repairs after the Reconquest of 1692. Espinosa also gives a circumstantial account[24] of Casañas' martyrdom in 1696. Casañas arrived in New Mexico in 1693 and proceeded to "San Diego de los Hemes, where the Church and Convento had been burned thirteen years earlier." Espinosa claims that repairs had been begun by missionaries on the site prior to Casañas' arrival. Casañas, however, "rebuilt his church with much ability, and repaired his humble *convento*." To repeat, neither was Giusewa destroyed by fire during the Revolt nor were repairs carried out after the Reconquest, to our present knowledge.

In short, whenever the location or history of "San Diego de los Jemez" is mentioned, the descriptions, referring variously to the river by that name, the canyon, a mesa, or a pueblo site, do not fit Giusewa. San José was the only other possibility.

Two important new studies,[25] using fresh source material, not only have confirmed this identification, but throw much light on the actual history of the mission at San José–Giusewa. Zarate Salmerón's work there surely began in 1621–22, and construction of the church may have begun during that winter.[26] Scholes also proves that the mission was either abandoned or sporadically ministered between 1623 and 1626, although some work was done there in 1626.[27] By 1658 the area had surely been abandoned.[28] Bloom points out that the site does not figure in the records for some time previous to 1638;[29] Scholes places the abandonment of the mission after 1632 and before 1639.[30] In short, the total life of the mission was at least ten years, and not more than seventeen.

The question arises: what is the origin of the fill found by Bloom in 1922,[31] consisting of charred wood and other debris, located between two floor levels three and one-half inches apart? The timbers studied by Stallings show no trace of fire, and the fire which gave rise to the fill discovered by Bloom must antedate the raising of the present walls, in which the dated timbers are embedded. Otherwise the fire producing the charred wood was part of the process of construction. It is well known that charcoal is an efflorescent substance, repelling water, and its use in foundations is a process of very great antiquity, intended to protect the structure from moisture at building level. San José, then, was either devastated by fire before

---

20. Ibid.

21. Twitchell, 1916, p. 356.

22. Idem, p. 357.

23. Espinosa, 1746, p. 35.

24. Idem, p. 283. To be sure, Espinosa is writing many years after the event, and quoting from Vetancurt. But his consistency in writing of these two widely separated events is reassuring.

25. Bloom and Mitchell, 1938. Scholes, 1938. See also Reiter, 1938, for a close summary of the present situation.

26. Scholes, 1938, p. 169.

27. Idem, p. 70.

28. Idem, p. 96.

29. Bloom and Mitchell, 1938, p. 97.

30. Scholes, 1938, pp. 98–99.

31. Bloom, 1923, p. 17.

the new timbers were laid, about 1625, or its charcoal floor is a refinement of construction.

San Diego[32] *de la Congregación (San Juan), Walatowa.* Following the abandonment of the mission at Giusewa, before 1639, the Jemez conversion was reduced to a single establishment, at San Diego de la Congregación. This pueblo, as we have seen, was probably founded in 1622 by Geronimo de Zarate Salmerón.[33] A year or two later, the establishment was ruined by fire, in an incident instigated by Governor Eulate, and the mission was temporarily abandoned.[34] In 1626 or 1628, the pueblo and mission were founded anew, to thrive as the center of operations among the Jemez until 1680.[35] Bloom has opined that San Diego occupied the site of the modern pueblo of the Jemez, called Walatowa.[36] A low mound just east of the ditch separating the modern rectory from the pueblo perhaps contains the foundations of this establishment.[37]

If this is really the site of San Diego de la Congregación, excavations there should yield valuable evidence on an important center of colonial missionary activity. San Diego was almost continuously occupied from 1626 or 1628, whereas San José functioned for very few years. Not only did the establishment at San Diego flourish during the seventeenth century, but it was rebuilt, possibly on the same site, in 1695, under the new name of San Juan de los Jemez.[38] Abandoned again during the revolt of 1696, it was repopulated in 1703,[39] and in 1706, it is reported that a church was being built,[40] although the advocacy of the mission was changed back to San Diego. Then, in 1709, Apaches raiding the Jemez pueblo destroyed the church.[41] By 1744, San Diego was once again established as a mission,[42] and in 1754, a sizable establishment was functioning.[43]

A detailed description of mission routine at San Diego in 1773 has survived.[44] The Indians prayed each morning in the churchyard, and again in the evening. At Mass, the Indians knelt in the church, the women being separated from one another by men, so that the women might not chatter. There is an indication of bitter conflict between the government and the missionaries at this time. The spirit and number of the Jemez Indians, who once had been "bold rebels," had deteriorated.[45]

In 1782, the site was reduced to a *visita,*[46] and the next mention of a church at San Diego occurs in 1833.[47] Simpson visited the building in 1849:[48] Kern's drawing (Fig. 172) shows the

32. Not to be confused with the nearby San Diego de al Monte, at Patokwa. Loew, 1876, p. 211, n. 1, thinks the name Walatowa (*Vallatoa*) may be the corruption of "Valladolid."

33. Scholes, 1938, p. 69. Reiter, 1938, p. 33.

34. Scholes, 1938, p. 68.

35. Bloom and Mitchell, 1938, p. 97.

36. Idem, pp. 93–97.

37. Idem, pp. 108–109.

38. Idem, p. 104. Espinosa, 1746, p. 35, gives 1693. Twitchell, 1917b, p. 48, speaks of a foundation on the "upper mesa."

39. Bloom and Mitchell, 1938, p. 107.

40. Hackett, 1937, p. 376.

41. Salpointe, 1898, p. 93.

42. Hackett, 1937, p. 405.

43. Idem, p. 464.

44. Idem, pp. 502–506.

45. Ibid.

46. Bancroft, 1889, p. 274.

47. Twitchell, 1914, p. 361.

48. Simpson, 1852, p. 20. "The church, an adobe structure, some one hundred by twenty-eight feet in plan, appeared very old, and was evidently wasting away under the combined influence of neglect and moisture. . . . A pilaster and arch arrangement, with crosses at intervals, characterized the side walls; and a number of paintings, all daubs, excepting the central one, the wall back of the chancel. . . . I noticed upon a projecting piece of the side pulpit a human skull and some bones, and in a side room, to which I could only peep in, some images and pictures."

ruined shell of a church, south of the pueblo, but Simpson describes in some detail another, intact church which he visited. The ruin figured by Kern[49] may be any one of the preceding churches, but we have no record corresponding to the intact structure viewed by Simpson himself. Lamy noted that the "cathedral ruins" could hardly be seen in 1874;[50] this unquestionably refers to the ruin depicted twenty-five years earlier by Kern. In 1874, the *convento* associated with this ruin was used as a schoolhouse.[51] Lamy also reported that a new church was built at Jemez in 1856,[52] and this is probably the fabric mentioned by Bourke in 1881,[53] which had recently collapsed, although the façade and steeple were left intact.

The present church (Fig. 173) at Walatowa occupies roughly the site indicated in Kern's drawing. Whether this new-looking structure incorporates anything of the older building, I was unable to determine. In any case, we have at Walatowa a continuous record of several churches and rebuildings; where these were located, and to what extent their remains will confirm the reasonable identifications made by Professor Bloom, should be ascertained by excavation.

3. THE EASTERN FRONTIER

Nuestra Señora de los Angeles de Porciuncula, Pecos. During the seventeenth century, the population of Pecos was among the greatest in New Mexico, and its religious establishment was correspondingly important.[54] It is not exactly known when the church was built, or by whom, although Benavides gives the *terminus ante quem* in his statement that the pueblo had "a very splendid [muy luzido] temple of distinguished workmanship and beauty."[55] Benavides does not say that the church was built during his term of office as Custodian, so that we may assume that it was already standing before 1625, when he entered New Mexico. Bandelier fixed the date at 1629, somewhat arbitrarily.[56]

The *convento* was furnished, as we learn in 1663, with a reception hall, provided with doors,[57] and in 1664 and 1666, the foundation was designated as Nuestra Señora de los Angeles, "a very good church, [with] provision for public worship, and organ and choir."[58] According to Vetancurt,[59] it was "a magnificent temple, adorned with six towers, three on each side, its walls so wide that services were held in their thickness." This picture evokes a church of the size and magnificence that are in evidence among the ruins of Pecos today (Fig. 30).

The history of the establishment during and after the Revolt of 1680 is unclear. De Vargas' entry on October 17, 1692, was peaceful,[60] and no mention is made in his journal of the condition of the church. The *Mercurio Volante* is equally silent.[61] Vetancurt, however, asserts that the church had been burned, and he gives no further details.[62] The burning of the churches did not necessarily complete their destruction. It is likely, at Pecos as well as at San Miguel in Santa Fe, that restorations were carried out late in the seventeenth and early in the eighteenth

49. Simpson, 1852, opposite p. 16.
50. Lamy, 1874, p. 25.
51. Ibid.
52. Ibid.
53. Bloom, 1938, p. 227.
54. Ayer, 1916, p. 231.
55. Idem, p. 22.

56. Bandelier, 1881a, pp. 37–133.
57. Hackett, 1937, p. 247.
58. Scholes, 1929, pp. 48, 53.
59. Vetancurt, 1697, p. 102.
60. Vargas, 1914a, p. 422.
61. Siguenza, 1932.
62. Vetancurt, 1697, p. 102.

centuries. In effect, the tree-ring data supplied by Stallings yield a terminal date shortly after 1695.[63] Father Alvarez' phrase, in 1706, that "the building of the church has been begun,"[64] is a formula he used indiscriminately, even in the case of Acoma, where the church was nearly intact after the Reconquest. Later in the eighteenth century, both Menchero[65] (1774) and Morfi[66] (1780) evoke the Pecos monument in terms of exceptional praise, unfortunately without specific detail.

In 1808, Pereyro found the church and priest's house in "deplorable condition." In 1822, the church was described as "almost entirely razed to the ground."[67] By 1837, the population of the pueblo had dwindled to eighteen adults. In 1840 the survivors removed to the pueblo of Jemez and the church was finally abandoned.[68] A few years later, the ruins were studied by

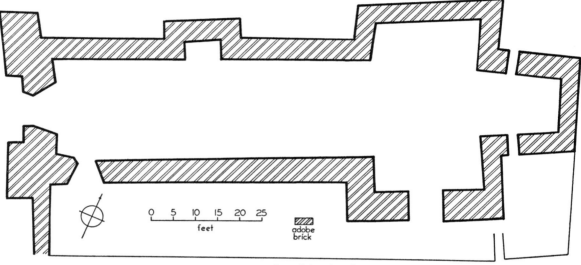

30. Pecos. Plan of the church.

the American military and reconnaissance expeditions,[69] and Lieutenant Emory published an excellent drawing of the church. This drawing (Fig. 116) yields many details which had been lost by the time Bandelier studied the ruin in 1881. Complementary to this drawing, a sketch by Schoolcraft[70] may be adduced, made about 1854. In 1860, the roof timbers were used as

63. Stallings, 1937, p. 5.

64. Hackett, 1937, p. 373.

65. Idem, p. 403.

66. Morfi, 1932, p. 93.

67. Twitchell, 1914, p. 94.

68. Bandelier, 1881a, pp. 124–125.

69. Hughes, 1907, p. 193. "The spacious temple, on whose altar the sacred Montezumian or Vestal fire was kept alive for so many successive ages was built of sun-dried bricks, as the tradition proceeds, more than three hundred years ago. . . . The interior of the temple, the division into compartments, the subterranean cells, the decorations of the altar, and the stone cisterns and tanks, display some taste, although the edifice is but the wreck

of what it has been, the turrets having tumbled to the ground." Emory, 1848, p. 30, gives a more detailed description. "The remains of the modern church, with its crosses, its cells, its dark mysterious corners and niches, differ but little from those of the present day in New Mexico . . . the walls of sun-dried brick, the rafters of well-hewn lumber, which could never have been hewn by the miserable little axes now used by the Mexicans. . . . The cornices and drops in the architrave . . . are elaborately carved with a knife." Abert, 1848, p. 30, likewise notes the presence of carved woodwork. "The ends of the rafters are carved in imitation of a scroll: the ground plan of the edifice is that of a cross."

70. Schoolcraft, 1854, p. 29.

corral posts by a resident of the neighborhood,[71] and in 1881 the priest's house had been reduced to shapeless mounds.[72] The façade had already collapsed at that time.

In 1915, the Department of Archaeology of Phillips Andover Academy, collaborating with the State Museum and private individuals in New Mexico, undertook to repair the ruin under the direction of J. L. Nusbaum.[73] Concrete foundations were poured and weakened walls and lintels were rebuilt. These restorations have saved the church from complete disintegration, although certain details of the plan and foundations have been lost thereby. Further excavations and repairs are currently in progress.[74]

San Cristobal. The ruined pueblo of San Cristobal was abandoned during the Revolt of 1680,[75] and probably never reoccupied. The religious establishment there consequently dates from the seventeenth century, when it figured perhaps as a *visita* of Galisteo.[76] Bandelier studied the ruin, and gave its measurements in 1892 (Fig. 52). These reveal that the monument has suffered very little during the last fifty years. Bandelier notes that other buildings stood to the south of the present ruin.[77]

The Salinas Pueblos. The Salinas area, named for the numerous salt lagoons in the vicinity, lies about twenty-five miles east of Albuquerque (Fig. 1), and includes a variety of climatic conditions. An eastern branch of the Tiwa tribes occupied a narrow strip along the eastern slope of the Manzano mountains, just west of a forested range rich with game. To the east of their pueblos, Chilili, Quarai, Tajique, lay the saline lagoons which constituted part of the tribal produce for trade with tribes far to the south in Chihuahua. Beyond the lagoons lay desert country, infested with the nomad Apache tribes whose incursions ultimately led to the abandonment of the entire area in the 1670's.[78] The area south of them, and adjoining them, was occupied by an eastern branch of another Rio Grande stock, the Piro tribes. This eastern branch was sometimes called Tompiros, a term incorrectly used by Benavides to include some of the Tiwa pueblos. The Piros were also called Salineros, because of their proximity to the saline lagoons. Their country, extending southward from Abó for about twenty-five miles, was far more desert than that of the eastern Tiwas, and the Piros perennially faced a water shortage. Abó alone was endowed with an adequate stream; Humanas possessed wells; the others, Tabirá and Tenabó, may have depended upon rain-water storage. All were evangelized in the seventeenth century, and missions and chapels were probably erected in all of them.[79]

(a) Nuestra Señora de Navidad, Chilili. As early as 1598, a chaplain in Oñate's entourage, starting from Pecos, began the conversion of the Indians at Quarai, Abó, Tenabó, and perhaps Humanas.[80] This evangelization, however, was of temporary character, and it has

71. Kidder, 1924, p. 15.
72. Bandelier, 1881a, pp. 123–125.
73. Kidder, 1924.
74. Ely, 1939.
75. Bancroft, 1889, p. 186. Twitchell, 1917, p. 513.
76. Vetancurt, 1697, p. 102.
77. Bandelier, 1892a, p. 104. "In 1882 the rear part . . .

was still standing to the height of about 4 meters. It is a chapel only, measuring 16.0 by 7.4 meters [52½ by 24¼ feet]. In front of it lies a churchyard and other buildings seem to have been appended to it on the south."
78. Ayer, 1916, p. 220.
79. Idem, pp. 214–215.
80. Idem, p. 215.

recently been established that the first permanent missionary activity among the Tiwas of the eastern frontier began in 1612, under the guidance of Friar Alonso Peinado, among the Indians of Chilili.[81] By 1616, Peinado was prepared to baptize his charges, and Friar Agustin de Burgos came to assist him in the work.[82] Peinado died at Chilili after 1617.[83]

A church at the site was dedicated to La Navidad de Nuestra Señora.[84] Exactly when it was built has not been determined. Modern Chilili is not located on the site of the seventeenth-century pueblo, but the outline of the ruins of this church were studied shortly before 1917 by N. C. Nelson of the American Museum of Natural History. Bandelier described it, furthermore, as a "small chapel."[85] Twitchell reports some peculiar treasure-hunting operations carried out there about 1900 by a Brazilian adventurer.[86]

(b) San Miguel, Tajique. During a visit to Tajique in 1935, I was told that the ruins of the church lay beneath a modern construction housing the general store of the village. Twitchell presents a confusing picture of the location and condition of the church at the time he was writing. In one place[87] he maintains that "there is nothing left of the original town or church but a mound overgrown with vegetation." Elsewhere he asserts that the ruins were plainly visible in his time.[88] Bandelier (Fig. 53) says, furthermore, that the "chapel" was built of adobe.[89]

If it were not that Chilili and Tajique were both served before 1662 by the same minister,[90] indicating that they were reasonably close to one another, one would be tempted, on the evidence of maps[91] and Governor Marin del Valle's expedition of 1759,[92] to suspect that Quarai and Tajique have become confused, the present Quarai really being Tajique, and the present Tajique really being Quarai. In effect, Vetancurt[93] and two eighteenth-century maps[94] indicate these reversed positions, Quarai being situated nearer to Chilili, the northernmost pueblo of the eastern branch of the Tiwas, than Tajique, which is shown located near Abó. Governor Marin del Valle set out from Santa Fe in 1759 to recover the remains of Friar Geronimo de la Llana, who, according to Vetancurt, died at Quarai in 1659.[95] Marin del Valle was acquainted not only with Vetancurt's text, but also with Friar Nicolas de Freitas' letter of 1706,[96] in which the latter relates that he disinterred De la Llana's remains in 1669, and removed them to a less humid place within the church at Quarai. Now Marin del Valle, coming from Santa Fe in 1759, and following Vetancurt, who placed Quarai north of Tajique, proceeded to the site now known as Tajique, thinking it was Quarai. Nothing was found there. Then an Indian recalled a story to the effect that when Quarai was abandoned in 1674, the inhabitants exhumed the beloved Friar de la Llana. Moving to Tajique, they

81. Scholes, 1937, p. 23.
82. Idem, p. 42.
83. Bandelier, 1892a, p. 256.
84. Vetancurt, 1697, p. 103.
85. Bandelier, 1892a, p. 255.
86. Twitchell, 1917a, p. 489.
87. Idem, p. 490.
88. Idem, p. 494.
89. Bandelier, 1892a, p. 258.
90. Hackett, 1937, p. 132.
91. Both maps were made by Bernardo de Miera y Pacheco. The first is painted on cloth, 85 by 111 cms.,

No. 1148, Direccion de Geografia, Hidrologia, y Meteo-rologia, Tacubaya, D.F., Mexico, executed about 1760 and dedicated to Governor Marin del Valle. The map has been published (Tamaron, 1937, p. 357). The second map is dated in 1779, and has been published by A. B. Thomas to accompany Morfi, 1932, p. 87.
92. Twitchell, 1917a, pp. 493–494.
93. Vetancurt, 1697, p. 103.
94. Note 5.
95. Vetancurt, 1697a, p. 75.
96. Twitchell, 1917a, p. 494. Bandelier, 1892a, p. 262.

presumably took his wooden coffin with them. The text states that the Indian, Ché, did not know what was done with the body, but Twitchell affirms that it was taken to Tajique.[97] In any case, in 1759, there was disagreement as to whether Quarai was Tajique, or vice versa, and this disagreement probably took place at the site now called Tajique. Marin del Valle then proceeded to the more southerly site, as given by his guide, Vetancurt, and there found the friar's bones in due order. Upon being returned to Santa Fe, the remains were interred in the *parroquia,* behind an inscribed slab stating that they had been found at *Quarai!*

The first question is this: did the inhabitants of Quarai really move the coffin to Tajique in 1674, or is the story an Indian fabrication made up extempore in 1759 and improved by Twitchell? Secondly, after the remains had been discovered and removed to Santa Fe, did Marin del Valle have any idea where Quarai really was? The answer to both these questions hangs upon the authenticity of the story of the removal of the coffin from Quarai to Tajique in 1674. If the Indian's story is a fabrication, modern Quarai is correctly named, and the inscription in Santa Fe is correct. If the story, however, is true, Quarai and Tajique must be renamed. This writer inclines to question Twitchell's version, although the manuscript "Dilixencias sobre la solizitud del cuerpo del venerable Pᵉ Fray Geronimo de la Llana," 1759, cited by Bandelier,[98] should be reviewed before this important point can be settled.

(*c*) La Concepción, Quarai. Reference has already been made to a possible confusion in the naming of the site known today as Quarai. However that may be, three fragments of wood from the monument by that name, studied by Stallings, give the cutting date 1630–31.[99] The date agrees, if we respect the present name for the ruin, with the theory that the mission establishment there was founded by the aged Estevan de Perea before 1633,[100] and it contradicts Hodge's assertion that Quarai was established by Geronimo de la Llana in 1642.[101] Geronimo de la Llana died there in 1659,[102] but Vetancurt[103] does not credit him with the construction of the church. That the establishment was of some importance is indicated by Vetancurt, who says that the church was furnished with "rich altars and vessels of silver."[104] In 1661, moreover, when Friar Nicolas de Freitas was guardian at Quarai, the establishment was maintaining a choir.[105]

The descriptions by Abert and Carleton[106] in the nineteenth century are particularly valuable for reconstructing certain features of the monument which no longer exist.

97. Twitchell, 1917a, p. 494.
98. Bandelier, 1892a, pp. 258–259.
99. Stallings, 1937, p. 5.
100. Hackett, 1937, pp. 129–130.
101. Ayer, 1916, p. 235.
102. Cuevas, 1928, p. 512.
103. Vetancurt, 1697, p. 103.
104. Vetancurt, 1697a, p. 75.
105. Hackett, 1937, p. 135.
106. Abert, 1848, p. 71. "Here there is yet standing the walls of a time-worn cathedral; it is composed entirely of stone, red sandstone; the pieces are not more than 2 inches thick. The walls are 2 feet wide, and the outer face dressed off to a perfectly plain surface. The ground plan presents the form of a cross . . . the rectangular projec-

tions that partly fill the angles formed by the arms, are 6 feet square. At the foot of the cross are rectangular projections, that measure 10 feet in the direction of the long axis, and 6 feet in the other direction; . . . the walls . . . rise to a height of 60 feet." Carleton, 1855, p. 302. "We found one room here . . . which was in a good state of preservation. The beams that supported the roof were blackened by age. They were square and smooth, and supported under each end by shorter pieces of wood carved into regularly curved lines and scrolls. . . . The earth upon the roof was sustained by small straight poles, well finished and laid in herring bone fashion upon these beams. . . . Every piece [of stone] . . . was in the same rough form which it had when it was broken from the quarry."

The University of New Mexico acquired the site in 1917,[107] and excavations (Fig. 27) were carried out there in 1934–35 with government assistance.[108]

(*d*) San Gregorio, Abó. Vetancurt[109] says that Friar Francisco de Acevedo built the church at "San Gregorio en Abbo." This missionary evidently came to New Mexico with Perea in 1629,[110] and his activity among the Piro pueblos must therefore date from after that year. Vetancurt claims that Acevedo died at Abó in 1644, although the name appears again, as of a living person, in 1661.[111]

Hodge[112] implies that the church at Abó was never completed, but that the unfinished structure was abandoned in 1672. A fragmentary roof timber from Abó, in the possession of J. G. Meem, of Santa Fe, and Stallings'[113] cutting date, 1646, for a timber from the west transept landing, confirm the view that the majority of the fabric had been completed before the middle of the seventeenth century, contrary to Hodge. It is also to be noted that the mission was well enough established by 1661[114] to acquire an organ, with proceeds from the sale of piñon nuts.

In the nineteenth century, Abert[115] and Carleton[116] described the ruins. An early view[117] of the ruin preserves a northwest aspect of the demolished sanctuary (Fig. 159), while Abert's[118] remarks supply information on lateral fenestration. Bandelier spent some days at Abó and prepared an important if inaccurate ground plan, which now resides in the Vatican Library (Fig. 49). A Lummis photograph,[119] copyrighted in 1890, shows the collapsed east transept standing nearly intact. The site of the ruin recently passed into the hands of the Regents of the University of New Mexico, and during 1938–39 repairs and excavation were begun under the direction of J. H. Toulouse, Jr.

(*e*) San Buenaventura, Humanas (Gran Quivira, Tabirá). Humanas, a pueblo frequently cited in seventeenth-century writings,[120] has recently been identified with the ruined settlement known as Gran Quivira National Monument.[121] For some time, Gran Quivira has also been known as Tabirá, following the suggestion made by Bandelier.[122] The recent identification rests upon the figures for the population of the Salinas pueblos in 1672.[123] These cite Humanas as the most thickly settled of the pueblos. The size of the ruin at Gran Quivira

107. Twitchell, 1917*a*, p. 499.
108. Ely, 1935, 1935*a*.
109. Vetancurt, 1697, p. 81.
110. Bloom, 1933*a*, p. 226.
111. Hackett, 1937, p. 146.
112. Ayer, 1916, p. 215.
113. Stallings, 1937, p. 5.
114. Hackett, 1937, p. 192.
115. Abert, 1848, p. 77.
116. Carleton, 1855, p. 300.
117. Abert, 1848, unnumbered plate.
118. Abert, 1848, p. 77.
119. Ayer, 1916, Plate XIV, opposite p. 33.
120. Hackett, 1937, *passim*.
121. Kubler, 1939. Mr. France V. Scholes has long

planned a work on the history of the Jumano Indians in the seventeenth century, in which this identification will be made. I was unaware of his research on the subject until after my note had appeared in print.

122. Bandelier, 1890, p. 131, was probably influenced by eighteenth-century maps, such as that of Miera y Pacheco in 1779, in which the only site shown south of Abó is Tabirá. The Miera y Pacheco map has been published to accompany A. B. Thomas, *Forgotten Frontiers*, University of Oklahoma, 1932.

123. Hackett, 1937, p. 298. Los Humanas had more than 500 families, Abó over 300 families, Quarai more than 200, and Chilili more than 100. Tabirá is not mentioned.

National Monument, together with the fact that it alone contains the remains of two churches, certified for Humanas in 1660,[124] makes the identification tenable.

Two widely separated campaigns of missionary activity mark the history of the pueblo, and each of them appears to have led to the construction of a church. Oñate's chaplain, Francisco de San Miguel, seems to have undertaken the conversion of the Humanas Indians after 1598.[125] About twenty years later, Benavides, by his own statement,[126] worked among the Humanas, and in 1629, a relatively durable conversion was effected by Friars Juan de Salas and Diego Lopez, who came to the Salinas from San Antonio de la Isleta.[127] Francisco de Letrado then worked at Humanas until 1631, and during his residence, he is said to have built a church.[128] The smaller chapel structure at Humanas, east of the large establishment, may possibly be this work of Letrado's (Figs. 31, 165). After Letrado's departure, no resident missionary figured at Humanas until about 1659.[129] During this time, the community was administered from Abó as a *visita* by Friar Francisco de Acevedo.[130] It also seems that the pueblo of Abó came to Humanas to worship in the chapel there during part of this time.[131] In 1659, however, a young friar, Diego de Santander, undertook to build a new church.[132] His plans were opposed by Governor Mendizabal in 1661,[133] and the church and *convento,* of which extensive remains subsist, were never finished, for in 1668, a famine carried away about one-fourth of the inhabitants,[134] and in 1672, the pueblo was finally depopulated by the Apaches.[135]

Bandelier, by means of archaeological reasoning, appears to have reconstructed this series of events in some detail, without recourse to documents,[136] but the question remains as to the stage of completion at which the construction was abandoned. Roof timbers belonging to the church were found in place in 1872 by Willison.[137] This observer may have mistaken the choir-loft joists for roof timbers, but if his notes are correct, the possibility exists that the church itself had been completed, while portions of the *convento* were left unfinished in 1672.

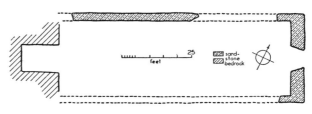

31. Humanas (Gran Quivira). Simplified plan of the chapel.

Humanas was apparently forgotten during the eighteenth century, until about 1778, when the name Quivira came to be attached to the ruins, apparently on the authority of a Jumano Indian living near El Paso, named Tio Juan Largo.[138] Governor Marin del Valle does not seem to have known the site during his expedition to recover the bones of Geronimo de

124. Hackett, 1937, pp. 135, 143.

125. Ayer, 1916, p. 272.

126. Idem, p. 20.

127. Vetancurt, 1697, p. 96.

128. Hodge, 1937, p. 91. Bandelier, 1892, p. 97. Hodge, 1937, n. 195.

129. Hackett, 1937, pp. 135, 145.

130. Idem, p. 146.

131. Idem, p. 143.

132. Idem, p. 146.

133. Idem, p. 216.

134. Idem, p. 272.

135. Idem, p. 298.

136. Bandelier, 1892a, p. 291.

137. Bandelier, 1881, pp. 30–31. "The carved timbers in the church are still in a good state of preservation; a portion of the roof still remains; some of the timbers must have weighed 3,000 pounds at the time they were brought to this place." These timbers were still in place in 1883 (Bandelier, 1889, p. 366).

138. Idem, p. 365.

Llana in 1759, nor do the maps of Miera y Pacheco record the name, Humanas. The earliest extensive notices of the ruin were published by Carleton[139] in 1855, and later by Bandelier,[140] citing Willison.

4. THE KERES PUEBLOS

Nuestra Señora de la Asunción, Zia. As early as 1614, Zia had a *convento*, where Peralta was held prisoner for some time at the request of Estevan de Perea.[141] Cristobal de Quiros, whom Benavides associates with the miraculous appearances of Maria de Jesus, 1620–31,[142] was guardian there in 1616.[143]

Adolf Bandelier believed Zia was completely destroyed in 1689 by Domingo Gironza Petriz Cruzate.[144] A careful reading of General de Vargas' journal of the campaign of 1692, however, allows the belief that the Zias reoccupied their pre-Rebellion pueblo, and repaired the church there. Upon first arriving at Zia, the General found the village ruined and abandoned. The following day, he proceeded to a village four leagues distant, on the Mesa of the Red Hill, occupied by the fugitives. After receiving their submission, he urged them "to return and inhabit their said village since the walls were strong and good and the church still has its nave and choir in good condition and all they needed was timber which I told them they could cut this coming moon, and they said they had nothing to cut it with, and I told them . . . that I would give them a new [outfit] so that they should have something with which to cut the said timbers for the church and *convento*."[145] No church ruins have been discovered in the neighborhood of Zia, so it may be assumed that the Zias returned to their pre-Rebellion village, and repaired the church, which is the one visible there today (Figs. 8, 79), at the orders of General de Vargas. During 1696, Zia did not participate in the widespread rebellion of that year, and General de Vargas used the site as his headquarters in the expedition against the rebellious inhabitants of Acoma.[146] In 1706, Father Alvarez, speaking of Zia, uses the rubber-stamp phrase, "The church is being built," with a slight variant, "It is now at a good height."[147] When Alvarez wrote, the pueblo was temporarily administered from Jemez, although it had a regular resident minister. By 1808, the *convento* stood vacant, although the church was still in good condition.[148] Bourke visited the church in 1881, and noted that the interior was rapidly decaying, and that it had a ceiling of "riven pine slabs," locally thought to be very old.[149]

San Estevan, Acoma. Productive missionary effort began at Acoma relatively late in the seventeenth century. In 1621,[150] the pueblo was still unconverted. Permanent indoctrination was initiated between 1623 and 1626, when Geronimo de Zarate Salmerón,[151] leaving the Jemez district, bent his efforts upon the Keres pueblos. Benavides[152] reports that a friar was

139. Carleton, 1855, p. 300.

140. Bandelier, 1881, pp. 30–33.

141. Scholes, 1937, p. 36.

142. Ayer, 1916, pp. 276–277.

143. Scholes, 1937, p. 42.

144. Bandelier, 1892a, p. 198. But Bandelier earlier stated, 1890, p. 267, his belief that perhaps Zia alone could "lay claim to real antiquity," of all the churches of New Mexico then in use.

145. Vargas, 1914a, pp. 429–431.

146. Twitchell, 1917b, p. 49.

147. Hackett, 1937, p. 376.

148. Pereyro, 1808.

149. Bloom, 1938, pp. 222–223.

150. Scholes, 1937, p. 79.

151. Zarate Salmerón, 1900.

152. Ayer, 1916, p. 27.

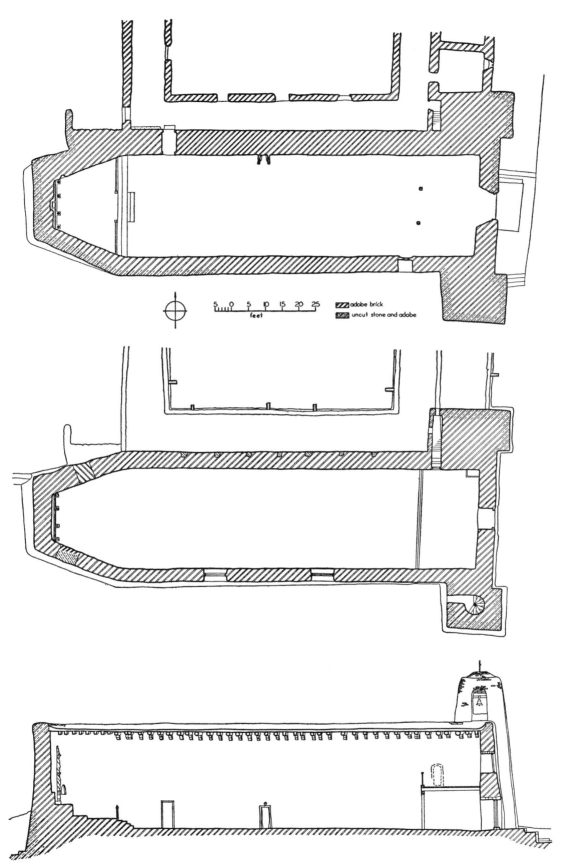

32. Acoma. *Above:* Plan at ground level. *Center:* Plan at window level. *Below:* Longitudinal section.

catechizing and indoctrinating the residents during his term of office, probably referring to Salmerón's slightly earlier work. This first campaign seems to have been abandoned, for Perea, arriving at Acoma in June, 1629, implied that the inhabitants were without religious care, and assigned Friar Juan Ramirez to the work. Hodge[153] speaks of a church which stood to the north of the present edifice. A few beams in a house of the north tier[154] are supposed to be all that remains of this early structure, which Hodge attributes to Juan Ramirez. I do not know Hodge's authority for the existence of such a structure, but his thesis[155] that the present church (Fig. 32) was erected after 1699 can readily be disproved.

In a petition of 1664, the following passage occurs: "The beautiful rock of Acoma has on its summit the church which is the most handsome, the paraphernalia of worship is abundant and unusual; [the church] has a choir and organ."[156] Clearly an establishment of some importance was built before 1664 and after 1629, for neither Benavides, Perea, nor Salmerón mentioned a church. General de Vargas supplies conclusive evidence that the present church at Acoma is substantially the same as that which existed there before the Revolt of 1680. In 1692,[157] the General noted that after taking the submission of the residents, he went to see the church dedicated to San Estevan. "I found it to be very large," he says, "and it seemed to me even larger than the convento of San Francisco in the Court [Mexico City], in its extent as well as in the height of its walls, which are almost a yard and a half in thickness; they stand firm in spite of the heavy rains which break the windows and skylights of the said church." This is doubtless the church built before the Revolt, as described in 1664. It was only slightly damaged, and after De Vargas' visit, the roof may have been rebuilt.[158] The General mentioned "skylights," probably referring to a transverse clearstory window, and this feature was eliminated either then or during some later campaign of reconstruction. Some windows in the sanctuary may have been pierced at the same time; these, however, have since been blocked up again (Fig. 58). Stallings,[159] using two fragments of wood, has shown that a building campaign probably occurred some years after 1781; more extensive investigations will certainly yield earlier tree-ring dates.

Villaseñor noted in 1748[160] that the mission was still active, maintaining a resident friar. In 1782, Morfi reported that the church and *convento* were among the finest in the country, and that the *convento* had room for twenty friars.[161] By 1782, the establishment had so declined in importance that it was reduced to a *visita* of the neighboring mission of Laguna.[162] In 1808, Pereyro noted the fine, spacious rooms of the *convento,* and in 1860, Domenech mentioned "two very pretty spires."[163] In 1890, Scott reported that the "south wall is wasting away, as are also its huge towers, once square."[164] In 1924, numerous repairs were made on the façade and towers by the Committee for the Preservation and Reconstruction of New Mexican Mission Churches. These included the remodeling of both towers, the repair of the façade, and replacing the dirt roof with a concrete slab.[165] The north tower was found defective, and

153. Idem, p. 251.
154. H.A.B.S., 36 NM 5, sheet 24.
155. Hodge, 1907, p. 10.
156. Scholes, 1929, p. 48.
157. Vargas, 1914a, p. 298.
158. Bloom, 1931, p. 191, n. 34.
159. Stallings, 1937, p. 5.
160. Villaseñor, 1748, p. 421.

161. Morfi, 1932, p. 104. Tamaron, 1937, p. 351, noted in 1760 that "la casa de cura es de alto, bien dispuesta."
162. Morfi, 1932, p. 104.
163. Domenech, 1860, p. 203.
164. Donaldson, 1893, p. 125.
165. Reuter, 1924–27, MSS.

Reuter rebuilt it, noting that work had been done there in 1902, by a native crew working under the local priest. The south tower was badly cracked, and while repairing it, Reuter discovered a winding staircase at its core (Fig. 106).

5. THE WESTERN OUTPOSTS

The Zuñi Pueblos

(*a*) La Purísima Concepción, Hawikuh.

(*b*) The church at Kechipauan.

(*c*) Nuestra Señora de la Candelaria (La Limpia Concepción, Nuestra Señora de Guadalupe), Halona.

THE seventeenth-century mission called La Purísima Concepción de Hawikuh is built of adobe (Fig. 50). Extensive excavations, which have not been published in any detail, were made there between 1917 and 1923 under the direction of J. L. Nusbaum. A large, continuous-nave church was revealed, with extensive conventual buildings.[166]

The nearby church at Kechipauan[167] is built of stone (Fig. 175), and resembles the chapel in the pueblo of Humanas (Fig. 165). No excavations have been made at this site.

A third church of some antiquity (Fig. 176) exists in the modern pueblo of the Zuñi (Halona), about fifteen miles northeast of Hawikuh. The dating of these three churches presents problems of some complexity. The evangelization of the Zuñi tribes was seriously begun in 1629, by Friar Roque de Figueredo, Friar Agustin de Cuellar, and a lay brother named Francisco de la Madre de Dios.[168] Their first house of worship was a dwelling purchased from the natives shortly after the friars' arrival in the settlement called Zibola. Between 1629 and February, 1632, the two unnamed missions mentioned by Benavides were built.[169] The exact location of one of these is uncertain, although Hodge, who identifies Zibola with Hawikuh,[170] places the other mission[171] at Halona, first mentioned in 1666.[172] In 1632, following the murder of Friar Francisco de Letrado at Hawikuh, the Zuñi district was abandoned by the Spaniards, probably until about 1660.[173] Scholes[174] has proved that an expedition to reëstablish the missions in 1636 never left Santa Fe, and a mission list of 1664,[175] after referring to the murder of the missionary, states that the 1,200 Indians in the district

---

166. Hodge, 1922; 1937, pp. 101-102.

167. I quote Mindeleff's description of the ruin (1891, p. 82). "The Spanish church in this pueblo was built of stone. . . . The building is well preserved, most of the walls standing 8 or 10 feet high, and in places 14 feet. This church was apparently built by Indian labor, as the walls everywhere show the chinking with small stones characteristic of the native work. . . . The ground plan of the church shows that the openings were splayed in the thickness of the walls, at an angle of about 45 dedrees. In the doorway, in the east end of the building, the greater width of the opening is on the inside; . . . in the window, on the north side, this arrangement is reversed. . . . The position of the beam-holes on the inner face of the wall suggests that the floor of the church had been

raised somewhat above the ground, and that there may have been a cellar-like space under it. No beams are now found, however, and no remains of wood are seen in the 'altar' end of the church." The suggestion of a "cellar-like space" is puzzling; Mindeleff may have mistaken the level of the choir-loft flooring timbers for the nave floor.

168. Bloom, 1933*a*, p. 229.

169. Ayer, 1916, p. 28.

170. Hodge, 1937, pp. 42-46, 87.

171. Idem, 90.

172. Scholes, 1929.

173. Vetancurt, 1697, p. 101.

174. Hodge, 1937, p. 114.

175. Scholes, 1929.

"have asked for ministers once more." Hodge believed that "internal evidence" proved that this report was drawn up shortly after 1632,[176] but his case lacks proof.

A mission report covering the years 1663–66[177] is the first account to give us information closely matching the material remains of churches in the Zuñi region. Nuestra Señora de la Candelaria at Halona was being served by the only friar in the region; a *visita* was dependent upon Halona, and so was the pueblo of La Purísima Concepción de Hawikuh, with its *visita*. Four sites, then, are involved, of which only one, Halona, was a functioning mission. The *visita* of Hawikuh was probably Kechipauan, which has a small stone church, closely resembling the chapel at Humanas. Vetancurt complicates the picture[178] with his mention of the church at Halona, serving two little *visita* churches, and the church at Hawikuh, where Letrado was murdered, and which was burned both in 1632 and again in 1680 (Fig. 174). Vetancurt fails to mention an earlier burning of the church at Hawikuh in 1672. The mission had a resident friar, Pedro de Avila y Ayala, after 1671. In 1672, however, this minister was murdered by Apaches who also set fire to the church.[179] Hodge,[180] following Bandelier, long maintained that Hawikuh was definitively abandoned in 1670. Recently, he has accepted Vetancurt's account.[181] It seems more than probable, then, that the extensive establishment at Hawikuh, excavated between 1917 and 1923,[182] was built during the first missionary occupation, by Figueredo, Cuellar, or Letrado, after 1629 and before 1632. The other establishment mentioned by Benavides may have been either at Kechipauan or at Halona, depending upon whether the missionaries spread out or remained close to Hawikuh. If the latter was the case, the chapel at Kechipauan would have been built during the earlier period, and its resemblance to the one at Humanas suggests its attribution to Letrado, who, we have seen, was active at Humanas in 1629–30. Either Kechipauan or Halona, however, was built following the reoccupation of about 1660, if we accept Benavides' statement that only two establishments were built in 1629–32. Hodge[183] arbitrarily assumes that Halona was built by Cuellar, adding that Kechipauan[184] was the work either of Figueredo or Letrado.

After 1680, the Zuñis retired to the summit of an isolated mesa known today as Towayalane, where General de Vargas found them living in 1692. The General was welcomed by the Indians, and was surprised to find a Christian altar, furnished with many pieces of mission equipment, carefully tended and maintained in the house of one of the women.[185] The Spaniards then turned back to Halona, which they found uninhabited, but in which it is implied that the church was still standing, although the *convento* was gone.[186] In 1699, the mission at Halona was begun anew, very probably utilizing the pre-Rebellion fabric, under the direction of Friar Juan de Garaycoechea.[187] The advocacy was changed to Nuestra Señora de Guadalupe, either in 1699 or at some later time, but a tragedy, in 1703, involving the massacre of three Spaniards in the church, caused the Indians to withdraw to the mesa again, staying there until the spring of 1705.[188] At this time they descended for good, settling in the

---

176. Hodge, 1937, p. 95.

177. Scholes, 1929.

178. Vetancurt, 1697, p. 101; cf. Maas, 1929, p. 88. Hodge, 1937, n. 212.

179. Hodge, 1937, p. 99.

180. Hodge, 1907, p. 539.

181. Hodge, 1937, pp. 106–107.

182. Hodge, 1922; 1937, pp. 101–102.

183. Hodge, 1937, p. 90.

184. Hodge, 1937, p. 96.

185. Vargas, 1914*a*, p. 305. Siguenza, 1932, pp. 78–80, 119–120.

186. Twitchell, 1917*b*, p. 44.

187. Bandelier, 1892*a*, p. 371.

188. Idem, p. 335.

present village of Zuñi (Fig. 43), which Mindeleff[189] has shown to coincide in part with the older, pre-Rebellion Halona, in which the church was presumably rebuilt in 1699. The older village lay on both sides of the Zuñi River, and the eastern parts of the settlement of 1705 coincide with the western half of Halona. The present church at modern Zuñi (Figs. 43, 176) stands just west of these blocks of houses. It is reasonable to assume that the decrepit fabric in evidence today is identical with that described in 1666, burned in 1680, rebuilt in 1699, and reoccupied finally in 1705. According to Father Alvarez, the mission was again in the charge of Friar Garaycoechea in 1706, and the advocacy of the establishment had become La Limpia Concepción de Halona.[190] By 1754,[191] the mission had been changed back to the advocacy of 1699, Nuestra Señora de Guadalupe. No change of name has been made since 1754. Morfi and Escalante administered the mission in 1780,[192] and Pereyro,[193] usually reliable, maintains that the church was rebuilt (probably repaired) in 1780. It had two rooms for the ministers, and a fresh altarpiece, painted under the direction of Escalante with local materials.[194]

Before 1846, the Indians are reported by Doniphan[195] to have expelled their priests, and in 1881, the church was crumbling, when Bourke[196] visited and described it. In 1891, Scott recorded the contemporary use that was being made of part of the church.[197]

The history of the three churches may briefly be summarized: *Hawikuh;* built about 1630, finally abandoned 1680. *Kechipauan;* probably built about 1630, finally abandoned 1680. *Halona;* built about 1660, rebuilt 1699, 1705, 1780.

6. The Lower Rio Grande

Nuestra Señora de Guadalupe del Paso, Juarez City (Mexico). In the seventeenth century the site of El Paso, Texas, formed an entrance to New Mexico from the south. The church there, in the old town known today as Juarez City, across the river in Mexico, was built in 1662-68 by Friar Garcia de San Francisco y Zuñiga and Friar Salvador de Guerra.[198] It unquestionably belongs to the style created by the missionaries to New Mexico. The adobe construction, the simple cruciform plan, transverse clearstory light, and limited lateral fenestration are distinct from anything farther south (Figs. 136, 177), while constituting the only intact seventeenth-century monument of the variety of Acoma, or the Salinas, or San José at Giusewa. All these either lack roofs, or have newer roofs. The church in Juarez City, however, preserves its seventeenth-century woodwork (Fig. 73). The structure is unique in that we possess the

189. Mindeleff, 1891, p. 88.

190. Hackett, 1937, pp. 376-377.

191. Morfi, 1932, p. 108.

192. Idem, p. 113.

193. Pereyro, 1808.

194. Morfi, 1932, p. 113. Pereyro, 1808.

195. Hughes, 1907, p. 312.

196. Bloom, 1936, p. 115. Zuñi: "11 paces in width, 42 in length, and about 30 feet in the clear inside. The windows never had been provided with panes and were nothing but large apertures barred with wood. The carvings about the altar had at one time included at least half a dozen angels as caryatides, of which 2 still remained in

position. The interior is in a ruined state, great masses of earth have fallen from the north wall; the choir is shaky and the fresco has long since dropped in great patches upon the floor. The presence of 5 or 6 different coats of this shows that the edifice must have been in use for a number of years." May 19, 1881.

197. An adobe annex at the southwest corner of the church, probably part of the *convento,* was being used for hangings. Criminals were suspended from the ends of the roof beams which projected over the entrance. Julian Scott, *apud* Donaldson, 1893, p. 129.

198. Scholes, 1929, pp. 196ff. Vetancurt, 1697, pp. 7-8; 1697*a,* p. 98. Hughes, 1914, p. 307.

written description drawn up at its dedication in 1668.[199] The detail of this document coincides closely with the existing monument. In 1706, Father Alvarez explicitly stated that the church retained its pre-Rebellion furniture, since the site was remote from the center of disturbance.[200] In 1754, the mission was described as the "flower of them all," with orchards and vineyards from which a local wine was produced.[201]

During the last fifty years, however, the edifice has been altered. A gabled roof was placed over the flat dirt terrace, the façade and tower were rebuilt, and the interior was remodeled. These changes may be dated from a comparison between photographs made in 1880 (Fig. 177), by Wittick, and more recent views of the church.

San Miguel (Nuestra Señora), Socorro. The possibility exists that the present church at Socorro (Figs. 74, 94), now dedicated to San Miguel, is substantially the same as that noted by Benavides in 1630 at the pueblo of Pilabo,[202] under the advocacy of Nuestra Señora del Socorro, which Hodge claims was built by Garcia de San Francisco y Zuñiga.[203] In 1692, General de Vargas entered Socorro, on December 9. His detailed description of the church once again allows the possible identification of an extant structure with a pre-Rebellion fabric. According to the General, the walls of the church at Socorro had fallen, but enough of them was still standing for him to determine that they had originally been "more than two yards and a half in thickness."[204] This account is complemented by that of Escalante, also in 1692, who remarked that the church was still standing, except the roof, which had been burned.[205] Bishop Tamaron, who visited New Mexico in 1760, gives evidence to prove that the site remained desolate for many more years. As he passed up the east bank of the Rio Grande, the ruins ("vestigios") of Socorro were visible across the river. Tamaron knew that the pueblo had been destroyed in the Revolt of the preceding

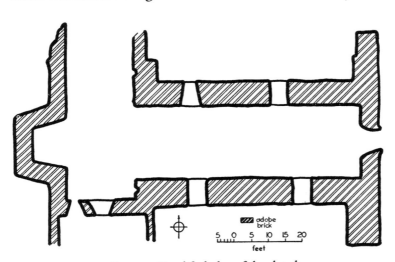

33. Socorro. Simplified plan of the church.

199. Scholes, 1929, pp. 196ff. "The woodwork in the church, in addition to being very strong and unusual, is excellently finished. The church has a beautiful arch. The nave is ninety-nine feet long and thirty-three feet wide; the transept measures twenty-eight feet by forty-five feet; and the chancel is twenty feet long and twenty-one feet wide on the side of the transept. The altar steps are very beautiful." Ocaranza, 1934, pp. 65–69, also cites this document. Ocaranza misconstrues certain architectural details.

200. Hackett, 1937, p. 376.
201. Idem, p. 460.
202. Ayer, 1916, p. 17. As with many other churches, Benavides claims that he built them himself. Such statements are true in the figurative sense, that Benavides was the *entrepreneur.*
203. Idem, p. 205.
204. Twitchell, 1917a, p. 353.
205. Cited from Bandelier, 1892a, pp. 241–242.

century, and he could see only the walls of the church and some peach trees.[206] The actual resettlement of Socorro took place in 1800, and the church was probably rebuilt shortly thereafter.[207] Bandelier maintained that the seventeenth-century pueblo of Pilabo actually lies beneath the modern town of Socorro.[208] The walls of the present church are nine feet thick in places, answering General de Vargas' estimate of two and one-half yards (Fig. 33).

In recent literature, the church at Socorro has been called San Miguel. When the change of name took place is not known. Twitchell referred to the church as San Miguel, "a very old structure, built about the middle of the eighteenth century."[209] The pitched roof and wooden towers have been added in recent years, sometime before 1916.[210]

San Agustin (San Antonio), Isleta. A church and *convento* of some importance were in existence at Isleta as early as 1626.[211] The question whether any part of the church fabric now standing (Figs. 84, 99) in the pueblo of Isleta was built before the Revolt of 1680 depends entirely upon the relation of the present pueblo to the pre-Rebellion settlement. Bandelier[212] states positively that the two sites are not congruent, but "very near" to one another on the west bank of the Rio Grande. If parts of the two settlements coincide, as at Halona, it is likely that the present church incorporates elements of the seventeenth-century structure. If, on the other hand, no parts of the two settlements coincide, two distinct churches are probably involved. In the former case, some evidence exists to prove that the older fabric not only was usable, but was actually put into condition again before the end of the seventeenth century. In 1681, Otermin[213] found the church burned and being used as a corral. General de Vargas,[214] however, noted in 1692 that the walls of the nave of the church were in good condition. Vetancurt[215] asserted in 1697 that the church built at Isleta by Friar Juan de Salas, and dedicated to San Antonio de Padua, had just received a new roof. Vetancurt, however, may have confused the northern and southern pueblos, both called Isleta.

Bandelier[216] maintained that the pueblo was not resettled until 1718, although proof may exist that the mission of San Antonio de la Isleta had a church in 1706.[217] Father Alvarez, who recorded this fact, was referring, perhaps erroneously, to the northern pueblo, and conspicuously omits his usual phrase to the effect that "the church is building." The pueblo also had a resident minister, serving the resettled Tiwas.

By 1744, the mission had acquired the name San Agustin de la Isleta, which it maintains to the present day.[218]

The church has been heavily rebuilt since 1881. The façade buttresses were added before 1910, and numerous additions have been made to them in recent years. The gabled roof was added after 1910. These reconstructions may be determined from photographs in the State Museum and in the Heye Foundation collections.

206. Tamaron, 1937, p. 333. "Se descubrieron a la otra banda del rio los vestigios del pueblo del Socorro, se mantienen las paredes de la iglesia y arboles de duraznos . . ." cuyo pueblo tambien se perdio con el reino."

207. Twitchell, 1914, p. 348.

208. Bandelier, 1892a, p. 241.

209. Twitchell, 1917a, p. 356.

210. Ayer, 1916, Plate II.

211. Scholes, 1929, p. 49. Ayer, 1916, p. 17. Bandelier, 1892a, pp. 233-234.

212. Idem, p. 234. Hackett, 1937, p. 139. Twitchell, 1917a, p. 111.

213. Hackett, 1916, p. 54.

214. Vargas, 1914a, p. 291.

215. Vetancurt, 1697, p. 99.

216. Bandelier, 1892a, p. 234.

217. Hackett, 1937, p. 377.

218. In 1744, Father Trigo referred to the mission as San Miguel de la Isleta, probably erroneously. Idem, p. 413. Tamaron, 1937, p. 352, refers to San Agustin, Isleta: "La iglesia es de un cañon, con un altar adornado."

CHAPTER II

POST-REBELLION MONUMENTS
1692–1846

1. Spanish Towns

SANTA FE. (*a*) San Francisco. The *parroquia,* or parish church serving Santa Fe, and dedicated to San Francisco, has occupied seven distinct structures since its establishment in 1610. The location of the first of these is uncertain, although it was probably built under the guidance of Friar Alonso Peinado.[1] It was an establishment of some size, with a *convento* dedicated to La Asuncion de Nuestra Señora.[2] The church had a transept, which is mentioned in an account of services held there in 1626 to receive the new Custodian, Alonso de Benavides.[3] Now Benavides referred somewhat later to this structure as a "poor hut," in connection with the new buildings erected to replace it during his term of office. It may be that Benavides actually undertook the new buildings; we do know, however, that during the period 1628–39, the *parroquia* was transferred to San Miguel,[4] and that construction on the actual edifice was not concluded until 1639.[5] Whether this third site for the *parroquia* occupied the same ground as the first, built in 1610, is uncertain, although Twitchell asserts that the present Cathedral occupies the pre-Rebellion *parroquia* site.[6] During the seventeenth century, the advocacy of the *convento* seems to have been changed, for it is cited in 1661 as the Immaculate Conception in Santa Fe.[7]

This establishment was burned in 1680, as we learn from Otermin's account of the siege of Santa Fe,[8] and must have suffered complete destruction during the years of independence, for General de Vargas made no mention of any remains when he entered Santa Fe in 1692.[9] San Miguel, as we have seen, was still in fair condition, but to provide a *parroquia,* and dwellings for the friars, Vargas was obliged to recondition parts of the Governor's Palace. In doing so, he unknowingly restored to church use a chamber which had been the military chapel of the garrison before 1680, then dedicated to Nuestra Señora de la Luz.[10] The *parroquia* was maintained here until 1714, falling into gradual decay.[11]

In 1714, a new *parroquia* was under construction, and it is again uncertain whether this edifice occupied the site of any earlier parish church. It is sure, however, that parts of this structure still survive (Fig. 179), incorporated with the stone Cathedral built by Archbishop Lamy late in the nineteenth century.[12] The fabric of 1714 is described by Tamaron in 1760.[13] Morfi mentions a chapel in 1782, dedicated to Nuestra Señora del Sagrario, as well as a

1. Scholes, 1937, p. 21.
2. Idem, pp. 99–102.
3. Ayer, 1916, p. 23.
4. Scholes, 1937, p. 150.
5. Hackett, 1937, p. 54.
6. Twitchell, 1925, p. 153.
7. Hackett, 1937, p. 231.
8. Idem, p. 333.
9. Vargas, 1914a.

10. Twitchell, 1914a, pp. 118–122; 1925, p. 59; 1911, p. 406. Wuthenau, 1935, pp. 178–179.
11. Twitchell, 1914, pp. 10, 73, 317.
12. Twitchell, 1912, p. 344, n. 272.
13. Tamaron, 1937, p. 335. "La iglesia parroquial . . . es grande, con su amplio cañon y crucero adornado de altares y retablos que todo se reconoció con la pila bautismal y demás que trae el ritual romano."

nearby *convento* where two or three friars resided. Sometime before 1797,[14] parts of the structure were nearly ruined, and their repair was undertaken by a devout citizen of Santa Fe, Antonio José Ortiz. Ortiz also erected a cruciform chapel dedicated to San José.[15] In 1799, the church appears to have collapsed,[16] and the same citizen repaired the fabric at his own expense, amounting to about 5,000 pesos.[17] These repairs consumed some time, for only in 1804[18] were the walls ready to receive the roof timbers. The church was then struck by lightning,[19] and Ortiz began anew, enlarging the plan and rebuilding the walls.[20] In 1808, Pereyro properly gave Ortiz credit for the rebuilding of nearly the entire edifice.

In 1826, the then extant *parroquia* (Fig. 117) was described at some length by Agustin Fernandez, then Vicar-General of the Archdiocese of Durango.[21] The length was given as "54 yards by 9½ in width, with two small towers. . . . Inside, communicating with the 'crucero' are two large separate chapels, the one on the north side dedicated to Our Lady of the Rosary, called also 'La Conquistadora,' and on the south side the other dedicated to San José." This north chapel is clearly the same as that mentioned by Morfi in 1782,[22] but dedicated to Nuestra Señora del Sagrario, under "La Conquistadora," the figure of the Virgin which accompanied Vargas in 1692, and which is claimed still to reside in the Cathedral. The south chapel, erected, as we have seen, by Ortiz, was cruciform and has since disappeared, being replaced by a newer adobe structure.[23]

According to Salpointe,[24] the parish church was in bad repair during the 1850's, and when Bishop Lamy assumed charge of the diocese, the *parroquia* had been transferred to the Castrense, the military chapel dedicated to Nuestra Señora de la Luz. In 1859, the Castrense was sold,[25] and the proceeds were used for the repair of the old parish church.[26] When the building of the Cathedral was initiated in 1869, the *parroquia* remained in use until the new structure was nearly complete; then the old adobe walls were torn down, within the new nave, and only the north chapel was left standing (Fig. 179), with its carved ceiling and the figure called "La Conquistadora."[27]

(*b*) Nuestra Señora de Guadalupe. This edifice (Fig. 180), located in the western part of Santa Fe, on the south bank of the river, does not find mention until 1821, when, according to Salpointe,[28] the church was visited by Agustin Fernandez. No such structure figures on the Urrutia map,[29] nor is it mentioned in Pereyro's exhaustive report of 1808. The church must therefore have been built between 1808 and 1821.[30]

14. Sena, 1938, p. 350.

15. Idem, pp. 350, 356.

16. Idem, p. 355.

17. Ibid.

18. Idem, p. 356.

19. Ibid.

20. Ibid.

21. Cited from Salpointe, 1898, pp. 160–161.

22. Stallings has studied specimens from the carved roof timbers of the north chapel: these range between 1745±25 and 1851+*x*. Stallings, 1937, p. 5.

23. According to Salpointe, 1898, p. 161, citing Fernandez, a south chapel was used by the Third Order of

St. Francis in 1826, and since it lacked the necessary furniture, its concession was revoked. It is possible that this was the chapel of San José, built by Ortiz in the eighteenth century, since traces of other chapels on the south side are not evident.

24. Idem, p. 204.

25. Twitchell, 1925, pp. 155–156.

26. Salpointe, 1898, p. 204.

27. Twitchell, 1912, p. 344, n. 272.

28. Salpointe, 1898, pp. 160–161.

29. Anonymous, 1914*a*, p. 332.

30. Twitchell, 1925, p. 156.

In 1935, however, I secured a boring from one of the carved choir-loft joists, and Stallings determined the date of the specimen at 1761±10.[31] The timbers of this group must therefore have been brought from another site, which it is tempting to identify with the Castrense. Twitchell thought this church, located until after 1859 on the south side of the plaza, was built between 1717 and 1719.[32] In any case, the Castrense was remodeled and rededicated to Nuestra Señora de la Luz about 1761,[33] with an altarpiece of stone, and, perhaps, the timbers which now figure in Nuestra Señora de Guadalupe. In effect, Abert, who visited the ruined Castrense in 1846,[34] says that the church had been in use until fourteen years previous, or 1832, and that the roof of the church had collapsed "some years previous" to 1846.

In 1881, Bourke visited the building and found it "dilapidated and timeworn."[35] Shortly before this, the church had been used by Protestants, and in 1881 it received the Catholic parochial rite.[36] In 1922,[37] fire destroyed the transept and sanctuary roof timbers, as well as the painted wooden steeple. The building was then repaired to the state in which it now exists.

San Felipe, Albuquerque. Founded in the spring of 1706, Albuquerque was immediately provided with a church, "capacious and appropriate," serving a population of 252 persons.[38] Part of the priest's house had been begun, probably under the direction of Friar Juan Minguez.[39] By 1754, the settlement had thinned out, the population taking up its residence in ranches about the countryside, and the church was used only on Sundays.[40] By the end of the century, the establishment had fallen in disrepair, and in 1793 the Indians of Valencia and Tomé were ordered to assist "as before in the construction of the new building."[41] The present fabric (Figs. 181, 182) probably dates (in part) from this campaign of reconstruction.[42]

Santa Cruz de la Cañada. In 1695, General de Vargas founded the Villa Nueva de Santa Cruz de los Españoles Mexicanos del Rey Nuestro Señor Don Carlos Segundo.[43] The original population was sixty families, of whom twenty came from Zacatecas in Mexico.[44] A chapel and a house for the priest were immediately built,[45] although it is evident that this first settlement stood on the south bank of the Santa Cruz River, whereas the modern town occu-

31. In correspondence, Stallings indicates that the timber "has 1751 for its last ring. There have been several rings cut from the outside. My estimation of the felling date (subject to revision as in all cases where outside rings are lacking) is 1761±10, and I believe my allowed range of 20 years extremely conservative in this case. That is, I believe the date much closer to 1751 than 1771."

32. Twitchell, 1925, pp. 156, 330.

33. Wuthenau, 1935, pp. 188–189. Tamaron, 1937, p. 336.

34. Abert, 1848, pp. 39–40.

35. Bloom, 1935a, p. 320.

36. Defouri, 1881.

37. Anonymous, 1927.

38. Bloom, 1935, pp. 48–50. Hackett, 1937, p. 379.

39. Candelaria, 1929, p. 274.

40. Hackett, 1937, p. 464.

41. Twitchell, 1914a, p. 351. "Es publica la desgracia de la caida de la Iglesia de Albuquerque, y tambien de la necessidad urgentissima de levantarla, y la poca facultad que reside en los que actualmente quedan de Parrochianos en ella. Por tanto arreglandome a la mas exacta equidad, mando que el Vecindario de Valencia San Francisco [Fernando?] y Tomé que ahora se segrega de ella, concurra como antes a la construccion, de aquel nuebo edificio con los proprios aussilios que le estaban enseñalados por su Alcalde mayor antecedentemente. Fernando de la Concha, Santa Fe, 18 de Febrero, 1793." Pereyro, 1808, gives 1790 for the rebuilding.

42. Prince, 1915, p. 243, enumerates the nineteenth-century additions made to the church.

43. Vargas, 1914b, p. 58.

44. Ibid.

45. Ibid.

pies the north bank. The move was effected some time before 1707.[46] The building of the present church was begun about 1733,[47] when a permit was issued to the inhabitants to build a new church, since their former one was in ruins. The building operation lasted until about 1748,[48] one of the longest on record in New Mexico. Menchero testifies that the "sumptuous church" was still building in 1744,[49] and Villaseñor wrote in 1748 that the church was being completed, probably that which Tamaron qualified in 1760 as large, but with little decoration.[50] In 1783, a new roof was built at the expense of Father Sebastian Fernandez,[51] and before 1798, the south chapel (Fig. 97), of the Third Order of Saint Francis,[52] was erected at the expense of Father Josef Corral.[53] The north chapel (Figs. 132, 138), dedicated to Nuestra Señora del Carmen, was in existence before 1798.[54] Also in 1808, the priest's house was "almost useless," and a new one, two stories high, with seven rooms, was built by Friar Ramon Antonio Gonzales.[55] Bourke described the church in some detail in 1881.[56] In recent years, since 1900, gabled roofs were imposed upon the church and its chapels. It is likely that these will be removed in the near future, and that the roof lines will be restored to their earlier condition.

2. SPANISH VILLAGES

Santa Rosa, Abiquiu. The various sporadic settlements in the neighborhood of modern Abiquiu formed an important district of the northwestern frontier of New Mexico during the eighteenth century. Although Hodge[57] believed Santa Rosa was but an earlier name for the settlement later known as Santo Tomás, proof exists that each of the names describes a different site. Santa Rosa is unquestionably the earlier of these. Mentioned in 1744[58] by Menchero, the settlement included twenty families of Spaniards, and was administered by the friar from San Ildefonso. Twitchell maintains that Santa Rosa was abandoned[59] before 1767,[60] and that a town named Santo Tomás was founded in 1754[61] upon lands previously uninhabited, belonging to one of the settlers of Santa Rosa. The location of Santa Rosa is thought to be at a place called La Puenta,[62] about three miles southeast of the modern Abiquiu. A roofless adobe church ruin stands at this spot (Figs. 34, 54, 86); a boring taken from the choir-loft joist in 1935 gave 1744±20 as the cutting date.[63]

Ranchos de Taos. A settlement existed at this site as early as 1744,[64] although the actual town was not built until 1779.[65] The church is of considerable size (Figs. 13, 123). Reliable docu-

46. Twitchell, 1914, p. 132.
47. Twitchell, 1914a, p. 202.
48. Hackett, 1937, p. 399.
49. Idem, p. 413.
50. Tamaron, 1937, p. 347.
51. Pereyro, 1808.
52. Imbentario, 1798.
53. Pereyro, 1808.
54. Imbentario, 1798.
55. Pereyro, 1808.
56. Bloom, 1936, pp. 250–251.
57. Hodge, 1907, p. 2.
58. Hackett, 1937, p. 399.
59. Elsewhere Twitchell cites the text of the Domin-

guez-Escalante journal of 1776. These travelers celebrated Mass at Santa Rosa de Abiquiu on July 30, 1776. Perhaps the fabric was still in usable condition. Twitchell, 1917, p. 524.
60. Twitchell, 1914, p. 162.
61. Idem, pp. 25–28.
62. Twitchell, 1917, p. 521.
63. Stallings, 1937, p. 5.
64. Hackett, 1937, p. 400.
65. Morfi, 1932, p. 97 (1780). "The settlement frames a square plaza, very capacious. Its houses were almost finished in 1779 with towers at proportionate distances for their defense."

mentary evidence for the date of its construction has not been found.[66] Tree-ring studies, however, indicate 1816±10.[67]

The concrete coping along the crest of the walls, the beams and spalls in parts of the nave, the floor, and the adobe lanterns of the towers were all added in recent years, by local labor under the supervision of Father Giraud, curate at Taos. The sanctuary and the transept were entirely roofed anew in 1930–31.[68]

El Santuario, Chimayo. The site was mentioned as early as 1695 by General de Vargas,[69] when a settlement was first effected there, and in 1706[70] the residents were ministered by a friar from San Juan. No church is shown at the site in the Miera and Pacheco map of 1779.[71] The first building operation there appears to have taken place early in the nineteenth century, when the present Santuario (Fig. 124) was erected, at the expense of Bernardo Abeyta.

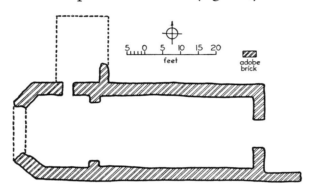

34. Abiquiu. Simplified plan of the ruined church.

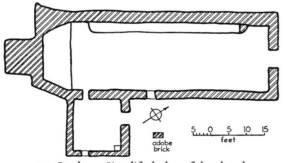

35. Cordova. Simplified plan of the church.

Prince[72] gives no authority for fixing the date of completion in 1816,[73] although the doors (Figs. 107, 108) leading into the nave from the narthex bear an inscription which reads, "Esta puerta Hiso Pedro José Corea el Año de Mil ocho cientos diciseis por solicitud del selago del Señor Domingues por debocion del R.P.F." The church has acquired the reputation of a miraculous site, and pilgrimages to secure the healing earth from the floor of the chapel dedicated to San Rafael are commonly recorded.[74]

San José, Trampas. A temporary mission was established at some point on the Trampas River as early as 1733, among the Jicarilla Indians.[75] Whether the modern site of the village of Trampas is identical with this mission seems impossible to determine. In 1751, however, the town of Santo Tomás Apostol del Rio de las Trampas was founded, with twelve families.[76] The Miera y Pacheco map of 1779[77] shows the symbol for a church at this site, and it is

66. Prince, 1915, p. 261, gives 1772.

67. Stallings, 1937, p. 5.

68. In conversation with Father Giraud, August, 1935.

69. Twitchell, 1917, p. 509.

70. Hackett, 1937, p. 374.

71. Morfi, 1932, p. 87.

72. Prince, 1915, p. 320.

73. Read, 1916. Walter, 1916a, p. 3. Walter suggested the Santuario was built some years after 1837.

74. Walter, 1916a. In recent years, the church was purchased anonymously, through the efforts of Mary Austin, and deeded to the Archdiocese of Santa Fe. Henderson, 1938, p. 123.

75. Hodge, 1907, p. 893.

76. Twitchell, 1914, pp. 289–293.

77. Morfi, 1932, p. 87.

therefore possible that the present structure (Figs. 25, 119) dates from the third quarter of the eighteenth century.[78]

In 1932, repairs were carried out by the Society for the Preservation of New Mexico Mission Churches,[79] consisting of new roof timbers, new bases for the towers, and a new balustrade and beam for the façade balcony.

Cordova. Father José Cubell of Santa Cruz told the writer in 1935 that he had once located papers giving the date of building of the church at Cordova in 1831. It was not possible to review these papers at the time. The building (Figs. 35, 113) appears originally to have been built as a private chapel. The east nave wall has a low bench of adobe the length of the interior (Fig. 183): its function is that of an interior buttress, and I was told by residents that it had recently been added, within the last ten years.

Chapel of San Miguel, La Bajada. In 1831,[80] a license was issued to erect a chapel in the settlement one league to the east of the pueblo of Cochiti. This is without doubt the present settlement of La Bajada. How soon the building operations were begun after the issue of the license is uncertain. The gabled roof was probably added in 1918.[81]

Peña Blanca. In 1780, Morfi[82] described the ranch of Nuestra Señora de Guadalupe de la Peña Blanca, situated midway between Cochiti and Santo Domingo. At that time the site was inhabited by only one family, but it is unquestionably the same location as the present settlement by that name.

Permission was given by the Bishop of Durango in 1831 to erect a church there.[83] About 1920, the church (Fig. 196) was altered by the addition of a new façade and gabled roof.[84]

San Miguel del Vado. One of the first permanent Spanish settlements in the Pecos valley was San Miguel del Vado, founded during the term of office of Governor Fernando Chacon, 1794–1805.[85] In 1805, a church was in construction, for a resident was accused of refusing an order to work on the construction.[86] This region, in the seventeenth and eighteenth centuries, was a frontier area, and had never maintained any other than an Indian population. In 1846, the adobe church (Fig. 188) was mentioned by Wislizenus.[87] This establishment was secularized in 1826.[88]

In 1866, the church underwent repairs, including the building of two new towers.[89]

78. Probably after 1760, if Tamaron's reference applies to the building of a church. "Se dejó licencia para que fabrícaran, licencia que tambien se trazó de suerte que quedará dentro de su cuartel cerrado que había de ser de treinta varas de larga con su crucero." In 1881, Bourke (Bloom, 1936, p. 274) recorded the advocacy as San José de Gracia.

79. Reuter, 1932. Reuter claims to have found proof in the village that the church was built early in the eighteenth century.

80. Archives of the Archdiocese, Santa Fe. Uncatalogued papers.

81. Anonymous, 1918, p. 51.

82. Morfi, 1932, p. 99.

83. Salpointe, 1898, pp. 164–165.

84. *Franciscan Missions of the Southwest*, VIII (1920), 30.

85. Twitchell, 1917a, pp. 206–207.

86. Twitchell, 1914a, p. 475.

87. Wislizenus, 1848, p. 18.

88. Salpointe, 1898, p. 160. Twitchell, 1912, p. 166.

89. Salpointe, 1898, pp. 208–209.

Cebolleta. This site, probably visited by Vargas in 1692,[90] was the seat of a temporary mission from 1744 to 1750,[91] populated with Navajo converts, by Friar Menchero,[92] and later ministered by Friar Manuel Vermejo.[93] A church was built, not by the Navajos, but by Laguna Indians forced into this service.[94] After the friar was driven out in 1750,[95] the Navajos refused to return, and in 1782,[96] Morfi reported the site vacant. The actual settlement was probably established early in the nineteenth century, although a garrison held the spot at the end of the eighteenth century.[97] The Navajos besieged the district in 1805,[98] and later in the century, Cebolleta was visited by the American armed forces on several occasions.[99] The town then had no Indian settlers, and consisted of Mexicans.[100] No documentation has been established for the building of the present church (Figs. 36, 194). In 1865, Bishop Lamy issued a permit to the Sena family of Cebolleta to build a private chapel,[101] although Stallings[102] gives $1814+x$ and $1836+10$ as cutting dates for two specimens taken from the choir loft in 1935.

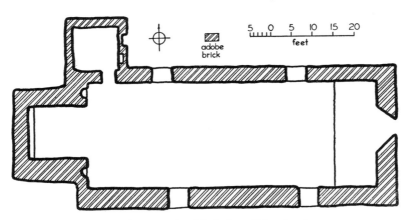

36. Sebogeta. Simplified plan of the church.

3. INDIAN PUEBLOS

San Felipe on the Black Mesa. The important mission founded by Cristobal de Quiñones before 1609[103] stood on the east bank of the Rio Grande, where Otermin visited it during the retreat of 1680.[104] In 1681, Otermin found the site abandoned, and the entire church had been demolished.[105] In 1693,[106] the Indians, fulfilling a promise to General de Vargas, returned to their pueblo, which, however, no longer occupied the pre-Rebellion site, but stood on the brink of the high mesa overlooking the west bank of the Rio Grande, about a mile north of the older location. There a church was built of adobe after 1694, of which substantial remains are still in evidence (Figs. 37, 47, 56). Bandelier[107] supposes this settlement and church were abandoned at the time of the Revolt of 1696. The event certainly occurred before 1706, when Father Alvarez reported that the pueblo had been moved down from the mesa to a new

90. Twitchell, 1917a, p. 347.
91. Hackett, 1937, p. 432.
92. Idem, p. 421.
93. Idem, p. 432.
94. Idem, p. 471.
95. Salpointe, 1898, p. 102.
96. Morfi, 1932, p. 104.
97. Twitchell, 1917, p. 374.
98. Ibid.

99. Twitchell, 1912, p. 217.
100. Idem, pp. 303–304.
101. Anonymous, 1935, p. 46.
102. Stallings, 1937, p. 5.
103. Vetancurt, 1697, p. 43; 1697a, p. 100.
104. Twitchell, 1914a, pp. 15ff.
105. Bandelier, 1892a, p. 190.
106. Ibid.
107. Idem, p. 191.

settlement, where a church was being built.[108] The adobe ruin on the mesa at San Felipe and the small structure at Patokwa were therefore contemporary, and represent a significant phase of post-Rebellion construction, characterized by small buildings, erected of adobe or stone, located among the pueblo buildings, constituting an integral part of the settlement.

San Diego de al Monte, Patokwa. Bloom believes that the church ruin located on the low mesa at the confluence of San Diego and Guadalupe canyons, at the site called Patokwa, is to be identified as San Diego de al Monte.[109] The ruins are unquestionably those of a church (Fig. 26), and Bloom's sources for the identification are compelling.[110] The evidence of the Miera y Pacheco map of 1779 may be added to his argument, where a ruined church is shown occupying a mesa site at the confluence of the canyons.[111] The designation on the map is "San Diego." Friar Francisco de Jesus

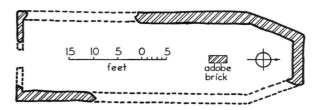

37. San Felipe on the Mesa. Plan of the church.

was assigned to this mission in 1694, with four soldiers, and the church was probably built at that time. Early in June, 1696, Francisco de Jesus was murdered there at the church door.[112] The Indians fled from the mission, and were joined by other Jemez Indians from the area, who were not resettled until after 1703.[113]

Santo Domingo. According to Bandelier,[114] Santo Domingo has occupied four distinct sites in historic time. At the first of these, a church was built about 1605, and Friar Juan de Escalona was buried there in 1607.[115] Located on the banks of the Galisteo River, this site was destroyed by a flood of which Bandelier does not give the date.[116] A second settlement, situated farther west, on the Rio Grande was also destroyed by floods. Moving a third time, the tribe was established once again a little farther east, on a site (Fig. 51) partly occupied by the present pueblo. A serious flood in 1886 demolished the religious establishment, and before 1890, the present church (Fig. 190) was built by Father Noel Dumarest.[117]

Several lines of evidence converge to give a fairly accurate picture of the establishment destroyed in the flood of 1886. Old photographs (Fig. 149) and sketches show a considerable church and *convento,* as well as a smaller church abutting the principal one. Bandelier has left a plan (Fig. 51) of the village, showing the churches and their relation to the pueblo buildings. A sketch by Moellhausen gives a rough impression of the façade in 1858.[118] Pike, who visited the pueblo in 1807, noted the mud-brick walls, the choir loft, as well as an "outside hall," and expressed surprise at the quality of the church furnishings.[119] It seems likely that this is the establishment which, in 1808,[120] was described as "new." Preceding it, a church

108. Hackett, 1937, p. 375.

109. Reagan, 1917, p. 31, suggested the church was San José.

110. Bloom and Mitchell, 1938, pp. 103–104.

111. Morfi, 1932, p. 87.

112. Espinosa, 1746, p. 35. Twitchell, 1916, pp. 356–357. Bloom and Mitchell, 1938, pp. 105–107.

113. Bloom and Mitchell, 1938, p. 107.

114. Bandelier, 1892a, pp. 186–187.

115. Vetancurt, 1697, p. 100.

116. According to Bandelier, no traces remain of this first establishment. 1892a, p. 187.

117. Poore, 1893, p. 109. White, 1935, p. 25, n. 59.

118. Moellhausen, 1858, Vol. I, opposite p. 336.

119. Pike, 1895, Vol. II, pp. 615–616.

120. Pereyro, 1808.

existed in the eighteenth century "two cuadras"[121] from the river bank, and which was "being built" in 1706.[122] It is most unfortunate that the dates of the destructive floods mentioned by Bandelier are not known,[123] for without them it is impossible to determine whether or not this eighteenth-century fabric incorporated anything of the pre-Rebellion structure.

The seventeenth-century edifice had a colorful history. In 1611,[124] the mission became the ecclesiastical capital of the province, and was later converted to military use by the friars in their opposition to the civil officers. Thus, in 1640,[125] it was charged that the church had been fortified, and the *convento* was supplied with munitions and military defenses.[126] In 1680,[127] the establishment contained an archive room and was known as one of the best missions in the province. But Otermin noted in 1681[128] that the church and *convento* had been demolished. The writing desks from the *convento* were found in one of the houses of the pueblo.[129] It appears, however, that by 1696 the establishment had been rebuilt. Plundered during the revolt of that year, it apparently was not repaired or rebuilt until 1706.[130] At least three separate establishments may be inferred: (1) the church built about 1605, and demolished in 1680–81; (2) a church built before 1696, and destroyed in 1886; and (3) the present church, built before 1890. This scanty architectural record seems to contradict the vague account of many floods.

San Felipe de Jesus, San Felipe. Father Alvarez states that the Indians were moved down from the Black Mesa some time before 1706,[131] and that the church and a new pueblo were then being built. Shortly thereafter, in 1707, according to Morfi,[132] the population was 330 persons. Salpointe[133] cites another building operation at San Felipe in 1736, under Friar Andrés de Seballos, involving the use of 84 *canales* or drain spouts, probably signifying a church of some size. The citations of 1706 and 1736 very probably refer to the site of the present pueblo. At any rate, the location is specifically stated in a report of 1754,[134] where San Felipe is placed on the same side of the river as Isleta; that is, the west bank, where the modern pueblo stands. In 1808, some rebuilding took place, including the construction of two new steeples (Fig. 191), probably under the direction of Friar José Rubi.[135]

San Lorenzo, Picuris. During the seventeenth century, the Picuris Indians were very numerous. Benavides[136] implies that a church and *convento* were standing in their pueblo prior to his arrival. Vetancurt[137] attributes the indoctrination of Picuris, if not the construction of the mission establishment, to Friar Ascencio de Zarate and Friar Martin de Arvide. According to Vetancurt,[138] the church was large ("muy capaz"), and was burned in 1680. The actual

121. Hackett, 1937, pp. 464–465.

122. Idem, p. 375.

123. Bandelier seems to have relied upon local tradition for these floods of which older documentary sources make no mention. 1892a, p. 187.

124. Scholes, 1937, p. 21, implies that indoctrination was not begun before this date at Santo Domingo.

125. Idem, p. 140.

126. Hackett, 1937, p. 217.

127. Vetancurt, 1697, p. 100.

128. Hackett, 1916, p. 67.

129. Twitchell, 1916, p. 67.

130. Hackett, 1937, p. 375.

131. Ibid.

132. Morfi, 1932, p. 97.

133. Salpointe, 1898, p. 96.

134. Hackett, 1937, p. 463.

135. Pereyro, 1808.

136. Ayer, 1916, p. 25. Scholes, 1929, p. 50.

137. Vetancurt, 1697, p. 101; 1697a, p. 24.

138. Vetancurt, 1697, p. 101.

course of events is unusually well documented. According to the testimony of a Picuris Indian[139] at El Paso in 1683, Luis Tupatu, who became governor of the northern pueblos for a short time during the Rebellion, found the church at Picuris "falling to ruins." He ordered the vessels and vestments to be collected in a box and hidden in a wall of the church near the altar, so that they might be safe either until the return of the Spaniards or until the objects should rot.

Hodge[140] maintains the pueblo was rebuilt "near its former site" in or near 1692. In 1696, General de Vargas found the church "extremely filthy."[141] The walls had been painted with Indian designs, and the door was broken, but no other major damage was noted. Whether the church noticed by the General is the same as the seventeenth-century fabric is difficult to determine.

Bandelier[142] points out that the Picuris Indians left their new settlement in 1704, returning in 1706, when a small church, without resident friar, was already in existence, if we may believe Father Alvarez.[143] During the decade 1740–50, the mission was restored, supporting eighty families and maintaining a resident minister, until at least 1754.[144] In 1759, however, Governor Marin del Valle found the pueblo in ruins,[145] when recovering the remains of Friar Ascencio de Zarate from the "ancient church,"[146] or what remained of the pre-Rebellion structure.

In 1782,[147] the mission was established once again, with a priest's house built in 1780, under the direction of Friar Fernandez.[148] Through this confusing record, it is difficult to determine how many separate edifices are involved, and what antiquity the present structure (Fig. 87) can claim, although it is improbable that the church now in use should antedate the Rebellion of 1680,[149] since the pre-Rebellion church was in ruins in 1759.

Santa Ana. Bandelier was unable to determine whether the present site of the pueblo of Santa Ana is identical with the pre-Rebellion village. The latter was alleged to have had a mission establishment at the time of the Revolt in 1680.[150] In 1687, a mesa settlement inhabited by these Indians was burned, and in 1692, General de Vargas found them occupying the Red Mesa, four leagues distant from Zia, together with the Zias.[151] The Santa Anas promised to return to their pueblo, presumably the pre-Rebellion establishment, and were found living there in 1693. In 1706, Father Alvarez[152] recorded that the Indians had a small church, with a resident friar. A bell found at Santa Ana in 1890 by Poore[153] bore the date 1710, and may have formed part of the equipment of this early eighteenth-century edifice. In 1734,[154] we learn that the church (Figs. 82, 128) was rebuilt, under the direction of Friar Diego Arias de Espinosa. It appears that the Indians were obliged to hire workmen from Pecos to manufacture the drain spouts for the church,[155] an indication of the decline in skill

139. Punsili, 1683, p. 5.
140. Hodge, 1910, p. 245.
141. Twitchell, 1917a, pp. 404, 423.
142. Bandelier, 1890a, pp. 181–182.
143. Hackett, 1937, p. 374.
144. Villaseñor, 1748, p. 419. Hackett, 1937, p. 403.
145. Salpointe, 1898, pp. 99–100.
146. Twitchell, 1917a, p. 491.
147. Morfi, 1932, pp. 95–96.

148. Pereyro, 1808.
149. Prince, 1915, p. 267, implied great antiquity.
150. Bandelier, 1892a, pp. 194–195.
151. Ibid.
152. Hackett, 1937, p. 376.
153. Donaldson, 1893, p. 109.
154. Salpointe, 1898, p. 96.
155. Ibid.

and training prevailing among the Indians, at least at Santa Ana. The establishment was mentioned in 1744[156] and again in 1754.[157] In 1808, the church was in "fair condition."[158]

In 1927 a new roof and windows were added, with funds raised by the Indians, and under the direction of the Committee for the Preservation and Restoration of New Mexican Mission Churches.[159]

San José, Laguna. This pueblo, formally established in 1699 by Governor Cubero,[160] appears to have been settled by Friar Miranda, with rebel Keres Indians, perhaps a year or two before 1699.[161] In 1706,[162] the mission had been established, although lacking all furniture, and the church was being built. The mission was administered from Acoma. In 1760, Bishop Tamaron noted the poor and small church building.[163] In 1782, the establishment acquired Acoma as its *visita*.[164] This fact does not necessarily reflect the growing importance of Laguna, or the decline of Acoma, so much as one aspect of the shrinking missionary enterprise. Abert visited the church in 1846, and at that time, just as today, the interior was "painted with curious Indian ornaments, in which they have used the pure red, blue, and yellow."[165] In 1851 Dr. ten Broeck[166] described the church as "quite a large building of stone, laid up in mud . . . surmounted by a wooden cross. It is long and narrow, and the walls are whitewashed in much the same style that the Indians paint their earthenware. The front is continued about ten feet above the roof, the whole overtopped by the cross, and in this wall are three arches, containing as many sized bells, whose tones are by no means orphean." In 1860, Domenech[167] reported that the church was half in ruins. The building was measured by the Historic American Buildings Survey in 1934 (Fig. 38) and extensive repairs were made by the Committee for the Preservation and Restoration of New Mexican Mission Churches. In 1936–37, the priest's house was remodeled.

Santo Tomás, Abiquiu. Several efforts were made during the eighteenth century to found a town in the neighborhood of Abiquiu (with *Genizaros,* or Indians who had been recovered from their captors).[168] An early settlement was established before 1747, when we first hear of it, but was abandoned in 1748, in consequence of Ute raids. In 1754, Governor Velez Cachupin commanded that the area be reoccupied, and a mission dedicated to Santo Tomás was founded and first administered by Friar Juan José de Toledo (or Tobedo),[169] upon land which had previously been uninhabited. In 1765, the site had about 800 inhabitants, constantly under attack from the Utes and the Navajos. Before 1770 the site had been abandoned, and Governor Mendinueta issued orders that its former inhabitants return to it.

Thus, we have three distinct periods of occupation: the location and advocacy of the first (?–1748) are unknown; the second was Santo Tomás, perhaps erected on another site; the

156. Hackett, 1937, pp. 400–404.
157. Idem, p. 463.
158. Pereyro, 1808.
159. Reuter, 1927.
160. Bandelier, 1892a, p. 294, n. 1.
161. Hackett, 1937, p. 469. Ayer, 1916, p. 251.
162. Hackett, 1937, p. 376.
163. Idem, p. 350.

164. Bancroft, 1889, p. 274.
165. Abert, 1848, p. 53.
166. Schoolcraft, 1854, pp. 72–74.
167. Domenech, 1860, p. 206.
168. Bandelier, 1892a, p. 54. Twitchell, 1917, p. 521; 1914, p. 162.
169. Ibid.

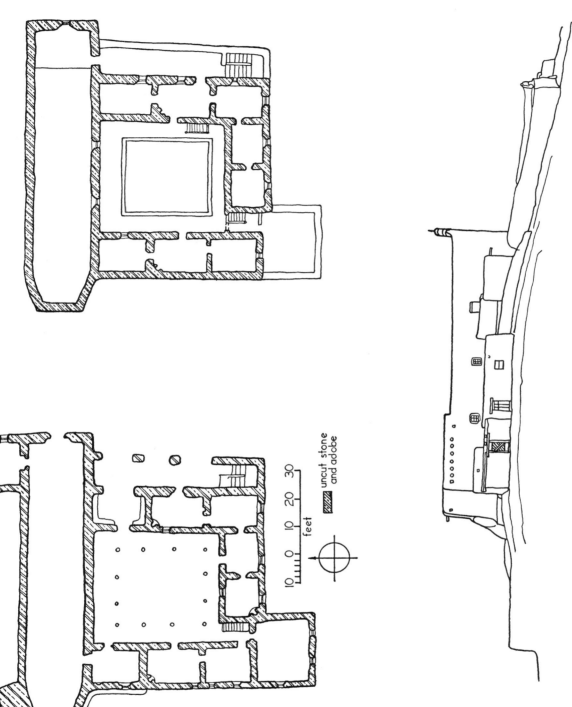

uncut stone
and adobe

feet

38. Laguna. *Above, left:* Plan at ground level. *Above, right:* Plan at window level. *Below:* Longitudinal elevation.

third, after 1770, evidently utilized the name and site of the second mission. Hence Santo Tomás probably dates from after 1754; in 1765, it formed part of the *alcaldia* of Santa Cruz,[170] and when the church was built is uncertain, although in 1808 it was described as being in good condition.[171] The old church (Fig. 39) has been supplanted (1934–38) by a new edifice built under the auspices of the Committee for the Preservation and Restoration of New Mexican Mission Churches. This new church is an excellent example of the current revival of the colonial style of New Mexico (Figs. 210, 211).

San Buenaventura, Cochiti. Bandelier[172] believed that the present pueblo of Cochiti stood upon nearly the exact site it occupied in 1598, when first visited by Oñate. It does not appear

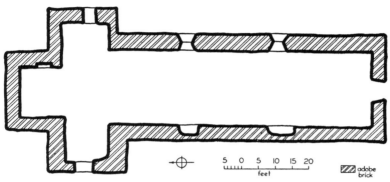

39. Abiquiu. Simplified plan of the church (destroyed 1937).

that Cochiti figured as an important mission during the seventeenth century, for in 1626,[173] it was a *visita* of Santo Domingo, and in 1666,[174] the *convento* was still served by a friar from Santo Domingo.

The pueblo was abandoned between 1683 and 1694,[175] although in 1706,[176] the "church was being built" and the village was provided with a resident friar. During the eighteenth century the village was continuously occupied, and enjoyed a relative stability of population.[177] In 1782,[178] the site was once again reduced to a *visita* of Santo Domingo. In 1819,[179] a request was filed to have a mason do work there, on the church building. The present church has been extensively remodeled since 1910, with a narthex (Fig. 40), a tin ceiling, and gabled roof. The basic fabric, however, possesses some antiquity, since tree-ring specimens from the anteroom yielded the cutting dates 1717 ± 20–$1744+x$.[180] Theoretically, parts of the

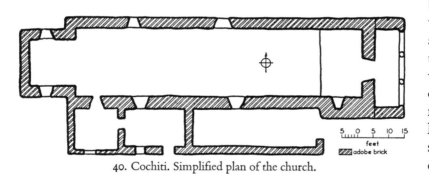

40. Cochiti. Simplified plan of the church.

170. Morfi, 1932, pp. 94–95.
171. Pereyro, 1808.
172. Bandelier, 1892a, p. 168.
173. Scholes, 1929, p. 47.
174. Idem, p. 54.
175. Bandelier, 1892a, pp. 168–170.

176. Hackett, 1937, p. 375.
177. Morfi, 1932, p. 99.
178. Bancroft, 1889, p. 281.
179. Twitchell, 1914a, p. 617.
180. Stallings, 1937.

church may have been built before the Rebellion, if Bandelier[181] was correct in assuming that the site has not been moved since the sixteenth century.

Bourke[182] described the church in 1881, noting that the ceiling was composed of "riven slabs," which had been replaced in the sanctuary with pine planks, painted with red, yellow, blue, and black designs of animals and Indians. An olla served as the font, and a general look of decay surrounded the building. In 1890, however, Poore[183] cited the good repair of the church, attributing this condition to the resident Mexican population.

San Diego (San Lorenzo), Tesuque. Hodge[184] asserts that the pueblo of Tesuque has occupied two distinct sites in historic time. The earlier, pre-Rebellion village lay three miles west of the present pueblo. In the seventeenth century, Tesuque figured as a *visita* of Santa Fe, and the mission establishment there was dedicated to San Lorenzo.[185] The friar was murdered and the church burned on August 10, 1680. In the eighteenth century, the advocacy, and perhaps the site, were changed. Tesuque became known as San Diego,[186] and a small church had been built there before 1706,[187] probably the same as that described by Morfi in 1782,[188] "entirely of adobe and very poor." In the latter decades of the Spanish dominion of New Mexico,[189] Tesuque had resident ministers, although the site had been a *visita* of Santa Fe during the eighteenth century,[190] just as before the Rebellion. During this time, early in the nineteenth century, Tesuque perhaps acquired the relatively large church of which no important traces remain, but which survives in an old photograph belonging to the Heye Foundation of New York City (Fig. 140). Carlos Vierra told me in 1935 that the foundations of this church are identical with the *atrio* of the present edifice, built since Vierra painted the older edifice in 1912–13.

San Geronimo, Taos. The pre-Rebellion establishment at Taos, destroyed once and for all in 1696, probably bears no relation to the ruined shell which now figures at that pueblo (Fig. 41). Always a center of disaffection, Taos destroyed the missionary enterprise there several times during the seventeenth century. An early foundation was suppressed there before 1626;[191] rebuilt, it was destroyed again in 1631 or 1639.[192] Under Mendizabal, efforts at reconstruction had to be

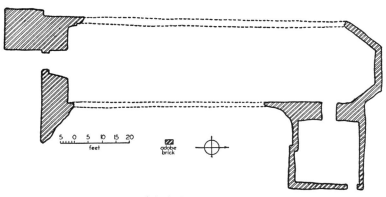

41. Taos. Simplified plan of the ruined church.

181. Bandelier, 1892, p. 168.
182. Bloom, 1938, p. 235.
183. Poore, 1893a, p. 106.
184. Hodge, 1910, p. 735.
185. Vetancurt, 1697, p. 100.
186. Twitchell, 1914, p. 40.

187. Hackett, 1937, p. 375.
188. Morfi, 1932, p. 92.
189. Twitchell, 1914a, pp. 533, 576.
190. Bancroft, 1889, p. 274.
191. Scholes, 1929, p. 50.
192. Vetancurt, 1697, p. 101. Scholes, 1937, p. 150.

abandoned,[193] and in 1680, friars were killed there,[194] as at many other pueblos. Whether any trace of the structure survived after 1692 is uncertain: in 1696, however, Vargas found the church in use as a stable, unfit for reconstruction, and ordered that it be torn down.[195]

In 1706, a new church was in construction, and this is probably the edifice of which the ruins stand west of the pueblo buildings.[196] Bishop Lamy reliably affirmed as much, on the evidence of the records he consulted in Santa Fe.[197] Tree-ring datings from the timbers of this ruin gave 1702+x and 1721.[198] Bishop Tamaron described the church in 1760 as "bien decente y capaz."[199] In 1846, a pitched battle at Taos resulted in the destruction of the monument by the American forces under General Price.[200] Enough of the ruin survives today to present a fair notion of the plan and façade disposition.

Nuestra Señora de la Concepción, Tomé. 1739 marks the formal settlement of Tomé,[201] although colonists had occupied the neighborhood since at least before the Rebellion. By 1746, the church and part of the *convento* had been built.[202] The original population consisted in part of *Genizaros,* or rescued Indian captives,[203] supplemented by thirty or forty Spanish families.[204] By 1769, the village was known only as a Spanish settlement.[205]

For as long as the site supported a mission, it was a *visita* of Isleta, six miles to the north.[206] According to Hodge[207] the town was destroyed by a flood in 1905. I believe the present church is rebuilt from the ruins of the eighteenth-century structure. The great thickness of the nave walls and the local tradition confirm this view. Another flood in 1920 caused the nave and façade to collapse; both were rebuilt. Part of the transept, and the sacristy, with its important collection of old wood sculpture, were built about 1875.[208]

CHRONOLOGICAL TABLE OF THE CHURCHES

THIS table includes buildings which have not been discussed separately in the preceding section. These are, for the most part, smaller buildings of recent construction, and older buildings of which no material remains subsist other than photographs or drawings. Some effort has been made, in the case of surviving churches, to indicate the history of previous churches occupying either the same site, or advocacy, or both. Each horizontal division pertains to a single church. Where several churches have occupied the same site, these are indicated vertically, in recessive chronological order, from top to bottom. Changes of exact location or advocacy are indicated wherever known. For churches not otherwise cited in the text, bibliographic indications are offered in the extreme right-hand column. The tree-ring dat-

193. Hackett, 1937, pp. 206, 161, 221.

194. Idem, pp. 330, 337.

195. Twitchell, 1917a, pp. 417, 421.

196. Hackett, 1937, p. 374.

197. Lamy, 1874, p. 25.

198. Stallings, 1937, p. 5.

199. Tamaron, 1937, p. 342.

200. Twitchell, 1909, p. 129.

201. Twitchell, 1917b, pp. 62–63. Candelaria, 1929, p. 278, gives 1740, from memory.

202. Ibid. Tamaron, 1937, p. 333, refers to Tomé in 1760: "Poblacion nueva . . . se ha fabricado ya una iglesia decente de treinta y tres varas de largo y ocho de ancho, con su crucero y tres altares, dedicada a la Purísima Concepción, con casa para el cura, que lo es el de la villa de Albuquerque."

203. Bandelier, 1890, p. 197.

204. Twitchell, 1917b, pp. 62–63.

205. Ibid.

206. Villaseñor, 1748, p. 416.

207. Hodge, 1910, p. 776.

208. Verbal communication from the resident minister, September, 1935.

ings are summary, representing a chronological center of gravity for a group of specimens, and they are all cited from Stallings, 1937, page 5. The table is in no way exhaustive of the religious architecture of New Mexico; it presents a minimum of information concerning each of the buildings relevant to this study.

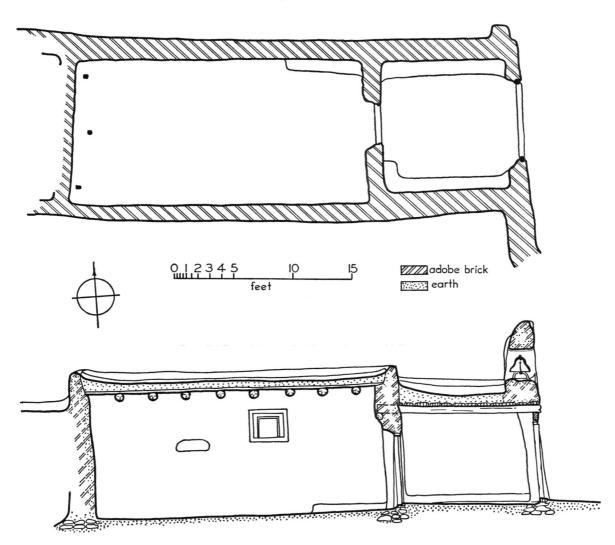

42. Talpa. *Above:* Plan at ground level. *Below:* Longitudinal section.

CHRONOLOGICAL TABLE OF THE CHURCHES

Name of Settlement	Building Dates for Extant Churches	Building Dates for Destroyed Churches	Changes of Name or Advocacy	Changes of Site
ABEYTAS	c. 1870			
ABIQUIU	Santo Tomás, 1934			
		c. 1770 c. 1938		Possible
		1754–c. 1770		
	Santa Rosa, c. 1744			
ABÓ	San Gregorio, c. 1630			
ACOMA	San Estevan, before 1644			
		Doubtful 1629		
ACOMITA	St. Anne, 1939–40			
ALBUQUERQUE	San Felipe, 1706			
BOSQUE	1892?			
CHILILI	La Navidad, c. 1616			
CHIMAYO	Santuario, early nineteenth century			
COCHITI	San Buenaventura, early eighteenth century?			Doubtful
		c. 1626–80?		
CORDOVA	After 1831			
EL PASO (Juarez City)	N. S. de Guadalupe, 1662–68			
EL RITO	1832			
EMBUDO	1809–16			
GIUSEWA	San José, c. 1626		"San Diego" (Bandelier)	
GRAN QUIVIRA	(See Humanas)			
HALONA	N.S. de Guadalupe de Zuñi, c. 1660		N.S. de Candelaria, in 1663–66; renamed La Limpia Concepción after 1706, but called N.S. de Guadalupe in 1699 and again in 1754	Possible but doubtful
HAWIKUH	La Purísima Concepción, c. 1630			
HUMANAS	San Buenaventura, 1659			

Dated Repairs of Churches	Tree-Ring Datings	Names of Builders	Names of Donors	Other Remarks	References
					Verbal communication from the sacristan
			Society for the Preservation of New Mexico Mission Churches		
Many (undated)				Bell in façade, dated 1744	
	1744±20			Abandoned 1767	
	1646			Abandoned 1672	
1692 1902 1924	1781+x 1870+x				
		Fr. Agnellus Lammert			
1793				Many nineteenth-century additions	
					Deed in Archives of Archdiocese, Santa Fe
		Fr. Alonso Peinado?		Abandoned c. 1672	
Gabled roof after 1916			Bernardo Abeyta		
1819 Roof, portico, c. 1910	1717±20 1744+x			Basic construction possibly seventeenth-century	
Recent additions				Private chapel	
Gabled roof, interior remodeling after 1880		Fr. Garcia de San Francisco, Fr. Salvador de Guerra		Unique seventeenth-century roof	
				Inscribed ceiling	
					Archives of Archdiocese, Santa Fe
Two floor levels	1625±2	Fr. Geronimo de Zarate Salmerón?		Abandoned 1632–39	
1699 1705 1780		Fr. Agustin de Cuellar? Fr. Juan de Garaycoechea, 1706		Crumbling in 1881	
Probably c. 1660				Abandoned 1680	
		Fr. Diego de Santander		Abandoned 1672. Church probably unfinished	

Name of Settlement	Building Dates for Extant Churches	Building Dates for Destroyed Churches	Changes of Name or Advocacy	Changes of Site
ISLETA	San Agustin, before 1629		San Antonio, c. 1629–80; San Agustin, early eighteenth century	Uncertain (Bandelier)
JEMEZ (*See* Giusewa, Patokwa, Walatowa)				
KECHIPAUAN	c. 1630?			
LA BAJADA	San Miguel, after 1831			
LAGUNA	San José, c. 1700			
LAS COLONIAS	After 1840			
LLANO QUEMADO	After 1900			
McCARTY'S	Santa Maria, 1932–33			
MESITA	Sacred Heart, 1935–36			
NAMBÉ		1725		
PARAJE	St. Margaret Mary, 1936			
PATOKWA	San Diego de al Monte, 1694			
PECOS	N.S. de los Angeles, before 1625			
PECOS PLAZA	1905			
PEÑA BLANCA	After 1831			
PICURIS	San Lorenzo, 1780?			Probable
		1692–1704		Possible
		Before 1625		
POJOAQUE	N.S. de Guadalupe, c. 1707			
QUARAI	La Concepción, before 1633			
RANCHOS DE TAOS	c. 1780			

Dated Repairs of Churches	Tree-Ring Datings	Names of Builders	Names of Donors	Other Remarks	References
(1697?) c. 1910 Many undated		Fr. Juan de Salas		Same fabric may have served both pueblos	
				Abandoned 1680	
Gabled roof about 1918					Archives of Archdiocese, Santa Fe, Uncatalogued papers
About 1860 1934 1936–37	1784+x 1810+x	Fr. Miranda			
				Corbels from Pecos church	Verbally communicated by W. S. Stallings, Jr.
				Altarpiece by Manuel Aragon	Communicated by Father Giraud
		Fr. Agnellus Lammert. John Meem			
		Fr. Agnellus Lammert			
Advanced decay 1890	1712+x 1739+x 1755±20		Governor Bustamante	Collapsed 1909. Dated joist owned by Mrs. Gerald Cassidy, Santa Fe	
		Fr. Agnellus Lammert			
		Fr. Francisco de Jesus?		Abandoned 1696	
c. 1692 1915 1939	1695+x			Abandoned 1840	
		Father Paulhan			
Façade and gabled roof 1920. Rebuilt 1860?					Salpointe, 1898, pp. 164–165
		Fr. Fernandez		This fabric may include portions of the structure of 1692	
				Perhaps reëstablished 1706	
		Fr. Ascencio de Zarate, Fr. Martin de Arvide		In ruins 1759	
				Abandoned after 1915 Timbers at Rancho Boquet	Hackett, 1937, p. 380. Prince, 1915, p. 269
	1630–31	Fr. Estevan de Perea		These remarks may pertain to the ruins at Tajique. Abandoned 1674	
Father Giraud 1904–34	1816±10			Altarpiece by Manuel Aragon	Communicated by Father Giraud

Name of Settlement	Building Dates for Extant Churches	Building Dates for Destroyed Churches	Changes of Name or Advocacy	Changes of Site
SALINAS (See Abó, Chilili, Humanas, Quarai, Tajique)				
SAN ANTONIO	1888?			
SAN CRISTOBAL	Before 1626			
SANDIA	San Antonio, c. 1890–95			North of modern town
		Projected 1748, completed before 1760	N.S. de Dolores de San Antonio de Sandia	West of modern town
		c. 1625?	San Francisco	
SAN FELIPE	San Felipe de Jesús, 1706			West bank of Rio Grande
		Before 1609		East bank of Rio Grande
SAN FELIPE ON THE BLACK MESA	1694			West bank of Rio Grande one mile north of modern pueblo
SAN ILDEFONSO	1905			Reoccupation of seventeenth-century site?
		c. 1706		One mile north of present site
		1692–96		
				Same as modern pueblo site
SAN JOSÉ DE CHAMA (Hernandez)	c. 1870?			
SAN JUAN	Church			
		An eighteenth-century structure?		
		1598	.	
	N.S. de Lourdes, 1912			
SAN MIGUEL DEL VADO	c. 1805			
SANTA ANA	1734			
		Before 1706		Present church may incorporate parts of this fabric
		Seventeenth-century establishment		Location undetermined
SANTA CLARA	1918			Probable
		1761		
		1706		
		Seventeenth century		

Dated Repairs of Churches	Tree-Ring Datings	Names of Builders	Names of Donors	Other Remarks	References
					Deed in Archives of Archdiocese, Santa Fe
				Abandoned 1680	
				Bell dated 1829	Hewett and Bandelier, 1937, p. 79
		Fr. Miguel Menchero		Abandoned c. 1891	
				Abandoned 1680	
Roof repairs, 1736. Steeples, 1808					
		Fr. Cristobal de Quiñones		Abandoned 1680	
				Abandoned after 1696, before 1706	
				Façade inscription	
Dilapidated in 1881				Destroyed c. 1910	
				Abandoned 1696	
				Destroyed 1680	
					Local information (verbal)
	1815±15 1843+x				Stallings, 1937, p. 5
				Destroyed 1680 or before?	Villagra, 1933, p. 150
Towers rebuilt, 1866					
1927	1729+x 1733+x	Fr. Diego Arias de Espinosa			
				Bell dated 1710	
				Destroyed 1680–92?	
				Doors come from older church	
				Cruciform church, in 1881	Bandelier, 1892a, p. 65. Bourke, 1936, p. 256
					Hackett, 1937, p. 374
					Ayer 1916, pp. 45ff.

Name of Settlement	Building Dates for Extant Churches	Building Dates for Destroyed Churches	Changes of Name or Advocacy	Changes of Site
SANTA CRUZ	1733–48			North bank of Santa Cruz River
		1695		South bank of Santa Cruz River
SANTA FE	San Miguel, after 1640			
		Before 1628		
	Cristo Rey, 1939–40			
	Cathedral, 1869			
		1714	San Francisco (*parroquia*)	Pre-Rebellion site?
		1692–1714		North tower of *palacio real*
		1628–39	Cited in 1661 as the Immaculada Concepción de N.S.	Uncertain
		1610–28	La Asunción de N.S.	Site unknown
		Nuestra Señora de la Luz (Castrense), 1759–60		
		Idem, before 1680		North tower of *palacio real*
		1717 or 1719?		South side of plaza
	Nuestra Señora de Guadalupe, 1808?–21			
	El Rosario, 1806–18			
SANTO DOMINGO	c. 1890			East of the pueblo
		c. 1808		On bank of Rio Grande
		c. 1696		"Two cuadras" from the river bank, in 1754
		c. 1605		On bank of Galisteo River
CEBOLLETA	Early nineteenth century			Probable
		1744–50		
SOCORRO	San Miguel, mid-seventeenth century?		Nuestra Señora del Socorro in seventeenth century	Possible but unlikely

Dated Repairs of Churches	Tree-Ring Datings	Names of Builders	Names of Donors	Other Remarks	References
New roof, 1783. Chapel of Third Order, before 1798, also south chapel. New *convento*, 1808	1789±20 1845+x				
				Abandoned before 1707	
1710–11 1730 1805 After 1873	1653+x 1737+x	1710: Agustin Flores de Vergara; Andres Gonzalez	Repairs of 1805: Antonio José Ortiz	Fabric may include portions of pre-1640 construction?	
				Destroyed 1640. *Parroquia* housed here 1628–39	
		John Meem			
		Antoine and Projectus Mouly			
1797–1804	1745±25 1851+x		Repairs 1797–1804 borne by Antonio José Ortiz	Only the north chapel (N.S. del Rosario) subsists	
			General de Vargas		
		Fr. Alonso de Benavides?		Destroyed 1680	
		Fr. Alonso Peinado?		Termed a "poor hut" by Benavides	
			Governor Marin del Valle	Sold in 1859; subsequently razed	
				Restored to use as *parroquia* by Vargas in 1692–1714	
				Incorporated with the remodeled structure of 1759?	
1922	1761±10 (choir-loft joist specimens)			Choir-loft timbers perhaps from Castrense, about 1832	
					Archives of Archdiocese, Santa Fe
		Father Noel Dumarest			
				Destroyed by flood 1886	
1706				Destroyed before 1808	
Fortified c. 1640		Fr. Juan de Escalona?		Demolished 1680–81	
Many (undated)	1814+x 1836±10				
		Fr. Menchero and Laguna Indians		Abandoned 1750	
Early nineteenth century		Fr. Garcia de San Francisco y Zuñiga		Abandoned from 1680 until 1800	

Name of Settlement	Building Dates for Extant Churches	Building Dates for Destroyed Churches	Changes of Name or Advocacy	Changes of Site
TAJIQUE	San Miguel, before 1650			Possible confusion with Quarai (*q.v.*)
TALPA	Chapel			
TAOS (Pueblo)	c. 1847?			Between house blocks
	San Geronimo, 1706			Western edge of pueblo
		Before 1626		Location unknown
TAOS (Town)	San Fernando, c. 1914			
		Unknown		
TESUQUE	San Diego, c. 1915			
		c. 1706		In *atrio* of present church?
		Seventeenth century	San Lorenzo	Three miles west of present pueblo
TOMÉ	Nuestra Señora de la Concepción, 1739–46			
TRAMPAS	San José, c. 1760			
TRUCHAS	In use 1852			
WALATOWA	San Antonio, 1919			
		1856		
		Before 1744	San Diego	Same as the church of 1706? Southern edge of pueblo?
		1706	San Diego	
		1695–96	San Juan	Unknown
		1626 or 1628	San Diego	Same as below? Mound near rectory?
		1622	San Diego	
ZIA	N.S. de la Asuncion, before 1614?			Affirmed by Bandelier, but unlikely
ZUÑI	(*See* Halona, Hawikuh, Kechipauan)			

Dated Repairs of Churches	Tree-Ring Datings	Names of Builders	Names of Donors	Other Remarks	References
				Abandoned 1672–74	
	1840±10			Ceiling inscription: built in 1851	H.A.B.S. 36 NM 10 (Fig. 42)
				Communicated by Father Giraud	
	1702+x 1721			Bombarded 1846	
1640–50 1692				Destroyed 1631 or 1639; razed 1696	
		Father Giraud			
				Razed c. 1914	
Enlarged in early nineteenth century?				Destroyed after 1913	
				Burned 1680	
Transept and sacristy, 1875 1905 Nave and façade, 1920					
1932	1791+x 1812+x				
New roof 1878 (inscription)					Archives of Archdiocese, Santa Fe
					Franciscan Missions of the Southwest (VIII), 1920, p. 45
				Collapsed c. 1881	
				In ruins 1874	
				Destroyed by Apaches 1709	
				Abandoned 1696	
				Abandoned 1680	
		Fr. Geronimo de Zarate Salmerón		Burned 1624	
Rebuilt 1692? 1706? 1923					

PART FOUR
HISTORICAL SUMMARY AND CONCLUSION

HISTORICAL SUMMARY AND CONCLUSION

I.

IN New Mexico the historic period embraces four hundred years. Once defined, the early formulas of construction and design account for all the monuments: innovations and departures were unknown until recent years. In Europe, during the same period, the style of religious architecture lived through vertiginous movements. The comparison indicates a difference in the rate of change. This difference naturally affects the validity of certain dating techniques. Where the rate of change is firm and constant, connoisseurship of style may assign the various kinds of execution to their relative positions in time. In New Mexico, the survey of architecture reveals few of the elements of an evolution of form: instead there are erratic minor variations from a frozen and immobile type. There are no timid, clumsy beginnings, followed by an ascending curve of invention and refinement. The friar-priests entered the new country with complex solutions developed from centuries of experience in monumental building. But rather than the differentiated, highly versatile materials of Western Europe, New Mexico offered a desolate paucity: wood without tools to work it, stone without equipment to move it, and clay without kilns to fire it. The labor available for building purposes was weak in numbers, lacking the special training and the architectural heritage of Europe, where constant experimentation with new materials and techniques and a rapid cycle of taste have always animated the movements of style. Sluggish fashions and technical conservatism usually characterize the frontier society and the peripheral area: in these terms, New Mexico was the provincial outpost in a state of chemical purity.

The period, therefore, that stands the most in need of critical examination is the seventeenth century, to the Revolt of 1680. It will be fitting to review the historical achievement of these few generations. The civil authority speaks for itself. A shoddy staff of rejected Europeans, a poor land, and the harassed population led to frictions, the massacre and subsequent anarchy, of the year 1680. The failure was by no means the fault of civilians alone, for the religious organization also contributed to the general ill will.[1] But the Church exerted an overwhelming influence for good in these formative years. The technological contribution of the friars was considerable. Immediate utility was a first consideration, and the friars sacrificed much to realize an ambitious revolution. The social and architectural program, usually entrusted to lone men, operating singlehanded in remote districts, was achieved with astonishing rapidity. Versatility and ingenuity in the personnel, to be sure, had been normal during the sixteenth century in Mexico, but the evangelization of New Mexico in the seventeenth century seems to constitute an especially brilliant missionary performance. The friars actually fulfilled the function of culture bringers in the range of their working knowledge, from stock breeding and horticulture to music and fine carpentry. Their equipment was negligible, and the instruments of work had to be contrived from raw materials on the

---

1. Scholes, 1937.

spot. Peculiar labor problems existed: these were solved to produce works of considerable magnitude in short order. In architecture, the local materials and techniques, although never finally abandoned, were made to approach the rarefied atmosphere of high style.

Conversely, of course, and not only in architecture, the forms of European life and style, when incorporated to the alien substance, lost edge and point; became, in fact, categorically novel experiments. The ancient technical habits of the Indians were not easily replaced with new ways of doing the same things. Thus, the Indians had long built the characteristic bee-hive dwellings or pueblos which have given their culture its name. Not only were they skilled in building these vast aggregate structures, but they had also solved, before the coming of Europeans, the relatively complex problem of roofing an area 40 to 60 feet in diameter, in the underground ritual chambers, where the center of the roof was supported by wooden pillars.[2] The introduction of programs and techniques peculiar to the Christian architecture of Europe did, however, entail the revision of many technical processes. Accustomed to rooms no higher than necessary for upright circulation, the Indians were taught to raise walls and roof to heights of 30 or 35 feet, thus enclosing a volume much larger than necessary for immediate needs. They were also taught to build towers, of which the vertical emphasis contradicted their own tendency to build in horizontal layers, inconspicuously, and following the lines of the landscape. Where they had left holes of mean size in the walls, the fenestration was organized and expanded. Other European elements were introduced: corridors, arches (which found no wide use), swinging doors, winding stairs, corbels, crenelations, and a new vocabulary of carved and painted ornament.

The number of seventeenth-century monuments available for comparative purposes is small. Giusewa, San Cristobal, Quarai, Abó, Humanas, Hawikuh, and Kechipauan exhaust the list of buildings untouched by subsequent restorations and additions. At Acoma, Pecos, Socorro, Zia, Isleta, San Miguel in Santa Fe, and El Paso, undetermined repairs in later periods have profoundly modified the original appearance and construction. It is possible, nevertheless, to use certain aspects of all these buildings in defining the style of the seventeenth century.

Adobe and sandstone are both used. Sandstone predominates among the pueblos in the Salinas region, and at Kechipauan, as well as at Giusewa, while adobe seems to have survived much longer in active use at Pecos, Acoma, San Miguel, Zia, Isleta, and El Paso.

Plans are both continuous and cruciform. It is to be remembered that their Mexican prototypes (Figs. 6, 64) in the sixteenth century rarely were provided with transepts, to simplify construction, and, perhaps, to refuse an enemy the protection of reëntrant corners. In New Mexico, the cruciform church, however, is common during the first generation of colonization, and its occurrence may be interpreted as a fusion between the defensive program of the sixteenth century and the Counter Reformation tendencies in plan and elevation during the seventeenth century in Mexico. The elevations, however, are severe, with dominant solids, few voids, and massive coherence, as in the Mexican models.

Roofs were uniformly constructed according to the familiar methods, as we gather from the testimony of documents, *viga* rests in the walls (Quarai), and the fragments of roofing still in place (Giusewa, Fig. 77). The beams were both round and square, with rich carving.

2. Kidder, 1924, p. 50.

There is no evidence that the roofing beams originally projected beyond the outer walls. Corbels and bed moldings were covered with a variety of carefully worked ornament (Fig. 73). Whether the original roofs showed any inclination, longitudinal or lateral, is not positively known, although a lateral inclination may be inferred from the necessity of drainage.

At Giusewa, Abó, Pecos, and Humanas, it is difficult to reconstruct the original system of fenestration. We do know, however, that at Acoma and Quarai there were transverse clearstory lights, and lateral fenestration in one wall of the nave. Abó and Pecos (Fig. 90) had windows in the transept. Windows were usually splayed and glazed with selenite.

In the sandstone monuments, floors were occasionally flagged (Quarai, Humanas). Packed adobe earth was probably the only flooring in adobe churches (Acoma, Hawikuh). The floor of the sanctuary was generally some steps higher than the nave or transept.

In elevation, the sanctuary (Fig. 32) was higher than the rest of the structure, to allow for overhead fenestration. The plan of the sanctuary was the polygonal shape common in Mexican fortress-churches.

Façades of the usual types occur: the balcony façade at Giusewa (Fig. 125), the towered façade with balcony at Pecos (Fig. 116), the unbroken fronts of the smaller churches of San Cristobal and the chapel at Humanas. Traces of the choir loft are still in evidence at Humanas, Quarai, Giusewa, and Hawikuh. At Quarai, access to it was most likely by stairs mounting from the *convento,* outside the church.

At Abó, Humanas (Fig. 12), and Quarai the baptistry and sacristy were at opposite ends of the building, and on opposite sides of the nave. Doorways were generally rectangular, widely splayed, and hung with doors fitting at top and bottom into pivot sockets. The buildings of the *convento* surrounded a central court and were occasionally two stories high (San Antonio de la Isleta).

To summarize the problem of possible deliberate irregularities of construction in the monuments of this period, we find that at Giusewa, Quarai, and Humanas the nave walls converge slightly toward the sanctuary, whereas at Abó, they diverge. At Acoma, the frequently rebuilt floor rises perceptibly toward the altar. Excepting at El Paso, which I was unable to measure, no evidence is available concerning the longitudinal deflection of roofs. In the monuments built of sandstone, to argue warping or settling of the fabric is an inadequate explanation for the lack of parallelism in the nave walls. To explain the phenomenon by asserting a defective skill in the native labor is also inadequate, when the irregularity appears with such uniformity.

In general, the least obvious but most significant trait of seventeenth-century architecture in New Mexico is its experimental character. The earliest stages of the style are lost: the first churches were probably impermanent shelters or converted dwelling spaces, as at San Gabriel, or San Juan before the founding of Santa Fe in 1610. It would be of extreme importance to know, nevertheless, by exact stages, how the transverse clearstory window attained the status of a definitive solution. This element, which is diagnostic for the New Mexican style, has no precedent elsewhere, unless it be in the problematic (Fig. 144) Beaumont drawing,[3] or in the terraced profiles of certain sixteenth-century churches of Mexico, where no functional difference of roof level actually exists for the purposes of fenestration.

---

3. *Supra,* p. 67. This drawing was probably executed in the eighteenth century. Toussaint, 1937, p. 14.

In the New Mexican churches of which ruins subsist, however, the transverse clearstory window is plainly evident, as a terminal stage of invention, always accompanied by other characteristic elements, such as the limited lateral fenestration, and the massive, unbroken sanctuary walls. Previous experiment must be postulated, although it cannot now be reconstructed.

Within the canon of this assembly, the seventeenth century offers a variety of divergent solutions to other problems. In terms of the plan, several unique experiments occur. Not only do the continuous-nave plan and the cruciform plan exist simultaneously, as at Acoma and Pecos, but at Giusewa and Abó the two forms occur in different modes of hybridization. Giusewa (Fig. 29) is a continuous, coffin-shaped nave, with chambers appended in place of transepts. At Abó (Fig. 4), the nave is a box, and the sanctuary, as well as the transepts, may be read as distinct, well-articulated additions to the basic unit of the nave. The thickness of the wall at all these churches is variable, and this dimension, ranging from the extreme width at Giusewa to the economical wall mass at Abó, mirrors a tentative, occasionally audacious approach to the problems of stability and permanence. At Giusewa again, the location of the single tower at the sanctuary not only breaks with all architectural tradition, but entails curious consequences in the massing of the edifice. At Abó, conventual buildings appear to abut both flanks of the church—a disposition which was rarely if ever repeated in New Mexico (and one which evokes the distant and splendid plan of the Escorial).

A similar variety of experiments may, of course, be read from the structure. At Abó (Fig. 14), the relatively thin curtain wall was maintained by wall buttresses, which finger the length of the west elevation in a heavy rhythm, recalling that of the church at Tepeaca in Mexico. The experiment was carried even farther, to the roof. At Abó the number of timbers was reduced to a minimum, but the size of each grew to huge proportions. The roof ceased to be a weft of slender elements spanning the nave, and became a wooden vault, scanned at wide intervals by the nine beams of the nave. At Pecos, furthermore, traces of arched construction subsist: roundheaded doorways (Fig. 101) led from the sanctuary to the subsidiary rooms installed in the reëntrant corners of the transepts, and it is possible that these were part of the seventeenth-century fabric.

A documentation which remains too scanty yields some material on the massing of the exterior elements of the churches. The six towers at Pecos, reported by Vetancurt, at the façade and transept corners, are unique among existing churches, unless an analogous arrangement existed at the fallen fabric of Abó. The sanctuary tower at Giusewa (Fig. 60) has no organic connection with the remainder of the structure, and it may have been an afterthought to use the platform provided by the hill into which the sanctuary nestles, but it testifies again to the free invention of the seventeenth-century builders, as yet bound to no endemic tradition, and faced with a program in which it was not too late to experiment. In the eighteenth century, solutions such as this—the use of a hillside to save wall, and as a tower base—simply do not occur.

The problems of internal massing connected with the transept have already been analyzed in some detail. It remains to determine a possible historical pattern for the seventeenth century in the history of this element. Here again, a preoccupation with variant, experimental solutions emerges. At Humanas (Fig. 12), the transept is a slight pulsation in the nave; at Abó (Fig. 4), it plays against the nave and sanctuary in a complex design; at Quarai (Fig. 27), the transept recalls Abó externally, but within, it is an ample, decisive cross vessel; at Giusewa there is no sign of a transept internally, although its semblance is presented on the west exterior, in the auxiliary construction of unidentified function.

Other experiments qualify the treatment of optical effect in these churches. The use of stone allowed a restricted vocabulary of moldings which was not accessible in the edifices of adobe brick. Thus at Quarai, a few slight, sharply profiled setbacks are evident on the exterior elevations. These establish horizontal accents which correct the dominant vertical corner profiles. At San Cristobal (Fig. 163), stone was used to produce rounded exterior corners, unique in New Mexico, yielding passages of modeling in light and shade. Inside the buildings, plastic values ranged from the rich surface texture (Fig. 73) of the carved timbers at El Paso (Juarez City) to the spacious rhythm of wide-set beams at Abó (Fig. 14). Little is known about seventeenth-century mural decoration, but the frescoes at Giusewa (Fig. 141) have no parallel in later wall decoration.

The foregoing mention of poorly preserved mural decoration provokes some speculation upon the nature of the many destroyed monuments preserved only in sparse textual notices. It is tempting to suppose many more experimental buildings, perhaps supplying the preparatory stages of the clearstory window invention. Other tentatives may have been in the direction of unprecedented, never-repeated roof silhouettes. It is likely that further examples of arched and perhaps even of domed construction have perished.

In any case, a level of abstraction may be defined at which all the churches of the seventeenth century are intimately related. The focal notion here is that of theatrical illumination, secured by the play between lateral and overhead fenestration (Fig. 98). This concept, within the limits of material and technique, controls the whole apparatus of design, for the illumination functions as a stylistic organizer: it is the principle animating the life of the style. Such factors as wall thickness and plan width are determined by the materials and the technique, but our organizing principle affects them too. Each of these determinants has, in a sense, its own sphere of influence: the clearstory window depends upon technique, but the massing is ultimately affected by the use of adobe, stone, and wood in a post-and-lintel construction.

Thus the definitive traits of seventeenth-century style emerge as follows: impermanent materials of limited plastic possibilities, clothing a simplified plan and a trabeated structure. The optical effects are controlled by baroque objectives of polar illumination and spatial unity. Within these limits, marked experimental tendencies are active, notably in terms of the structure and the massing. It remains to discuss a stylistic designation for the monuments of this period.

In a paper delivered before the International Congress of Americanists in 1935,[4] Dr. E. L. Hewett referred to the monuments of this period as constituting an "archaic"[5] mission style, of which the background was as yet untraced. But from the first formulation of the style to the recent decades of architectural activity, New Mexico has maintained the status of a provincial area, isolated from the currents of change which were effective in metropolitan centers of the Spanish world. The phenomena of regional survivals of an older artistic tradition, altered only by progressive simplification and reduction, characterize the arts of New Mexico, and there never occurred a period in which the original formulas were elaborated to

4. Hewett, 1938, pp. 53–67.　　　　　　5. Idem, p. 57.

a greater complexity and refinement of style. Now the term "archaic," when precisely used, does not signify mere chronological priority. As a term in the history of art, "archaic" has no significance whatever unless it describes phenomena that are both unprecedented and genetic, in the sense of inaugurating a life cycle of stylistic events. Thus, the term is legitimately used only when both of two conditions are present in the situation it describes: (1) The works in question incorporate for the first time a satisfactory solution to some major problem in the synthesis of form and matter. (2) Not only must this solution be unprecedented, but it shall be followed by kindred and dependent solutions of an increasing complexity of formal relationships. These are generally termed classic, mannerist, academic, and baroque, in chronological order, and the life cycle of style described by these terms must be clearly evident, uncontaminated by major interferences, before the terms themselves may properly be used. For if mere chronological priority is taken as the basis for archaic style, then anything becomes archaic with relation to its predecessors: Bernini is archaic with relation to Houdon; and conversely, a true archaic style will not be recognized as such in a mechanical system of priority, where the term loses shape and becomes a synonym for "older." In stylistic method, then, the term "archaic" is improperly applied to the seventeenth-century mission buildings of New Mexico, although the first of the essential conditions—an original solution to the problem of the synthesis of form and matter—is present in the resolution effected between baroque form and the materials of an aboriginal culture. The missing factor is the subsequent stylistic elaboration of the primary solution.

2.

For the purposes of a study such as this, the Revolt of 1680–92 opens up a chronological void. Such voids rarely occur in history. The complete withdrawal of the colonial program following the massacre, and its sudden renewal twelve years later, create two distinct periods. The notion of period is usually an artificial, abstract scansion of historical continuity: here, however, history really ceases; the prehistoric rolls into view and the interlude is like a dream in which submerged childhood memories explode upon the consciousness. The current personality seems to be sloughed off; actually, nevertheless, the return to a previous state of being is deeply conditioned by more recent formation and acquisitions. After 1680, the Indians undertook a process of cultural purification: European traits and skills, when consciously recognized as such, were often banned from personal and communal use.[6] The consciousness of a tribal unity and cultural heritage, and the emergence of Popé, a dislocated personality with absolute pretensions,[7] are related phenomena. With these for data, a cul-

6. Twitchell, 1914a, p. 57.

7. Popé, a San Juan Indian, organized the Revolt with two other Indians, Alonso Catiti and Francisco Tanjete, at the pueblo of Taos, where they claimed supernatural powers. The story of the outbreak of the Rebellion on August 10, 1680, and the retreat of the Spaniards to El Paso is well known (Hackett, 1911, 1912). Relieved of one set of oppressors, the Indians allowed Popé and his followers to establish a new tyranny. Popé appeared, for instance, at Zia, with Catiti and a Picuris Indian named Luis Tupatu. The Zias welcomed them, throwing corn meal upon them, and accommodating them in the house usually reserved for the Governor or the Custodian.

Popé rode a black mule and wore a headdress consisting of bull's horns reaching to the points of his shoulders. He took credit for expelling the Spaniards, and promised endless peace to the tribes, for he claimed to have built stone walls around New Mexico, which reached from the earth to the heavens. And if the Spaniards should pass these walls, he, Popé, could summon the darkness and destroy their weapons (Interrogation, 1689, p. 2). Popé was deposed before 1683, and the government was divided between Luis Tupatu in the north, and Alonso Catiti in the south (Punsili, 1683, p. 7). Some time later, Popé was again established in power, and he died before 1692. (Interrogation, 1689, p. 6).

tural purge might be guessed, even in the absence of further information. Hence the Spanish God was declared dead, baptism was effaced by bathing in rivers, and the Indians burned their rosaries. New kivas were built, and monogamy was abandoned.[8] Curious controversies arose, whether or not the peach tree was an importation, and over the recognized utility of the horse.

The church architecture, of course, suffered. Although the Spaniards had departed, their visible works remained, threatening the silhouette of each village. And the church was never merely a shelter or a visible object: it was the tangible projection of an alien sensibility, and like a seashell, it embraced and evoked the form of its absent maker. Sometimes the churches were destroyed, then again they were respected. The record contains specific details. At Sandia, for instance, a systematic effort was made to burn the church. Straw, scattered over the floor, served as kindling.[9] At Picuris, however, the church was unharmed, and in 1683, Luis Tupatu, one of the leading personalities of the Revolt, ordered the fabric to be maintained without further damage.[10] Elsewhere, the Spaniards themselves destroyed churches during the sporadic attempts to reconquer New Mexico in 1681, 1683, and 1689.[11]

In general, the churches survived the Rebellion in relatively good condition. Roofs, windows, and furniture were destroyed, but the stone or adobe shells stood intact. The extent of damages at San Miguel in Santa Fe, at Acoma, and possibly also Zia and Socorro gives some measure of the rate of decay. At San Miguel in 1692, and at Acoma, the roof and skylights alone stood in need of repair. Zia was also in fair condition, and the structure at Socorro remained a landmark well into the eighteenth century.[12] This documentation, ironically, gives us a firmer estimate of the durability of the edifices than we can guess from more peaceful periods, for during the crisis, records were more copious and detailed in this respect than at any other time during the seventeenth century.[13] The visible remains of European architecture in 1692 are important, since the renewal of the colonial enterprise, with its new staff, depended upon them for instruction. Repairs followed the pattern of extant buildings, which served also as models for new construction.

3.

THE Reconquest of New Mexico in 1692 was followed by a wave of European penetration much more intense than anything experienced during the earlier period. Santa Cruz, for instance, founded in 1695 by General de Vargas, was populated with 80 families, of whom 20 came from Zacatecas in Mexico.[14] Santa Fe was resettled, and Albuquerque was founded in 1706 as a Spanish town.[15] In addition, many Spaniards took up lands along the Rio Grande, and other cultivable areas of New Mexico were settled more thickly than at any time during the seventeenth century. In 1706, Governor Cuervo y Valdez asked His Majesty for the establishment of a new presidio "at a middle station along the road from El Paso to Santa Fe."[16] Although nothing seems to have come of this last project, the Spanish administration was

8. Twitchell, 1914a, p. 57.

9. Idem, p. 18.

10. Punsili, 1683, p. 5.

11. Hackett, 1916. Vargas, 1914.

12. *Supra,* pp. 98.

13. Hackett, 1937, pp. 327–365. Twitchell, 1914a, pp. 3–109; 1917a, pp. 340ff. Vargas, 1914a.

14. Vargas, 1914b, p. 58.

15. Hackett, 1937, p. 379.

16. Idem, p. 381.

clearly intent upon securing a firmer hold of the territory than it had enjoyed in the seventeenth century. Precise population figures for the early part of the eighteenth century are not now available, but the redistribution of white or European settlers may be gathered from occasional records, as in 1744, when Santa Fe was inhabited by 127 families, of whom few were Indians, "because they do not like to live with the Spaniards."[17] The population of Santa Cruz, furthermore, had increased to 100 families in 1744, and the smaller settlements throughout the province each sheltered 8 to 46 families.[18] El Paso, in 1744, had a garrison of 40 soldiers, considerably larger than any seventeenth-century establishment of which we have record. In general, it does not seem likely that the total European population was substantially increased. An estimate for the years 1677–80 indicates a white group of 2,500 to 3,000 persons;[19] in 1744, New Mexico contained 752 families, which, if the average family included five persons, amounts to about 3,800 people.[20] The significant factor, rather than numbers, is the intensive settlement of a more limited area.

On the other hand, the Indian population had dwindled before and during the Revolt. The Salinas pueblos were never resettled, and several of the remaining eastern pueblos were abandoned after the Revolt, such as San Lazaro, San Marcos, and San Cristobal. Thus the total area occupied by Indians had shrunk, although the practice of the *reducción,* used by the early missionaries, was not resumed, excepting for occasional efforts, such as the settling of Moquis at Sandia in 1747[21] and the founding of a few new pueblos, such as Laguna in 1699,[22] or the Apache settlements at Cebolleta and Encinal in the middle of the eighteenth century.[23]

The organized effort to reoccupy New Mexico, and to make the reoccupation permanent, was characterized by intense building activity. This, however, was categorically different from the primitive period in the early years of the seventeenth century. Abundant traces of the previous establishments remained, and many of these were in condition to be repaired. Thus, in 1706,[24] rebuilding had been begun at Pecos, Taos, San Juan, San Ildefonso, Santa Clara, Nambé, Santo Domingo, San Felipe, Zia, Acoma, and in the Zuñi district, at Halona. Churches were already in use at Picuris, Santa Cruz, Santa Fe, Tesuque, Santa Ana, Senecu, and Isleta. In the Indian pueblos, it may be inferred that native labor was used; at Zia, on October 23, 1692, General de Vargas ordered the Indians to cut timber for the church "during the coming moon."[25] It is to be noted, however, that the order was not issued by a friar, to whom the spiritual care of the pueblo had been entrusted, but by a secular person of military and civil authority. In the Spanish towns, building activity was also initiated by civil authorities, rather than by the churchmen. General de Vargas, for instance, built a church for the friars in Santa Fe, at his own expense, before 1703,[26] and it was Vargas again, not the friars, who ordered the repair of San Miguel in 1692, issuing axes, mules, and other equipment for the purpose from the military stores. The actual repair of this church did not occur until 1710, under the administration of Governor de la Peñuela, and the funds for it were raised by Agustin Flores de Vergara. Europeans composed the building crew, and from beginning to end, it was an operation from which the assistance of friars or Indians was notably

17. Idem, pp. 388–389.
18. Ibid.
19. Idem, p. 18.
20. Idem, p. 25.
21. Idem, p. 472.

22. Idem, p. 29n.
23. Idem, p. 432.
24. Idem, pp. 369ff.
25. Vargas, 1914a, p. 431.
26. Vargas, 1914b, p. 62.

absent.[27] In the pueblo of Nambé (Fig. 198), the church was erected in 1729 at the expense, not of the friars, but of Governor Bustamante.[28] In 1759–60, the first secular church in New Mexico was built, at the expense of the pious Governor Marin del Valle, and it was Marin del Valle again, not the friars, who undertook the expedition of 1759 to recover the remains of Friar Geronimo de la Llana in the Salinas area.[29] Much later, the building of the Santuario at Chimayo was another example of civil and private enterprise in the matter of church construction.[30] It was a private citizen of Santa Fe, finally, who bore the cost of the radical repairs to the *parroquia* in Santa Fe at the end of the eighteenth century.[31] On the whole, this phenomenon of civil enterprise and responsibility for religious buildings was unprecedented in New Mexico. Where the friars had initiated and realized the missionary program in the seventeenth century, the civil government constituted a violent opposition. In the eighteenth century, however, the direction of architecture seems to have passed to civilian hands, at least in European settlements, and not infrequently in Indian villages.

The style of construction and design, however, underwent no serious alterations with the transfer of initiative. The passive influence upon style, exerted by the burned and abandoned shells of churches, cannot be overestimated. Where these were still serviceable, the impulse to reinvent any of the elements of form found no expression. In the construction of new buildings, furthermore, the influence of existing example further stifled any tendency toward renewal of style. Hence, the apparent Europeanization of certain population areas in New Mexico was not attended by any marked increase in the technical and formal Europeanization of the style. In a sense, the converse proposition seems to prevail. The new settlers succumbed so completely to the existing style that one can speak of their "Indianization."

Obvious exceptions to such a process may of course be noted. In the Spanish towns, a tendency to locate the church in the center of the plaza is evident, as at Albuquerque. On the whole, moreover, spacious churches were erected only in the European towns. Santa Cruz, the *parroquia* of Santa Fe, and Ranchos de Taos are the churches which continue the splendid tradition of Giusewa or Quarai. In the pueblos, the churches were built more simply, closer to the ground, and without the lavish ornament of the preceding century. Both types, however, clearly show a decline in the quality of workmanship, principally in ornamental woodwork[32] and in finish of masonry. The sandstone spalls for wall construction are completely replaced by adobe clay. In adobe, the interior wall surfaces are uneven. The nave walls rise in convex or concave planes, and the corners are rounded in an irregular fashion.

With regard to plans, it is generally true that the cruciform churches are built only in the

---

27. Kubler, 1939a.

28. Dated choir-loft joist (Fig. 110), in possession of Mrs. G. Cassidy, Canyon Road, Santa Fe.

29. *Supra,* p. 88.

30. Prince, 1915, p. 320.

31. Sena, 1938.

32. This is not to mean decline in richness and variety of ornament, but in quality of line and elegance of execution. The woodwork at San Miguel in Santa Fe (1710) is extremely rich, but the line and composition of the ornament are far cruder than in the graceful corbels

and sumptuous *vigas* of Our Lady of Guadalupe in El Paso (1668).

Early in the nineteenth century a school of skillful wood carvers emerges in the Sangre de Cristo mountains, northeast of Santa Fe. At Chimayo (Figs. 107–108), Truchas, and Trampas, there are church doors, pulpits, and furniture decorated with handsome geometrical patterns, delicate moldings, and floral motives of considerable virtuosity of execution. It is tempting to associate with this renaissance the name of James Pursley, of Kentucky, who arrived in Santa Fe in 1805, to exercise his trade as a carpenter. Pike, 1895, Vol. II, pp. 757–758.

Hispanic settlements. In the pueblos, the continuous-nave church is typical (San Felipe, Santa Ana). In matters of construction, if, as we have supposed, the thicker wall supplied a fulcrum for handling the roof timbers, it may be inferred that the technique was improved in large European towns, since the nave walls are not only of equal width at Santa Cruz and Ranchos de Taos, but they are also much thinner than seventeenth-century walls.[33] In the pueblos and in small Mexican villages, however, the thicker wall persists.

The familiar system of fenestration undergoes certain modifications in the later churches. Reveals and window sills are clumsily constructed with irregular outlines. In the nineteenth century, the clearstory window is often suppressed, either during repairs to an older fabric, or in the building of a new church (Chimayo, Fig. 22; Cordova; La Bajada).

In European towns, large churches are built like those of the seventeenth century, while in the pueblos, the height of the nave is generally much less than the width. The resultant volumes are broad and tranquil, as if the Indians had reasserted their timeless preference for long, low structures which echo the lines of the landscape. The irregularities of construction in the eighteenth century show much less than the elusive uniformity noticed in monuments of the seventeenth century. The nave walls converge erratically, at either end of the nave. The inclination of the roofs and floors is likewise erratic, although many modern measurements, without excavation, are worthless in view of the many remodelings each church has undergone. In the towns settled by Europeans, the tendency exists to develop additional chapels from the ends of the transepts, as at Santa Cruz (Fig. 9), Socorro, or the *parroquia* in Santa Fe. These chapels sometimes constitute actual extensions of the cross vessel, at Socorro and the *parroquia,* or else they are separate chambers. In either case, the exterior massing of the church is profoundly altered.

The façades in European towns are generally without balcony, flanked by well-developed towers of considerable height. The ornamental Mexican parapet was common before the addition of gabled roofs. With few exceptions, as at Trampas (Fig. 119), the balconied façade is restricted to the pueblos, where the timbers, balusters, and wall surfaces are painted in bold earth colors with nature symbols peculiar to the Pueblo mythologies. A type of façade of which the occurrence in the seventeenth century is not certain is now found in the Indian pueblos: the plain end-wall façade with the choir-loft joists projecting to form a balcony or platform, as at Nambé (Fig. 198), San Ildefonso (Fig. 122), or Pojoaque (Fig. 205). Whether this arrangement was originally in use at Giusewa or Humanas cannot now be determined.

At San Ildefonso (Fig. 111), Santa Ana (Fig. 148), Santo Domingo, and Isleta (Fig. 99), examples of a structure probably used as an open chapel were built. Here again, the seventeenth-century precedent is not certain, but probable.

All churches of this period are heavily buttressed (Fig. 84), in contrast to the monuments of the preceding century. It seems as if the work of the second period were less careful and less durable, although the methods and disposition of the elements are the same. The principal movements of style consist in decreased skill and elegance of execution, and in the differentiation of the types of churches in the towns and pueblos.

Near the end of the second period of European occupancy, the religious affairs of the

33. Note the use of scaffolds at San Miguel in 1710. Kubler, 1939a, p. 12.

province were approaching a state of material and spiritual disintegration. In 1832, a visitor from Mexico reported that the churches were "almost destroyed, and most of them are surely unworthy of being called the temples of God. . . . There is an absolute deficiency of ministers, for almost all the curacies and missions of the territory are vacant."[34]

4.

WITH the American occupation of New Mexico in 1846, and the arrival of Bishop Lamy in Santa Fe in the summer of 1851,[35] new influences began to modify the architecture of Indian and Mexican settlements. The position of Bishop Lamy was at first a difficult one. His diocese had abruptly been wrenched from stagnation; in the terms of the Church, it was no longer to continue as a peripheral outpost of the Spanish world, but as a focus and point of diffusion in the Anglo-Saxon continent. Hence the Bishop, who originated in Auvergne, faced several antagonisms. Not only was he foreign to the Spanish-speaking population as a Frenchman and as a member of the secular clergy, but his faith, position, and authority were alien to the faith of the many new settlers from the United States. Notwithstanding these difficulties, the Bishop was successful in consolidating the Church, and he maintained the peace among factions. In the process, his attitude toward the traditional church architecture of New Mexico was, on the whole, negative. Shortly after his arrival in Santa Fe, a question arose over the disposal of the Castrense, built during Governor Marin del Valle's term of office in the eighteenth century. Rather than antagonize the government by making an issue of the preservation of old structures, the Bishop wrote, in 1851,[36] that he "would much rather see every church building in New Mexico destroyed than that one finger should be raised against the civil authorities." Lamy's objectives were clearly of a higher order than that of producing a style-conscious architecture, but it cannot be denied that his administration effected the mutilation by improvement which has denatured so many of the monuments treated in this study. In the construction of new churches, furthermore, plain serviceability was the first consideration of the new churchmen.

By 1865, the Bishop had accomplished much building; his report on the activity of the first fourteen years of his vicarship mentioned the building of forty-five churches and chapels, and the repair of eighteen or twenty.[37] In this work, the French training and taste of the Bishop and the French priests are clearly evident. The most notable works of his time were the Cathedral in Santa Fe, built of stone by French architects, in "Romanesque" style,[38] and the chapel of the Order of the Sisters of Loretto (1873–75), adapted from the Sainte Chapelle in Paris. The style of these and other churches built during the second half of the nineteenth century participates in the eclectic revivalist tendencies which then controlled architecture in Europe and America. In repairs, the taste of the day led to the imitation of medieval forms in wood and adobe; pointed windows, spires, and gabled roofs became the fashion.

Beside the French revivalist churches and repairs, the seventeenth-century formula of building persists, however weakened. In Taos pueblo, for instance, after the destruction of

34. Barreiro, 1928, p. 162.

35. Twitchell, 1912, pp. 329–330.

36. Twitchell, 1917a, p. 13, n. 373.

37. Twitchell, 1912, p. 342.

38. Cornerstone laid in July, 1869. Twitchell, 1925, p. 364.

the old church by an American bombardment in 1847,[39] a smaller church was built with the usual flat roof, earth floor, the characteristic clearstory window, and limited lateral fenestration.[40] At Santo Domingo pueblo, the church destroyed by the flood of 1886[41] was replaced by a traditional edifice, with clearstory window and balconied façade (Fig. 190).

In other localities where the tradition persisted, certain modifications of structure occur. At Santa Clara pueblo (Fig. 70), at San Antonio and Llano Quemado,[42] the sanctuary is apsidal, on a semicircular plan. This formation may have been introduced by the French priests from their own country. In colonial New Mexico, however, the apse was nonexistent.

At San José de Chama, near Española, the clearstory window and the choir loft are omitted.[43] Here, as well as at Abeytas (Fig. 193) and Bosque (Fig. 194),[44] there is an evident tendency to imitate the generous proportions of the traditional cruciform church on a plan of smaller dimensions.

Striking is the sharp definition of corners and edges (Fig. 200), accountable by the newness of the fabric, and perhaps as an imitation of the angularity of brick and stone construction. Carved ornament is rare: the beams are undecorated, and the occasional corbels are crudely fashioned.

Among natives of the country, the tendency since 1900 has been more and more away from the tradition, to formless structures without local style. Since 1920, however, when the Committee for the Preservation and Restoration of New Mexican Mission Churches was organized, the repair and construction of churches in the regional manner has been encouraged, as at Abiquiu. Father Agnellus Lammert's handsome constructions at McCarty's, Mesita, Paraje, and Acomita constitute a remarkable revival of seventeenth-century building practice. In Santa Fe, a new church of similar character, the Cristo Rey, has recently been completed, following the designs of John Meem. These buildings are usually modeled after San Felipe, Acoma, or Laguna. They constitute an architectural phase of the general southwestern revival of local craftsmanship and regional art (Figs. 207–219).

The question may be asked whether or not religious architecture is a residual art in New Mexico as it seems to be elsewhere in occidental countries. The presence of a devout Mexican population favors the continuance of a religious architecture of sorts. The excellent church at Hernandez (San José de Chama) might be taken as an example of the possibilities here (Fig. 72). On the whole, however, churches in the Mexican villages are produced with little attention to monumental form. The "archaeological" churches of recent years are few in number, and they are partly produced under a stimulus from outside, secular sources. The Penitente *morada* structures use the simplest of domestic forms: were the existence of the cult not threatened from within and without, it is theoretically possible that a future architecture might evolve from it.

39. Burton, 1913, pp. 176–209.

40. Lamy, 1874. Documentation of the buildings of this period is at present very scanty, and it is consequently impossible to give detailed histories.

41. Prince, 1915, p. 186.

42. Santa Clara (Fig. 70): rebuilt in 1918 on the site of an older church (Fig. 204). The doors of the present edifice come from the older building. San Antonio (Fig. 199): date and history unknown. Llano Quemado: date and history unknown. In the last two churches, the newness of the masonry and timbers suggests a fairly recent date.

43. Date unknown. Construction looks recent.

44. Abeytas: about 1870, according to the sacristan of the church. Bosque: 1892. Deed in Archives of Archdiocese.

5.

THE traditional religious architecture of New Mexico is, in the last analysis, a translation of the forms of stone and dynamic structure into those of friable material and static structure. The architecture has an exotic harmony, within which a few familiar phrases may be detected, but as an entity the style is unique, strongly conditioned by the semiarid environment, the peripheral society, and the historical isolation of New Mexico. The seventeenth-century adaptation of adobe to baroque form, and vice versa, constituted a stylistic end term. The later history of architecture in colonial New Mexico is comparable to that of the tissue which, divorced from its host, goes on proliferating, always identical with itself, until the favorable conditions in which it thrives are suppressed.

APPENDIX

BIBLIOGRAPHY

PLATES

INDEX

APPENDIX

THE Douglass method of tree-ring analysis has been used in archaeological investigations in the Southwest since about 1923. Dr. A. E. Douglass, of the University of Arizona, established in 1913 a system of dating modern specimens of wood, which depends upon the fact that the width of the ring-growths in the cross section of a tree trunk varies according to annual weather conditions. It was demonstrated that all specimens from a definable area show a characteristic ring pattern in which, although the actual width measurement of a given ring may vary in each specimen, the relative width of the rings in the pattern remains constant. Dr. Douglass also affirmed the probability that a given ring sequence, with its characteristic variations, is never exactly duplicated in time. The chronology for a given weather area was erected by matching the configuration of the central rings of one tree with the configuration of rings near the bark of another tree known to have grown previously. By this means a continuous sequence of ring patterns was prepared. It was then necessary to make a detailed chronology of each weather area. The Rio Grande chronology was established by W. S. Stallings, Jr.[1] The datings of the wood specimens from the church ruin at Giusewa and elsewhere were made from this chronology. The accuracy of the datings[2] depends upon the sensitivity of the ring-growth process, the determination of the variable amount of sapwood, and the presence of the rings near the bark in the specimen.

The relation of these studies to archaeological research is obvious.[3] Beams from which no outer rings are missing give the precise date of cutting the timber, and indicate the date of construction of the wall in which the timber was found.

The dates from Giusewa.[4] Material collected August, 1930, under auspices of the University of New Mexico. Research on material supported by Laboratory of Anthropology. Many of the timbers are worn, some badly; and those not worn have been adzed. With a single exception (JM 23), rings have been lost in one manner or the other on the outsides of the specimens, thus rendering the exact cutting dates impossible of determination. In certain of the specimens the loss is undoubtedly small, probably less than three years' growth. In the one specimen which retains a part of the original outside (at a knot) the configuration of the last rings is distorted, with the result that allowance must be made for possible error in the ring sequence. However, from an examination of the better-preserved specimens, and the grouping of the dates of the last rings present on these specimens, we can say with confidence that the timbers, as a group, very probably were felled within a year or two of 1625.

All the specimens are round timbers in sound condition. None shows evidence of having been subjected to fire. Ten of the specimens are Douglas Fir (*Pseudotsuga taxifolia*), known to the Spaniards as the *Pina real,* or royal pine; the other specimen (JM 25) is western yellow pine (*Pinus ponderosa*).

A listing of the material follows on page 148.

NUESTRA SEÑORA DE GUADALUPE (SANTA FE)

In a letter, Mr. Stallings communicates the following information (1936). "The core from the adzed viga under the choir has 1751 for its last ring. There have been several rings cut

---

1. Stallings, 1933, pp. 803–806.
2. Douglass, 1934.
3. Douglass, 1937. Stallings, 1937.

4. This information, in its present form, was kindly communicated by Mr. W. S. Stallings, Jr., of the Laboratory of Anthropology, Santa Fe, New Mexico.

from the outside. My estimation of the felling date (subject to revision as in all cases where outside rings are lacking) is 1761 plus or minus 10, and I believe my allowed range of 20 years extremely conservative in this case. That is, I believe the date much closer to 1751 than 1771. The 20-year range should take care of the felling date with a very small chance of error."

GIUSEWA

Specimen	Provenance	Outside Dated Ring	Estimated Number Rings Lost Outside
JM 4	Window lintel, east "transept"	1590	Many
JM 5	" " " "	1577	Many
JM 6	" " " "	1588	Many
JM 7	Window lintel, west "transept"	1611	Several
JM 17	Balcony beam, façade	1622	Very few
JM 18	" " "	1621	Very few
JM 19	" " "	1622	Very few
JM 20	" " "	1618	Few
JM 21	" " "	1574	Many
JM 22	" " "	1620	Few
JM 23	Beam projecting from east side of church, exterior	1622	Very few
JM 25	Beam projecting from north wall, east "transept"	1624	Very few

RANCHOS DE TAOS

Specimen	Description	Outside Dated Ring	Estimated Number Rings Lost Outside
RG 636	Adzed round beam	1776	Many
RG 637	" " "	1808	Few
RG 638	" " "	1807	Very few
RG 639	" " "	1806	Very few

BIBLIOGRAPHY

ABERT, J. W.

    1848   Report of the secretary of war, communicating . . . a report and map of the examination of New Mexico. Washington, 1848.

ALCEDO, A. DE

    1788   Diccionario geografico-historico de las Indias Occidentales o America, Vol. III. Madrid, 1788.

ANONYMOUS

    1914   Notes—reviews—communications. *Old Santa Fe,* Vol. I, p. 335. Santa Fe, 1914.

    1914*a*   Joseph de Urrutia. *Old Santa Fe,* Vol. I, p. 332. Santa Fe, 1914.

    1918   Editorial review. *Franciscan Missions of the Southwest,* No. 6, p. 51. St. Michael's, 1918.

    1927   *Santa Fe New Mexican,* Tuesday, June 27, 1927.

    1935   Document written by the archbishop is discovered. *El Palacio,* Vol. XXXVIII, p. 46. Santa Fe, 1935.

    1936   Kivas found in Quarai monastery. *El Palacio,* Vol. XL, p. 122. Santa Fe, 1936.

    1937   University buys Abó ruins. *El Palacio,* Vol. XLIII, p. 120. Santa Fe, 1937.

    1937*a*   Many mural paintings at Awatovi. *El Palacio,* Vol. XLII, pp. 52–53. Santa Fe, 1937.

    1937*b*   Archbishop Gerken preserves archives. *El Palacio,* Vol. XLIII, pp. 103–104. Santa Fe, 1937.

    1938   Pecos repairs begun. *El Palacio,* Vol. XLV, pp. 82–83. Santa Fe, 1938.

    1938*a*   Bandelier drawings found. *El Palacio,* Vol. XLIV, pp. 165, 166. Santa Fe, 1938.

    1938*b*   Abó mission repair begun. *El Palacio,* Vol. XLIV, pp. 167–168. Santa Fe, 1938.

ATL [GERARDO MURILLO]

    1924   Iglesias de Mexico. Las cupulas. Publicaciones de la secretaria de hacienda, Vol. I. Mexico, 1924.

    1927   Iglesias de Mexico. Publicaciones de la secretaria de hacienda, Vol. VI. Mexico, 1927.

AYER, E. A. B.

    1916   The memorial of Fray Alonso de Benavides, 1630. Chicago, 1916.

AYRES, A. B.

    1926   Mexican architecture. New York, 1926.

BANCROFT, H. H.

    1889   History of Arizona and New Mexico. San Francisco, 1889.

BANDELIER, A. F.

    1881   Historical introduction to studies among the sedentary Indians of New Mexico. *Papers of the Archaeological Institute of America,* Vol. I. Cambridge, 1881.

    1881*a*   A visit to the aboriginal ruins in the valley of the Rio Pecos. *Papers of the Archaeological Institute of America,* Vol. I, pp. 33–135. Boston, 1881.

    1889   Quivira. *The Nation,* Vol. 49, pp. 348–349, 365–366. New York, 1889.

    1890   Final report of investigations among the Indians of the southwestern United States. *Papers of the Archaeological Institute of America. American Series,* Vol. III. Cambridge, 1890.

    1890*a*   Contributions to the history of the southwestern portion of the United States. *Papers of the Archaeological Institute of America,* Vol. V. Cambridge, 1890.

    1892   An outline of the documentary history of the Zuñi tribe. *Journal of American Ethnology and Archaeology,* Vol. III, pp. 1–115. Cambridge, 1892.

    1892*a*   Final report of investigations among the Indians of the southwestern United States. *Papers of the Archaeological Institute of America. American Series,* Vol. IV. Cambridge, 1892.

    1895   Report of the U.S. commission to the Columbian exposition at Madrid, 1892–1893. Washington, 1895.

    1910   Introduction to the documentary history of the Rio Grande pueblos of New Mexico. *Papers of the School of American Archaeology,* No. 13. Cambridge, 1910.

BARREIRO, A.

    1928   Ojeada sobre Nuevo Mexico; translated and edited by L. B. Bloom. *New Mexico Historical Review,* Vol. III, pp. 73–96, 145–178. Santa Fe, 1928.

BENAVIDES, A. DE. *See also* AYER, 1916

    1634   Memorial a la sanctitad de urbano 8 nro señor acerca de las converciones del Nuevo Mexico hechas en el. MS., 1634. Photostatic copy of original (Archivio de Propaganda Fide, Rome) in Huntington Library, San Marino, California.

BERNARD, A.

    1928   Petits édifices d'Espagne. 6th series. Paris, 1928.

BLOOM, L. B.

    1913   New Mexico under Mexican administration 1821–1846. *Old Santa Fe,* Vol. I, pp. 3–49, 131–175. Santa Fe, 1913.

    1914   New Mexico under Mexican administration 1821–1846. *Old Santa Fe,* Vol. I, pp. 235–287, 347–368. Santa Fe, 1914.

    1914a New Mexico under Mexican administration 1821–1846. *Old Santa Fe,* Vol. II, pp. 3–56, 119–169. Santa Fe, 1914.

    1915   New Mexico under Mexican administration 1821–1846. *Old Santa Fe,* Vol. II, pp. 223–277, 351–380. Santa Fe, 1915.

    1923   The Jemez expedition, 1922. *El Palacio,* Vol. XIV, pp. 15–20. Santa Fe, 1923.

    1928   A glimpse of New Mexico in 1620. *New Mexico Historical Review,* Vol. III, pp. 357–389. Santa Fe, 1928.

    1929   Instruccion a Peralta por Vi-Rey. *New Mexico Historical Review,* Vol. IV, pp. 178–187. Santa Fe, 1929.

    1929a When was Santa Fe founded? *New Mexico Historical Review,* Vol. IV, pp. 188–194. Santa Fe, 1929.

    1930   The royal order of 1620. *New Mexico Historical Review,* Vol. V, pp. 288–298. Santa Fe, 1930.

    1931   A campaign against the Moqui pueblos, 1716. *New Mexico Historical Review,* Vol. VI, pp. 158–226. Santa Fe, 1931.

    1933   Bourke on the southwest, 1860. *New Mexico Historical Review,* Vol. VIII, pp. 1–30. Santa Fe, 1933.

    1933a Fray Éstevan de Perea's *Relación. New Mexico Historical Review,* Vol. VIII, pp. 211–235. Santa Fe, 1933.

    1934   Bourke on the southwest, II–V. *New Mexico Historical Review,* Vol. IX, pp. 33–77, 159–183, 273–289, 374–430. Santa Fe, 1934.

    1935   Albuquerque and Galisteo, 1706. *New Mexico Historical Review,* Vol. X, pp. 48–50. Santa Fe, 1935.

    1935a Bourke on the southwest, VI–VII. *New Mexico Historical Review,* Vol. X, pp. 1–35, 271–322. Santa Fe, 1935.

    1935b A trade invoice of 1638. *New Mexico Historical Review,* Vol. X, pp. 242–248. Santa Fe, 1935.

    1936   Bourke on the southwest, VIII–X. *New Mexico Historical Review,* Vol. XI, pp. 77–122, 188–207, 217–282. Santa Fe, 1936.

    1938   Bourke on the southwest, XIII. *New Mexico Historical Review,* Vol. XIII, pp. 192–238. Santa Fe, 1938.

BLOOM, L. B., and MITCHELL, L. B.

    1938   The chapter elections in 1672. *New Mexico Historical Review,* Vol. XIII, pp. 85–119. Santa Fe, 1938.

BOLTON, H. E.

    1916   Spanish exploration in the southwest, 1542–1706. New York, 1916.

    1917   The mission as a frontier institution in the Spanish American colonies. *American Historical Review,* Vol. XXIII, pp. 42–61. Santa Fe, 1917.

BOURKE, *see* BLOOM

BREW, J. O.

    1937   The first two seasons at Awatovi. *American Antiquity,* Vol. III, pp. 122–137. Menasha, Wisconsin, 1937.

    1939   Preliminary report of the Peabody Museum Awatovi Expedition of 1937. *American Antiquity,* Vol. V, pp. 103–114. Menasha, Wisconsin, 1939.

BRUTAILS, J. A.

    1900   Archéologie du moyen âge. Paris, 1900.

BURTON, E. B.

    1913   The Taos rebellion. *Old Santa Fe,* Vol. I, pp. 176–209. Santa Fe, 1913.

CANDELARIA, J.

    1929   Noticias 1776; with translation. *New Mexico Historical Review,* Vol. IV, pp. 294–297. Santa Fe, 1929.

CAREY, P. S.

1860   Chancels. *Notes and Queries,* Series 2, Vol. X, pp. 312–313. London, 1860.

1861   Choirs and chancels. *Notes and Queries,* Series 2, Vol. XI, pp. 55–56. London, 1861.

CARLETON, J. H.

1855   Diary of an excursion to the ruins of Abó, Quarra, and Gran Quivira, in New Mexico. *Ninth Annual Report of the Smithsonian Institution,* pp. 296–316. Washington, 1855.

CASTAÑEDA, P. DE N.

1904   Translation of the narrative of Castañeda; edited by G. P. Winship. New York, 1904.

CHENEY, S., and CANDLER, M.

1935   Santos. *Parnassus,* Vol. VII, pp. 22–24. 1935.

CUEVAS, M.

1922   Historia de la iglesia en Mexico, Vol. II. Tlalpam, 1922.

1928   Historia de la iglesia en Mexico, Vol. III. El Paso, 1928.

DAVIS, W. W. H.

1857   El gringo: or, New Mexico and her people. New York, 1857.

1869   The Spanish conquest of New Mexico. Doylestown, 1869.

DEFOURI, J. H.

1881   MS. Journal. Archives of the Archdiocese, Santa Fe, New Mexico.

1887   Historical sketch of the Catholic church in New Mexico. San Francisco, 1887.

DEHIO, G., and BEZOLD, G.

1901   Die kirchliche Baukunst des Abendlandes, Vol. II. Stuttgart, 1901.

DOMENECH, E. M.

1860   Seven years residence in the great deserts of North America, Vol. I. London, 1860.

1860a Seven years residence in the great deserts of North America, Vol. II. London, 1860.

DONALDSON, T.

1893   Moqui Indians of Arizona and Pueblo Indians of New Mexico. *11th Census of the United States, Extra Census Bulletin.* Washington, 1893.

DOUGLASS, A. E.

1934   Accuracy in dating. *Tree Ring Bulletin,* Vol. I, pp. 10–12, 19–21. 1934.

1937   Tree rings and chronology. *University of Arizona Bulletin.* Physical Science Bulletin No. 1. Tucson, 1937.

DUTTON, B. P.

1938   The Jemez mountain region. *El Palacio,* Vol. XLIV, pp. 133–143. Santa Fe, 1938.

ELY, A. G.

1935   The excavation and repair of Quarai mission. M.A. thesis. University of New Mexico. Unpublished.

1935a The excavation and repair of Quarai mission. *El Palacio,* Vol. XXXIX, pp. 133–144. Santa Fe, 1935.

1939   Field work at Pecos. *El Palacio,* Vol. XLVI, pp. 124–126. Santa Fe, 1939.

EMORY, W. H.

1848   Notes of a military reconnoissance from Fort Leavenworth in Missouri, to San Diego, in California. . . . Washington, 1848.

ENLART, C.

1919   Manuel d'archéologie française, Vol. I. Paris, 1919.

1920   Manuel d'archéologie française, Vol. II. Paris, 1920.

ESPINOSA, I. F. DE

1746   Chronica apostolica, y seraphica, Vol. I. Mexico, 1746.

EYRE, T. T.

1935   The physical properties of adobe used as a building material. *University of New Mexico Bulletin, Engineering Series,* Vol. I, No. 3. Albuquerque, 1935.

FALCONER, T.

1930   Letters and notes on the Texan Santa Fe Expedition 1841–1842. New York, 1930.

FEWKES, J. W.

   1898   Archaeological expedition to Arizona in 1895. *Seventeenth Report of the Bureau of American Ethnology*, Part 2, pp. 519–744. Washington, 1898.

FISHER, R. G.

   1937   The Jeddito Project of Peabody Museum. *El Palacio*, Vol. XLIII, pp. 97–101. Santa Fe, 1937.

FORREST, E. R.

   1929   Missions and pueblos of the old southwest. Cleveland, 1929.

GAGE, T.

   1928   The English-American, a new survey of the West Indies. London, 1928.

GARCIA GRANADOS, R.

   1934   Huejotzingo. La ciudad y el convento franciscano. Mexico, 1934.

   1935   Capillas de indios en Nueva España (1530–1605). *Archivo Español de Arte y Arqueologia*, Vol. XXXI, pp. 3–27. Madrid, 1935.

GILLET, L.

   1929   L'art dans l'Amérique latine. In: André Michel, *Histoire de l'art*, Vol. VIII, Part 3, pp. 1019–1096. Paris, 1929.

GOODYEAR, W. H.

   1896   Optical refinements in mediaeval architecture. *Architectural Record*, Vol. VI, pp. 1–20. New York, 1896.

   1896a   Perspective illusions in mediaeval Italian churches. *Architectural Record*, Vol. VI, pp. 163–183. New York, 1896.

   1902   Architectural refinements in Italian churches. *Journal of the Archaeological Institute of America*, 2d series, Vol. VI, pp. 166–196. Cambridge, 1902.

GREGG, J.

   1933   Commerce of the prairies. Dallas, 1933.

GUNN, J. M.

   1917   Shat-Chen. History, traditions, and narratives of the Queres Indians of Laguna and Acoma. Albuquerque, 1917.

H.A.B.S. *See* HISTORIC AMERICAN BUILDINGS SURVEY

HACKETT, C. W.

   1911   The revolt of the Pueblo Indians of New Mexico in 1680. *Quarterly of the Texas State Historical Association*, Vol. XV, pp. 93–147. Austin, 1911.

   1912   Retreat of the Spaniards from New Mexico in 1680, and the beginnings of El Paso. *Quarterly of the Texas State Historical Association*, Vol. XVI, pp. 137–168, 259–276. Austin, 1912.

   1916   Otermin's attempt to reconquer New Mexico, 1681–1682. *Old Santa Fe*, Vol. III, pp. 44–84, 103–132. Santa Fe, 1916.

   1937   Historical documents relating to New Mexico, etc., Vol. III. Washington, 1937.

HALLENBECK, C.

   1926   Spanish missions of the old Southwest. New York, 1926.

HALSETH, O. S.

   1924   Report of repairs on Zia mission. *El Palacio*, Vol. XVI, No. 1, pp. 9–12. Santa Fe, 1924.

HAMMOND, G. P.

   1926   Don Juan de Oñate and the founding of New Mexico. *Historical Society of New Mexico. Publications in History*, Vol. I. Santa Fe, 1926.

   1927   Don Juan de Oñate and the founding of New Mexico. *Historical Society of New Mexico. Publications in History*, Vol. II. Santa Fe, 1927.

HAMMOND, G. P., and REY, A.

   1929   Luxan's narrative of the Espejo expedition, 1582–1583. *The Quivira Society*, Vol. I. Los Angeles, 1929.

HENDERSON, A. C.

   1938   E. Dana Johnson. *New Mexico Historical Review*, Vol. XIII, pp. 120–125. Santa Fe, 1938.

HERRICK, C. L., and JOHNSON, D. W.

   1900   The geology of the Albuquerque sheet. *Bulletin of the Scientific Laboratories of Denison University*, Vol. X, pp. 230–233. Granville, 1900.

HEWETT, E. L.

1906   Antiquities of the Jemez plateau, New Mexico. *Bulletin 32, Bureau of American Ethnology.* Washington, 1906.

1938   Hispanic monuments. *El Palacio,* Vol. XLV, pp. 56–67. Santa Fe, 1938.

1938a   The frescoes of Kuaua. *El Palacio,* Vol. XLV, pp. 21–28. Santa Fe, 1938.

HEWETT, E. L., and BANDELIER, A. F.

1937   Indians of the Rio Grande Valley. *Handbooks of Archaeological History.* University of New Mexico Press, Albuquerque, 1937.

HISTORIC AMERICAN BUILDINGS SURVEY

1934.   U.S. Department of interior; Office of national parks, buildings and reservations; branch of plans and designs; drawings of Acoma, Chimayo, Laguna, Ranchos de Taos, Santa Fe (San Miguel), and Talpa Chapel.

HODGE, F. W.

1907   Handbook of American Indians north of Mexico. *Bulletin 30, Bureau of American Ethnology,* Vol. I. Washington, 1907.

1910   Handbook of American Indians north of Mexico. *Bulletin 30, Bureau of American Ethnology,* Vol. II. Washington, 1910.

1918   Excavations at Hawikuh, New Mexico. *Smithsonian Miscellaneous Collections,* Vol. 68, No. 12, pp. 61–72. Washington, 1918.

1922   Recent excavations at Hawikuh. *El Palacio,* Vol. XII, No. 1, pp. 1–11. Santa Fe, 1922.

1937   History of Hawikuh, New Mexico, one of the so-called cities of Cibola. Los Angeles, 1937.

HOLZAPFEL, H.

1909   Handbuch der Geschichte des Franziskanerordens. Freiburg i/Br., 1909.

HUGHES, A. E.

1914   The beginnings of Spanish settlement in the El Paso district. *University of California, Publications in History,* Vol. I, No. 3, pp. 295–392. Berkeley, 1914.

HUGHES, J. T.

1907   Doniphan's expedition; edited by W. E. Connelley. Topeka, 1907.

HULL, D.

1916   Castaño de Sosa's expedition to New Mexico in 1590. *Old Santa Fe,* Vol. III, pp. 307–322. Santa Fe, 1916.

IMBENTARIO

1798   Imbentario en que se manifiesta el estado en que ala presente se halla la Fabrica de la Igla y Capillas de esta Micion de la Villa de Sta. Cruz de la Cañada. MS., Archives of the Archdiocese, Santa Fe.

INTERROGATION

1689   Interrogation of a Zia warrior, Bartolome de Ojeda, at El Paso, on August 25th, 1689. MS. translation. Henry E. Huntington Library, San Marino, California.

JAMES, T.

1916   Three years among the Indians and Mexicans. Saint Louis, 1916.

JONES, H.

1932   Uses of wood by the Spanish colonists in New Mexico. *New Mexico Historical Review,* Vol. VII, pp. 273–292. Santa Fe, 1932.

KEECH, R. A.

1933   The Saline pueblo strongholds. *El Palacio,* Vol. XXXIV, pp. 1–13. Santa Fe, 1933.

KENDALL, G. W.

1844   Narrative of the Texan Santa Fe expedition. 2 vols. New York, 1844.

KIDDER, A. V.

1924   An introduction to the study of southwestern archaeology. New Haven, 1924.

KUBLER, G.

1939   Gran Quivira-Humanas. *New Mexico Historical Review,* Vol. XIV, pp. 418–421. Santa Fe, 1939.

1939a   The rebuilding of San Miguel at Santa Fe in 1710. *Contributions of the Taylor Museum.* Colorado Springs, 1939.

KUENSTLE, K.
1926 Ikonographie der Heiligen. Freiburg i/Br., 1926.

LAMY, J. B.
1874 Short history of the pueblo Indians of New Mexico, sent to General C. Ewing by the Bishop of Santa Fe. MS. February 25th, 1874. Archives of Archdiocese, Santa Fe.

LANE, W. C.
1928 Letters 1852–1854; edited by R. P. Bieber. *New Mexico Historical Review,* Vol. III, pp. 179–203. Santa Fe, 1928.

LASTEYRIE, R. DE
1905 La déviation des axes des églises. *Bulletin Monumental,* Vol. LXIX, pp. 422–460. Paris, 1905.

LEYBA, E.
1933 The church of the twelve apostles, Trampas. *New Mexico,* Vol. XI, p. 19. Santa Fe, 1933.

LOEW, O.
1876 Lieut. G. M. Wheeler's Zweite Expedition nach Neu-Mexiko und Colorado, 1874. *Petermann's Geographische Mittheilungen,* Vol. XXII, pp. 209–217. Gotha, 1876.

LUMMIS, C. F.
1893 The Spanish pioneers. Chicago, 1893.

LUXAN, D. P. DE
1929 Expedition into New Mexico made by Antonio de Espejo 1582–1583; translated, with introduction and notes by G. P. Hammond and Agapito Rey. The Quivira Society, Los Angeles, 1929.

MAAS, O.
1929 Misiones de Nuevo Mejico; documentos del archivo general de Indias. Madrid, 1929.

MACGREGOR, L.
1935 Cien ejemplares de plateresco mexicano. *Archivo Español de Arte y Arqueologia,* Vol. XXXI, pp. 31–45. Madrid, 1935.

MAGOFFIN, S. S.
1926 Down the Santa Fe trail and into New Mexico 1846–1847. New Haven, 1926.

MÂLE, E.
1927 Art et artistes du moyen âge. Paris, 1927.
1932 L'Art religieux après le Concile de Trente. Paris, 1932.

MEXICO, SECRETARIA DE EDUCACION PUBLICA
1933 Three centuries of Mexican colonial architecture. New York, 1933.

MINDELEFF, V.
1891 A study of pueblo architecture: Tusayan and Cibola. *Eighth Report of the Bureau of Ethnology.* Washington, 1891.

MOELLHAUSEN, B.
1858 Diary of a journey from the Mississippi to the coasts of the Pacific. 2 vols. London, 1858.

MORFI, A. DE
1932 A geographic description of New Mexico, 1782. In: *Forgotten Frontiers;* edited and translated by A. B. Thomas. Norman, Oklahoma, 1932.

MORLEY, S. G.
1915 Santa Fe architecture. *Old Santa Fe,* Vol. II, pp. 278–301. Santa Fe, 1915.

MOTOLINIA, T. DE B.
1858 Historia de los Indios de la Nueva España. *Colección de documentos para la historia de Mexico,* Vol. LIII, pp. 1–249. Madrid, 1858.

NEWCOMB, R.
1937 Spanish colonial architecture in the United States. New York, 1937.

Nissen, H.

    1906   Orientation. Studien zur Geschichte der Religion, Vol. I. Berlin, 1906.

    1907   Orientation. Studien zur Geschichte der Religion, Vol. II. Berlin, 1907.

    1910   Orientation. Studien zur Geschichte der Religion, Vol. III. Berlin, 1910.

Noel, M., and Torre Revello, J.

    1934   Arquitectura virreinal. *Estudios y documentos para la historia del arte colonial*, Vol. I. Buenos Aires, 1934.

Nuttall, Z.

    1921   Ordinances concerning the laying out of new towns. *Hispanic American Historical Review*, Vol. IV, pp. 743–753. Baltimore, 1921.

Ocaranza, F.

    1934   Establecimientos franciscanos en el misterioso reino de Nuevo Mexico. Mexico, 1934.

Perea, *see* Bloom, 1933*a*

Pereyro, J. B.

    1808   Census of the population of New Mexico. MS. Archive 1191. Public Survey Office, Santa Fe. December 30, 1808.

Pike, Z. M.

    1895   The expeditions of Zebulon Montgomery Pike; edited by Elliot M. Coues. 3 vols. New York, 1895.

Pino, P. B.

    1812   Exposición sucinta y sencilla de la provincia del Nuebo Mexico. Cadiz, 1812.

Poore, H. R.

    1893   Moqui pueblo Indians of Arizona and pueblo Indians of New Mexico. *11th Census Report of 1890*. Washington, 1893.

    1893*a* Condition of sixteen New Mexican Indian pueblos. *11th Census Report of 1890*. Washington, 1893.

Porter, A. K.

    1909   Medieval architecture, Vol. II. New York, 1909.

Prince, L. B.

    1915   Spanish mission churches of New Mexico. Cedar Rapids, 1915.

    1915*a* Spanish mission churches of New Mexico. *Journal of American History*, Vol. IX, pp. 487–561. New York, 1915.

Punsili.

    1683   Confession and declaration of Juan Punsili, a Picuris Indian, before the Governor and Secretary at El Paso del Norte on the 20th August 1683 relating to the causes, organization of the Rebellion of 1680 and condition of the people in the pueblos, their leader, their dissentions, their oppressions, and their resentment all certified under the hand of the Governor and Secretary and the interpreters. Translated from the original manuscript by Samuel Ellison, Sept. 18th, 1884. Henry E. Huntington Library, San Marino, California. MS. Doc. 50.

Read, B.M.

    1916   El Santuario de Chimayo. *El Palacio,* Vol. III, No. 4, pp. 81–84. Santa Fe, August, 1916.

Reagan, A. B.

    1917   The Jemez Indians. *El Palacio,* Vol. IV, No. 2, pp. 25–72. Santa Fe, April, 1917.

Reiter, P.

    1938   The Jemez Pueblo of Unshagi, New Mexico. With notes on the earlier excavations at "Amoxiumqua" and Giusewa. 2 vols. University of New Mexico Press, 1938.

Reuter, B. A.

    1924   MS. report on repairs at Acoma, to the committee for the preservation and reconstruction of New Mexican mission churches. September 17, 1924. Files of J. G. Meem, Santa Fe.

    1926   MS. report on repairs at Acoma, to the committee for the preservation and reconstruction of New Mexican mission churches. August, 1926. Files of J. G. Meem, Santa Fe.

    1927   MS. report on repairs at Acoma, to the committee for the preservation and reconstruction of New Mexican mission churches. May, 1927. Files of J. G. Meem, Santa Fe.

1927a MS. report on repairs at Santa Ana, to the committee for the preservation and reconstruction of New Mexican mission churches. October, 1927. Files of J. G. Meem, Santa Fe.

1927b MS. report on repairs at Santa Ana, to the committee for the preservation and reconstruction of New Mexican mission churches. November, 1927. Files of J. G. Meem, Santa Fe.

1932   MS. report on repairs at Trampas, to the committee for the preservation and reconstruction of New Mexican mission churches. May, 1932. Files of J. G. Meem, Santa Fe.

RICARD, R.

1933   La "conquête spirituelle" du Mexique. Essai sur l'apostolat et les méthodes missionnaires des Ordres Mendiants en Nouvelle-Espagne de 1523–24 à 1572. Paris, 1933.

RILEY, L. A.

1925   Repairs to the old mission at Acoma. *El Palacio,* Vol. XVIII, pp. 1–9. Santa Fe, 1925.

RITCH, W. G.

1885   Aztlan. N.p., 1885.

ROBERTS, F. H. H.

1935   A survey of southwestern archaeology. *Annual Smithsonian Report,* No. 3373, pp. 507–533. Washington, 1935.

1937   Archaeology in the southwest. *American Antiquity,* Vol. III, pp. 3–33. Menasha, 1937.

RUXTON, G. F. A.

1849   Adventures in Mexico and the Rocky Mountains. London, 1849.

SALPOINTE, J. B.

1898   Soldiers of the Cross. Notes on the ecclesiastical history of New Mexico, Arizona, and Colorado. Banning, California, 1898.

SCHOLES, F. V.

1928   Manuscripts for the history of New Mexico in the National Library in Mexico City. *New Mexico Historical Review,* Vol. III, pp. 301–323. Santa Fe, 1928.

1929   Documents for the history of the New Mexico missions in the seventeenth century. *New Mexico Historical Review,* Vol. IV, pp. 45–58. Santa Fe, 1929.

1930   The supply service of the New Mexico Missions in the seventeenth century. *New Mexico Historical Review,* Vol. V, pp. 93–116. Santa Fe, 1930.

1932   Problems in the early ecclesiastical history of New Mexico. *New Mexico Historical Review,* Vol. VII, pp. 32–75. Santa Fe, 1932.

1935   Civil government and society in New Mexico in the seventeenth century. *New Mexico Historical Review,* Vol. X, pp. 71–111. Santa Fe, 1935.

1935a The first decade of the Inquisition in New Mexico. *New Mexico Historical Review,* Vol. X, pp. 195–241. Santa Fe, 1935.

1937   Church and state in New Mexico 1610–1650. *Historical Society of New Mexico, Publications in History,* Vol. VII. Albuquerque, 1937.

1937a Notes on Sandia and Puaray. *El Palacio,* Vol. XLII, pp. 57–59. Santa Fe, 1937.

1938   Notes on the Jemez missions in the seventeenth century. *El Palacio,* Vol. XLIV, pp. 61–71, 93–102. Santa Fe, 1938.

SCHOOLCRAFT, H. R.

1854   Historical and statistical information, respecting the history, condition and prospects of the Indian tribes of the United States, Vol. IV. Philadelphia, 1854.

SECRETARIA DE EDUCACION PUBLICA, MEXICO.

1933   Tres siglos de arquitectura colonial. Mexico, 1933.

SEDGWICK, M. K.

1927   Acoma, the sky city. Cambridge, 1927.

SENA, J. D.

1938   The chapel of Don Antonio José Ortiz. *New Mexico Historical Review,* Vol. XIII, pp. 347–359. Santa Fe, 1938.

SENTER, D.

1934   The work on the old Quarai mission. *El Palacio,* Vol. XXXVII, pp. 169–174. Santa Fe, 1934.

SHEA, J. D. G.

1855 History of the Catholic missions among the Indian tribes of the United States. New York, 1855.

SIGUENZA Y GONGORA, C. DE

1932 Mercurio Volante; translated, with introduction and notes by I. A. Leonard. The Quivira Society, Los Angeles, 1932.

SIMPSON, J. H.

1852 Journal of a military reconnaissance, from Santa Fe, in New Mexico, to the Navajo country, made . . . in 1849. Philadelphia, 1852.

SISTER MARY LOYOLA

1939 The American occupation of New Mexico. *New Mexico Historical Review,* Vol. XIV, pp. 34–75, 143–199, 230–286. Santa Fe, 1939.

SITGREAVES, L.

1854 Report of an expedition down the Zuñi and Colorado Rivers. Washington, 1854.

SPELL, L. M.

1927 Music teaching in New Mexico in the seventeenth century. *New Mexico Historical Review,* Vol. II, pp. 27–36. Santa Fe, 1927.

STALLINGS, W. S., JR.

1933 A tree ring chronology for the Rio Grande district in northern New Mexico. *Proceedings of the National Academy of Sciences,* Vol. XIX, No. 9, pp. 803–806. Baltimore, 1933.

1937 Southwestern dated ruins: I. *Tree-Ring Bulletin,* Vol. IV, No. 2, p. 5. Tucson, 1937.

TAMARON Y ROMERAL, P.

1937 Demostracion del vastisimo obispado de la Nueva Viscaya—1765. *Biblioteca Historica Mexicana,* Vol. 7, Mexico, 1937.

TERRASAS, J. T.

1821 Ynbentario. yglesia parroquial de Sta Cruz de la Cañada. MS. April 20, 1821. Archive of the Archdiocese, Santa Fe.

TICHY, M. F.

1936 Observations on the mission uncovered at Puaray. *El Palacio,* Vol. XLI, pp. 63–66. Santa Fe, 1936.

TOULOUSE, J. H., JR.

1937 Two artifacts from Jemez. *El Palacio,* Vol. XLIII, pp. 107–108. Santa Fe, 1937.

1937a Excavations at San Diego mission, New Mexico. *New Mexico Anthropologist,* Vol. II, No. 1, pp. 16–18. Albuquerque, 1937.

1938 The mission of San Gregorio de Abó. *El Palacio,* Vol. XLV, pp. 103–107. Santa Fe, 1938.

TOUSSAINT, M.

1927 Iglesias de Mexico. Publicaciones de la secretaria de hacienda, Vol. VI. Mexico, 1927.

1932 La Cronica de Michoacan. *Nuestro Mexico,* Vol. I, pp. 7–8, 77. Mexico, 1932.

1935 Supervivencias goticas en la arquitectura mexicana del siglo XVI. *Archivo Español de Arte y Arqueologia,* Vol. XXXI, pp. 47–66. Madrid, 1935.

1937 La relacion de Michoacan. *Anales del Instituto de Investigaciones Esteticas,* Vol. I, pp. 3–14. Mexico, 1937.

TWITCHELL, R. E.

1909 The history of the military occupation of New Mexico from 1846 to 1851. Denver, 1909.

1911 The leading facts of New Mexican history, Vol. I. Cedar Rapids, 1911.

1912 The leading facts of New Mexican history, Vol. II. Cedar Rapids, 1912.

1914 The Spanish archives of New Mexico, Vol. I. Cedar Rapids, 1914.

1914a The Spanish archives of New Mexico, Vol. II. Cedar Rapids, 1914.

1916 The Pueblo revolt of 1696—extracts from the journal of General de Vargas. *Old Santa Fe,* Vol. III, pp. 333–373. Santa Fe, 1916.

1917 The leading facts of New Mexican history, Vol. III. Cedar Rapids, 1917.

1917a The leading facts of New Mexican history, Vol. IV. Cedar Rapids, 1917.

1917b The leading facts of New Mexican history, Vol. V. Cedar Rapids, 1917.

1919 Spanish colonization in New Mexico in the Oñate and De Vargas periods. *Historical Society of New Mexico. Publications*, No. 22. Santa Fe, 1919.

1925 Old Santa Fe. The story of New Mexico's ancient capital. Santa Fe, 1925.

VARGAS, D. DE

1914 The last campaign, 1704. *Old Santa Fe*, Vol. II, pp. 66–72. Santa Fe, 1914.

1914a The reconquest of New Mexico, 1692. Extracts from the journal of de Vargas. *Old Santa Fe*, Vol. I, pp. 288–307, 420–435. Santa Fe, 1914.

1914b Justification, 1703. *Old Santa Fe*, Vol. II, pp. 58–65. Santa Fe, 1914.

VERNEUIL, M. P.

n.d. Dictionnaire des symboles, emblèmes et attributs. Paris, n.d.

VETANCURT, A. DE

1697 Chronica de la provincia del Santo Evangelio de Mexico. Quarta parte del Teatro Mexicano de los successos religiosos. Mexico, 1697.

1697a Menologio franciscano de los varones mas señalados. Mexico, 1697.

VIERRA, C.

1918 New Mexico architecture. *Art and Archaeology*, Vol. VII, p. 37. Washington, 1918.

VILLAGRA, G. P. DE

1933 History of New Mexico, 1610; translation by Gilberto Espinosa; introduction and notes by F. W. Hodge. The Quivira Society, Vol. IV, Los Angeles, 1933.

VILLASEÑOR Y SANCHEZ, J. A.

1748 Theatro americano; Segunda parte. Mexico, 1748.

VIOLLET-LE-DUC, E. E.

1854 Dictionnaire de l'architecture, Vol. III, pp. 226–237. Article "Chœur." Paris, 1854.

WAGNER, H. R.

1924 The Spanish southwest, 1542–1794. Berkeley, 1924.

1937 The Spanish southwest. The Quivira Society, Los Angeles, 1937.

WALTER, P. A. F.

1916 The cities that died of fear. *Papers of the School of American Research*, No. 35. Santa Fe, 1916.

1916a A New Mexico Lourdes. *El Palacio*, Vol. III, No. 2, pp. 3–27. Santa Fe, January, 1916.

WEBB, J. J.

1931 Adventures in the Santa Fe trade 1844–1847. Glendale, California, 1931.

WEISE, G.

1933 Studien zur spanischen Architektur der Spaetgotik. Reutlingen, 1933.

WHITE, L. A.

1932 The pueblo of San Felipe. *Memoirs of the American Anthropological Association*, No. 38. Menasha, 1932.

1935 The pueblo of Santo Domingo, New Mexico. *Memoirs of the American Anthropological Association*, No. 43. Menasha, 1935.

WINSHIP, G. P.

1896 The Coronado expedition, 1540–1542. *Fourteenth Report of the Bureau of American Ethnology*, Part 1, pp. 329–613. Washington, 1896.

WISLIZENUS, A.

1848 Memoir of a tour to northern Mexico, connected with Col. Doniphan's expedition in 1846 and 1847. Washington, 1848.

WÖLFFLIN, H.

1926 Renaissance und Barock. 4th ed. Munich, 1926.

WOOD, S., and JACKSON, W. H.

1894 Ancient missions and churches of America. Chicago, 1894.

Wuthenau A. von

1935   The Spanish military chapels of Santa Fe and the reredos of Our Lady of Light. *New Mexico Historical Review*, Vol. X, pp. 175–194. Santa Fe, 1935.

Yarrow, H. C.

1879   Notice of a ruined pueblo and an ancient burial place in the valley of the Rio Chama. *Report upon United States geographical surveys west of the one hundredth meridian*, Vol. VII, pp. 362–365. Washington, 1879.

Zarate Salmerón, G. de

1856   Relaciones de todas las cosas . . . desde el año de 1538 hasta el de 1626. *Documentos para la historia de Mexico, Tercera Serie*. Mexico, 1856.

1899   Relacion. Translation by C. F. Lummis. *Land of Sunshine*, Vol. XI, pp. 336–346. Los Angeles, 1899.

1900   Relacion. Translation by C. F. Lummis. *Land of Sunshine*, Vol. XII, pp. 39–48, 104–113, 180–187. Los Angeles, 1900.

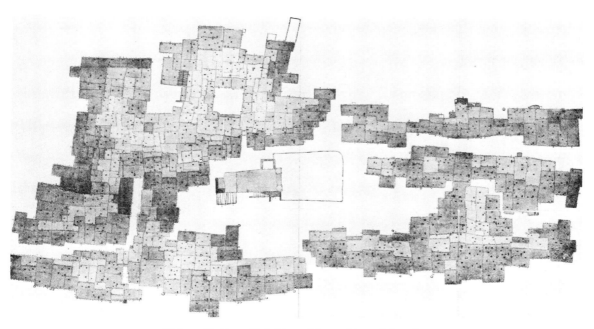

43. Halona (Zuñi pueblo). Plan of the pueblo and church. 1891.

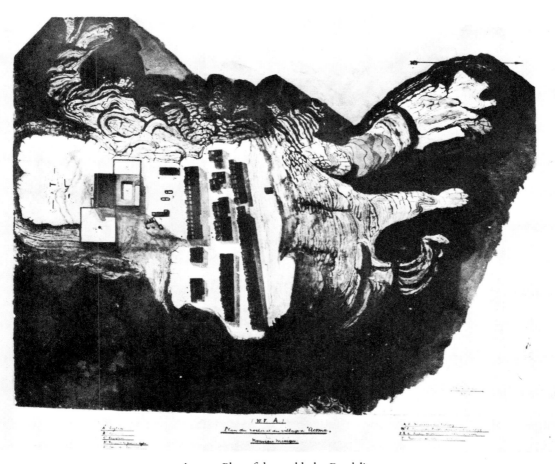

44. Acoma. Plan of the pueblo by Bandelier.

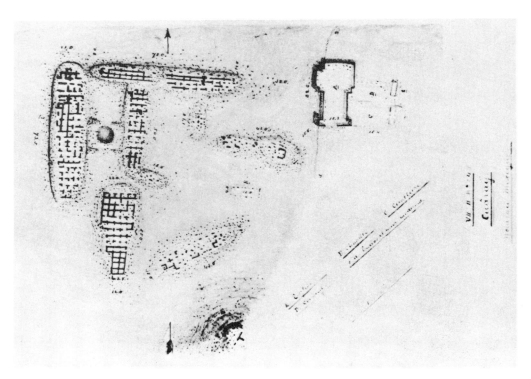

45. Quarai. Plan of the pueblo by Bandelier.

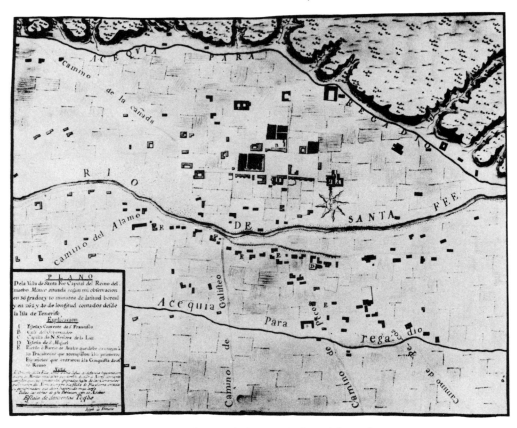

46. Santa Fe. Plan by Joseph de Urrutia. Late eighteenth century.

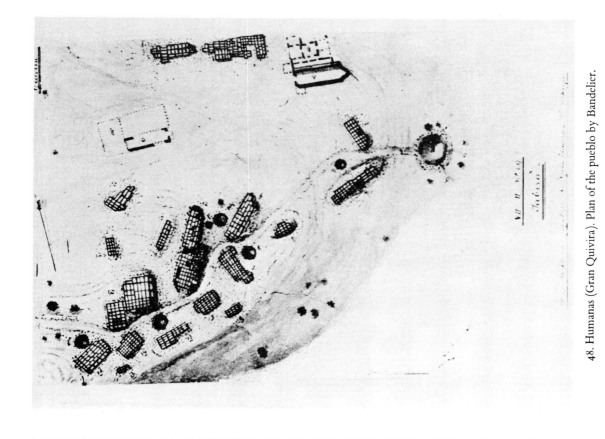

48. Humanas (Gran Quivira). Plan of the pueblo by Bandelier.

47. San Felipe on the Mesa. Plan of the pueblo by Bandelier.

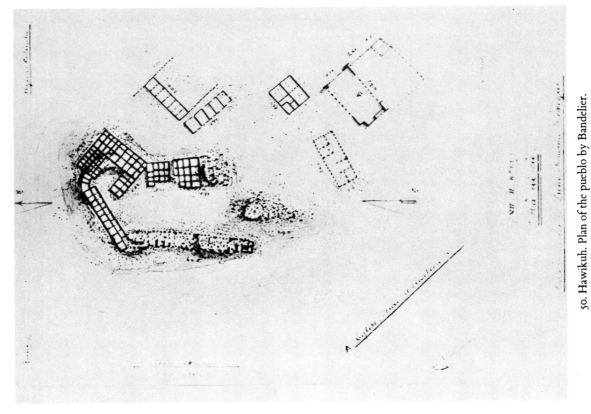

50. Hawikuh. Plan of the pueblo by Bandelier.

49. Abó. Plan of the pueblo by Bandelier.

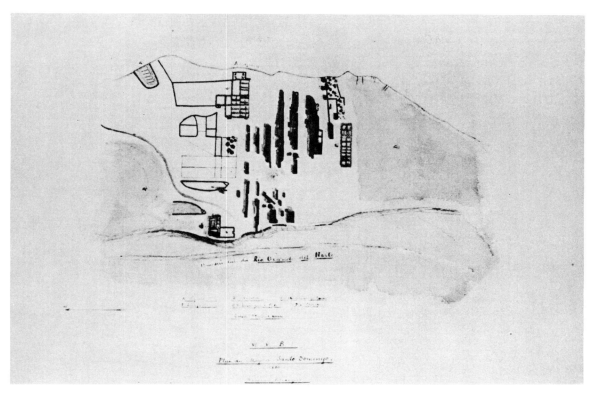

51. Santo Domingo. Plan of the pueblo by Bandelier, in 1880.

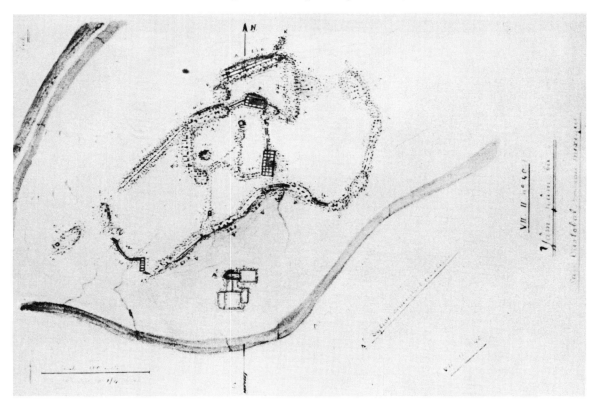

52. San Cristobal. Plan of the pueblo by Bandelier.

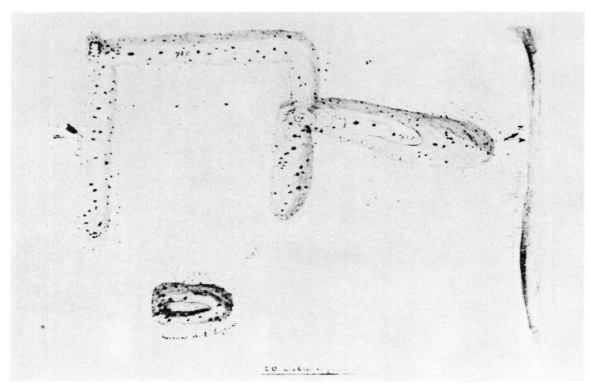

53. Tajique. Plan of the pueblo by Bandelier.

54. Santa Rosa de Abiquiu. North nave wall. 1937.

55. Pecos. The nave in 1881, looking east.

56. San Felipe on the Mesa. The nave from the south. 1935.

57. Isleta. The church from the northeast, about 1910.

58. Acoma. The church from the southwest. 1937.

60. Giusewa. The nave and tower from the south. 1937.

59. Abó. The church from the southwest. 1937.

61. Kechipauan. The church from the southeast, about 1919.

62. Abó. View from the southwest, after excavation and repair. 1940.

63. Abó. The west nave wall. 1935.

64. Tlaquiltenango, Mexico. The church from the south. 1936.

65. Albi, France. The Cathedral from the southeast.

66. Pecos. The church from the northeast. 1881.

67. Acoma. The north tower and courtyard. 1937.

68. Quarai. The nave from the south. 1935.

69. Santa Ana. The sanctuary from the northwest. 1938.

70. Santa Clara. The apse from the southwest. 1935.

71. Trampas. The nave and sanctuary. 1937.

72. San José de Chama (Hernandez). The nave. 1937.

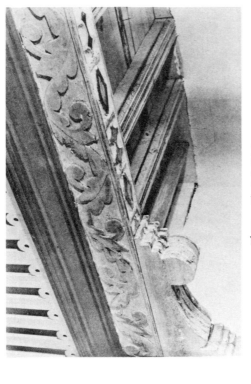

75. El Rito. Choir-loft joist. 1937.

76. Trampas. Choir-loft soffit. 1937.

73. Juarez, Mexico. Roofing detail. 1931.

74. Socorro. Ceiling at transept. 1937.

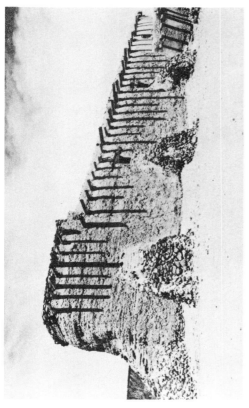

78. Santa Ana. The church from the southwest. 1938.

80. Tula, Mexico. The church from the northwest. 1936.

77. Giusewa. Roofing fragment. 1922.

79. Zia. The church from the northeast, about 1910.

81. Chimayo. The Santuario from the north. 1937.

82. Santa Ana. The church from the south. 1938.

83. Ranchos de Taos. The sanctuary from the west. 1939.

84. Isleta. The sanctuary from the southwest, about 1910.

85. Humanas (Gran Quivira). The ruins from the northwest.

86. Santa Rosa de Abiquiu. The nave from the east. 1937.

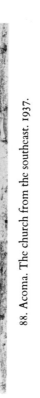

88. Acoma. The church from the southeast. 1937.

90. Pecos. The church from the southeast. 1881.

87. Picuris. The church from the south. 1935.

89. Santa Ana. Interior toward entrance. 1938.

92. Humanas (Gran Quivira). Sacristy window. 1937.

91. Santa Cruz. The sanctuary. 1937.

95. Isleta. The transverse clearstory window. 1937.

96. Trampas. The transverse clearstory window. 1937.

93. Santa Ana. The transverse clearstory window. 1938.

94. Socorro. The transverse clearstory window, from within roof. 1937.

97. Santa Cruz. The south chapel.

98. Zia. The sanctuary interior. 1938.

99. Isleta. The façade, about 1881.

100. Humanas (Gran Quivira). The main doorway. 1937.

101. Pecos. Arched doorway to sanctuary. 1935.

102. Santa Cruz. The south tower belfry. 1910.

103. Trampas. Doorway to baptistry.

104. Hawikuh. Doorway in *convento*. 1919.

105. Santa Clara. Main door. 1910.

106. Acoma. South tower staircase. 1933.

107. Chimayo. Door from narthex to nave. 1937.

108. Chimayo. Door from narthex to nave. 1937.

110. Nambé. Choir-loft joist. 1935.

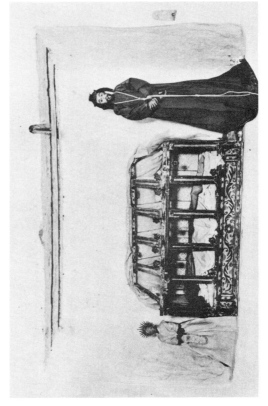

112. Santa Cruz. The Holy Sepulcher.

109. Acoma. Doorway to *convento.* 1937.

111. San Ildefonso. The open chapel (destroyed), about 1900.

113. Cordova. The sanctuary. 1937.

114. Laguna. The church from the east. 1881.

115. Santa Cruz. The façade. Before 1885.

116. Pecos. The church ruins, in 1846.

117. Santa Fe. The parish church, in 1846.

118. Giusewa. The church from the southwest. 1937.

119. Trampas. The façade. 1937.

121. Cochiti. The church, about 1910.

122. San Ildefonso. The church (destroyed), about 1899.

120. Santa Cruz. The façade. 1937.

123. Ranchos de Taos. The façade. 1939.

124. Chimayo. The façade. 1937.

127. Santa Fe. San Miguel, the façade, about 1880.

128. Santa Ana. The façade, about 1910.

125. Giusewa. The ruins, in 1852.

126. Truchas. The façade, about 1910.

131. Trampas. The nave and choir loft. 1937.

132. Santa Cruz. The choir loft in the north chapel, about 1910.

129. Laguna. The nave and choir loft. 1937.

130. Zia. The choir loft. 1938.

133. Taxco, Mexico. The church from the north.

134. Tlamaco, Mexico. The façade.

135. Calimaya, Mexico. The façade.

137. Santa Ana. The sanctuary. 1938.

138. Santa Cruz. The sanctuary of the north chapel, about 1910.

136. Juarez, Mexico. The nave and sanctuary, about 1880.

140. Tesuque. The façade (destroyed), about 1900.

141. Giusewa. Fragment of wall decoration in the church. 1922.

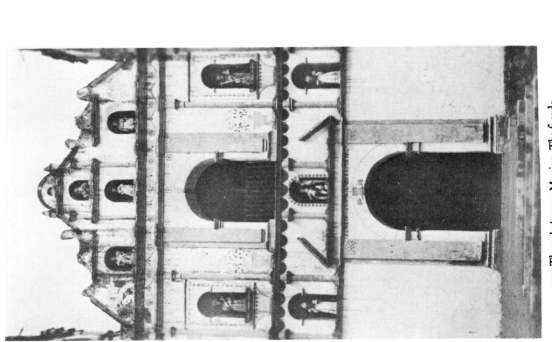

139. Tlacochahuaya, Mexico. The façade

142. Laguna. The sanctuary. 1937.

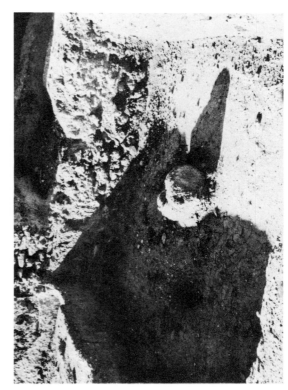

146. Giusewa. The baptistry. 1937.

144. Church in Michoacan, Mexico, according to Beaumont.

143. Zia. Wall painting in the nave. 1938.

145. Zia. The sacristy, about 1910.

150. Quarai. The sunken chamber in the *convento*. 1935.

148. Santa Ana. The open chapel. 1938.

147. Acoma. The patio walk, north range. 1937.

149. Santo Domingo. The church, destroyed in 1886.

152. Santa Fe. The sanctuary of San Miguel, exterior, in 1881.

151. Santa Fe. The sanctuary of San Miguel, in 1881.

153. Giusewa. The nave interior from the north. 1937.

154. Quarai. The church from the west. 1937.

156. Pecos. The sanctuary interior.

158. Las Colonias. Corbels in the sanctuary, from Pecos. 1931.

155. Pecos. The north transept interior. 1935.

157. Pecos. Roofing timbers. 1931.

159. Abó. The sanctuary from the northwest, in 1846.

161. Abó. The façade from the southwest. 1940.

160. Abó. The nave from the south. 1940.

162. Abó. The sanctuary from the north. 1940.

165. Humanas (Gran Quivira). The chapel doorway from the southwest. 1935.

166. Humanas (Gran Quivira). The nave from the east. 1937.

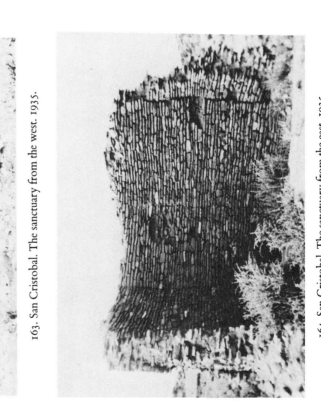

163. San Cristobal. The sanctuary from the west. 1935.

164. San Cristobal. The sanctuary from the east. 1935.

167. Zia. The church from the south, in 1899.

168. Zia. The façade from the east, about 1910.

169. Zia. The façade from the east. 1938.

170. Acoma. General view of the rock and pueblo, in 1881.

171. Acoma. The nave and sanctuary. 1940.

172. Walatowa (Jemez). The pueblo and church, in 1849.

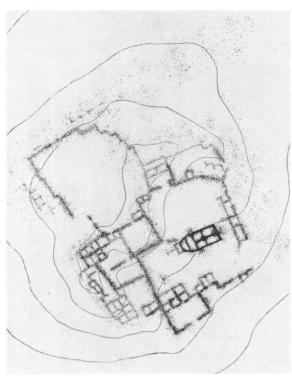

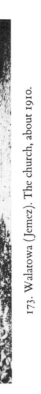

173. Walatowa (Jemez). The church, about 1910.

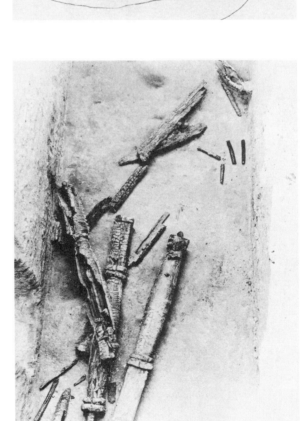

174. Hawikuh. Charred wood from the *convento*, lower room 30B. 1919.

175. Kechipauan. Plan of the pueblo and church. 1891.

177. Juarez, Mexico. The church from the east. 1880.

179. Santa Fe. The parish church, north chapel roof. 1933.

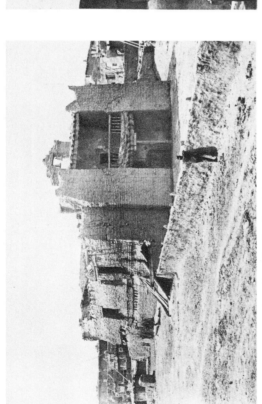

176. Halona (Zuñi). The church from the east. 1881.

178. Isleta. The church interior, in 1881.

181. Albuquerque. San Felipe from the southwest, about 1855.

183. Cordova. The nave. 1937.

180. Santa Fe: N.S. de Guadalupe from the northeast. 1881.

182. Albuquerque. San Felipe. 1881.

184. Ranchos de Taos. The nave. 1937.

185. Ranchos de Taos. The sanctuary. 1937.

186. Chimayo. View of the narthex from the nave. 1937.

187. Chimayo. The nave. 1937.

188. San Miguel del Vado. The town and church, in 1846.

190. Santo Domingo. The church from the southwest, about 1910.

191. San Felipe. The church from the northeast, about 1910.

189. Acoma. The nave. 1940.

193. Abeytas. The nave. 1935.

195. Sebogeta. The nave. 1935.

192. Abeytas. The church from the east. 1935.

194. Bosque. The church from the south. 1935.

196. Peña Blanca. The nave, about 1910.

197. Santo Domingo. Door panel.

198. Nambé. The church, about 1909.

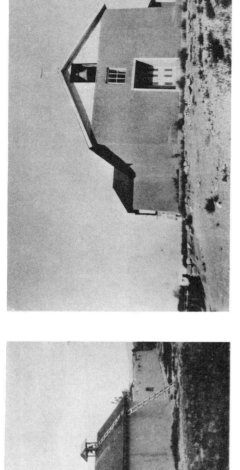

199. San Antonio. The apse. 1931.

200. Sandia. The church from the south. 1935.

201. San Juan. The church (destroyed), about 1900.

202. Talpa. The chapel from the east.

204. Santa Clara. The sanctuary (destroyed), about 1910.

206. San Fernando de Taos. The church (destroyed), about 1855.

203. Santa Clara. The church (destroyed), about 1910.

205. Pojoaque. The church (destroyed).

207. Santa Fe. The façade, Cristo Rey. 1940.

208. Santa Fe. The nave, Cristo Rey. 1940.

209. Santa Fe. The Castrense altarpiece of 1760. 1940.

210. Abiquiu. The nave corbels. 1940.

211. Abiquiu. The church from the southeast. 1940.

214. McCarty's. Santa Maria. 1940.

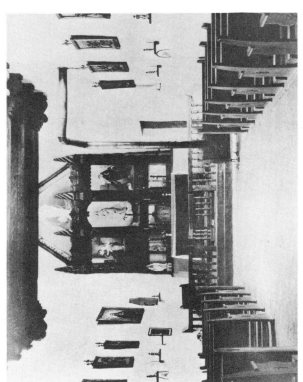

215. McCarty's. The nave, Santa Maria. 1940.

212. Paraje. St. Margaret Mary, from the southeast. 1940.

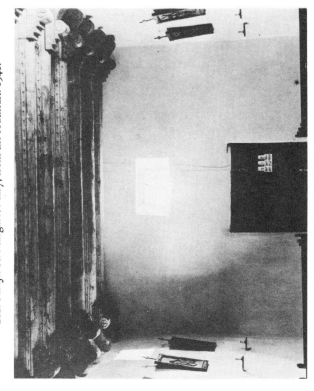

213. Paraje. St. Margaret Mary. The nave. 1940.

218. Mesita. Sacred Heart. From the southeast. 1940.

219. Mesita. Sacred Heart. The clearstory window. 1940.

216. Acomita. St. Anne, from the east. 1940.

217. Acomita. St. Anne, from the northwest. 1940.

INDEX